高级英语视听说教程

◎ 王涛 孙书兰 刘健刚
邢国垣 柳建玲 编著

东南大学出版社
·南京·

内 容 简 介

《高级英语视听说教程》是研究生英语系列教材之一,是针对非英语专业硕士研究生的实际水平而编写的。本教程以听说为主,视为辅,选材广泛,内容涉及求职、教育、餐饮、健康、节日、旅游、体育、婚姻、购物、科技、环保、社会文化等方面,具有很强的知识性、实用性和趣味性。全书共有 20 个单元,每单元一个专题,包括长短对话、短文、访谈或讲座等,练习形式多样,有多项选择、简答、填空、正误判断等,均有利于提高学生运用英语语言的实际能力。本教程适合各类非英语专业硕士研究生以及具有中等以上英语水平的读者自学使用。

图书在版编目(CIP)数据

高级英语视听说教程 / 王涛等编著. — 南京:东南大学出版社,2011.9

研究生英语系列教材

ISBN 978-7-5641-2930-9

Ⅰ.①高… Ⅱ.①王… Ⅲ.①英语—听说教学—研究生—教材 Ⅳ.①H319.9

中国版本图书馆 CIP 数据核字(2011)第 166629 号

高级英语视听说教程

编　　著	王　涛　孙书兰　刘健刚　邢国垣　柳建玲		
责任编辑	李　玉	责任印制	张文礼
文字编辑	周　菊	封面设计	王　玥

出版发行　东南大学出版社
出 版 人　江建中
社　　址　南京市四牌楼 2 号　　邮　编　210096
经　　销　全国各地新华书店
印　　刷　南京京新印刷厂
开　　本　787mm×1092mm　1/16
印　　张　14.75
字　　数　360 千字
版　　次　2011 年 9 月第 1 版　2012 年 10 月第 2 次印刷
书　　号　ISBN 978-7-5641-2930-9
印　　数　3001—6000 册
定　　价　42.00 元

(凡因印装质量问题,可直接向读者服务部调换。电话:025-83792328)

出版说明

《高级英语视听说教程》由东南大学外国语学院研究生英语教研室组织编写，是研究生英语系列教材之一。此教程是在充分考虑了非英语专业硕士研究生的实际水平的基础上编写而成的，其指导思想是根据《研究生英语教学大纲》和《考试大纲》所确定的听力以及加大口语教学的要求，尽可能满足当前研究生英语听说教学的需要。本教程适合各类非英语专业硕士研究生以及具有中等以上英语水平的读者自学使用。本系列教材还包括《高级英语读写译教程》。

《高级英语视听说教程》共有20个单元，可供两个学期使用。每单元有 Door to Wisdom, Join in the Dialogue, Listen and Discuss, Watch and Debate, Extracurricular Listening 等五个部分，除第一部分是纯口语表达、第五部分纯听力理解之外，其他三部分都设有听力训练和口语实践，听力素材有长短对话、短文、访谈、讲座等，口语表达活动都是围绕本单元的话题展开，使听力素材可直接用于口语实践，使学生在课堂上就能巩固所学的知识。

单元主题明确，每单元围绕一个话题展开，话题包括初次见面、喜怒哀乐、教书育人、求职应聘、城乡生活、饮食健康、节日庆祝、度假旅游、体育活动、人格特点、购物消费、人与环境、社会问题、多元文化、自然灾害、科学技术、投资理财、太空探索等，内容丰富，具有时效性、知识性、实用性和趣味性。练习形式多样，有多项选择、简答、填空、正误判断等，以期培养学生在听懂的基础上进行分析、总结、归纳，从而提高学生使用英语语言的实际能力。

全书20个单元中的前四部分分别由邢国垣（第1、6、14、18、19单元）、柳建玲（第2、4、8、10、11单元）、王涛（第3、15、16、17、20单元）、刘健刚（第5、7、9、12、13单元）负责编写，第五部分由孙书兰负责编写。

本教程在编写过程中得到了东南大学外国语学院和东南大学出版社的鼎力支持和热情关怀，他们在教材编写过程中提出了宝贵建议，在此一并表示诚挚的谢意。

尽管我们在本书的编写中尽了最大的努力，但由于水平有限，加之时间紧迫，恐难以做到尽如人意，错误和疏漏之处在所难免。热忱欢迎各位同行和广大读者朋友在本书的使用过程中给我们提出批评并加以指正。

编　者

2011.8

目 录

Unit 1　Communication Is the Key to Success ……………………………………… (1)

Unit 2　Emotions Have Taught Mankind to Reason ……………………………… (7)

Unit 3　Education Is the Transmission of Civilization …………………………… (12)

Unit 4　Work to Become, Not to Acquire ………………………………………… (20)

Unit 5　While There's Life, There's Hope ………………………………………… (25)

Unit 6　Life Well Spent Is Long …………………………………………………… (32)

Unit 7　All Holidays Can Be Good Times ………………………………………… (40)

Unit 8　Travel Is More Than the Seeing of Sights ……………………………… (47)

Unit 9　Sports Are a Microcosm of Society ……………………………………… (52)

Unit 10　Character Is Long-Standing Habit ……………………………………… (59)

Unit 11　Love Is the Fruit of Marriage …………………………………………… (65)

Unit 12　Money Isn't Everything ………………………………………………… (70)

Unit 13　Success Is Sweet ………………………………………………………… (77)

Unit 14　No Environment = No Development …………………………………… (84)

Unit 15　Problems Are the Price of Progress …………………………………… (92)

Unit 16　Cultural Diversity Shapes National Character ……………………………… (100)

Unit 17　Calamity Is Man's True Touch-Stone ……………………………………… (109)

Unit 18　Science and Technology Revolutionize Life ……………………………… (117)

Unit 19　Best Is Cheapest ……………………………………………………………… (125)

Unit 20　The Present Is Pregnant with the Future ………………………………… (134)

Scripts and Keys ………………………………………………………………………… (142)

 **Communication Is the Key to Success**

Part I Door to Wisdom

Read, think and interpret your understanding of the following proverbs and well-known sayings.

1. Everything that irritates us about others can lead us to an understanding of ourselves.

—Carl Gustav Jung

2. While nothing is easier than to denounce the evildoer, nothing is more difficult than to understand him.

—Feodor Mikhailovich Dostoyevsky

3. Distrust can be contagious. But, so can trust.

—Robbins Stacia

4. If men could only know each other, they would neither idolize nor hate.

—Elbert Hubbert

5. A good conversationalist is a good listener.

—Dale Carnegie

Part II Join in the Dialogue

Native English speakers tend to use first names to address persons they meet, however familiar, whatever the occasion. As in any other culture, titles like Doctor, Professor are important for one's social identity. For gender egalitarian, the title "Mrs." is often replaced by "Ms" to show the recognition of women's equal status to men's. Meeting each other, people use small talks as a way of starting a conversation. For example, they talk about the weather before discussing what's new in life and work, in person, on telephone, or even on the Internet.

Dialogue 1

Glossary

be on a visit 访问   put sb. up 接待,提供膳食
egalitarian 平等   status 地位

Ex. 1   Listen to the following dialogue and choose the best answer to each of the questions you will hear.

1. A. business meeting   B. grocery shopping
   C. wedding ceremony   D. fancy dress party
2. A. Two.   B. Three.   C. Four.   D. Five.
3. A. Formal.   B. First formal and then informal.
   C. Informal.   D. At first informal and then formal.
4. A. They are long lost friends.   B. They are old workmates.
   C. They are guest and hostess.   D. They are totally strangers.
5. A. In a company's Research Department.
   B. In a company named "Fifty-Gears".
   C. In a travel agency of the city.
   D. In a couple of shopping malls.
6. A. A few years.   B. A few months.   C. A few weeks.   D. A few days.

Ex. 2   Make dialogues on the following topics.

1. How do you behave when you meet or are introduced to someone for the first time? Talk about people's manners in their first meetings. Consider possible differences between cultures in the mention of names, opening small talk, physical contact, and so on.
2. Discuss the situation where you are invited to a business reception and need to meet some new business partners. Make a list of your preparation like the following. Add more items you think necessary into it.
   (1) self-introduction—name, position, working experiences, etc.
   (2) small talk—travel, accommodation, weather, etc.
   (3) further contacts—achievements, interests in cooperation, etc.

Dialogue 2

Glossary

relieve 放心,松口气   babysit 照看(孩子)

Communication Is the Key to Success

Unit 1

embarrassing 令人为难的　　　mislead 误导
Metamorphosis by Ovid 古罗马奥维德剧作《变形记》

Ex. 1 Listen to the following dialogue and choose the best answer to each of the questions you will hear.

1. A. Drive her mother to the theater.　　B. Take care of her little brother.
   C. Come to the theater with her.　　　D. Help her prepare for a class presentation.
2. A. He was difficult to understand.　　 B. He made her laugh.
   C. He seemed well prepared.　　　　　D. He seemed nervous.
3. A. It was a funny incident.
   B. He has made the same mistake before.
   C. He is worried that it will happen again.
   D. The woman should be more honest with him.
4. A. To baby sit her little brother.　　　B. To study with Joe.
   C. To see a play.　　　　　　　　　　D. To watch a video.

Ex. 2 Make dialogues on the following topics.

1. Remarks with similar literal meanings may cause quite different responses in different cultures. For example, questions like "Did you have lunch already?" could mean an invitation to a meal in Britain or the United States, while in China, it could mean you are simply greeting someone you see. Practice the pair work of making proper offers and responses. Try to be clear, direct and polite as well, and avoid misunderstandings.
2. While preparing an invitation, we need to clarify the information as much as possible for proper arrangements. Now prepare some invitations and then, make and respond to/decline the invitations in turn.

Part III　Listen and Discuss

Passage 1

Ex. 1 Listen to the following passage and choose the best answer to each of the questions you will hear.

1. A. As the result of the moisture in the Earth's atmosphere.
   B. As the result of the Earth's rotation.
   C. As the horizontal movement of air.
   D. As the vertical movement of air.
2. A. It's the ultimate cause of winds.　　　B. It causes vertical movements of air.
   C. It reduces differences in air pressure.　D. It's used to predict weather patterns.
3. A. Air pressure.　　　　　　　　　　　B. Temperature.
   C. Humidity.　　　　　　　　　　　　 D. Wind direction.

4. A. How winds affect temperature.

   B. Reasons for sudden increases in wind.

   C. The origin of storm systems.

   D. How vertical air movements influence weather.

Ex. 2　Make dialogues on the following topics.

1. Describe the climate of the place where you live or study. Do you like it? Why or why not?
2. Form pairs and comment on the advantages or disadvantages of weather forecasts in the past and today. Take notes and list your ideas in comparison and contrast.

Passage 2

Ex. 1　Listen to the following passage and choose the best answer to each of the multiple questions you will hear.

1. A. He made no hopeful policy and helped solve no problem.

   B. He made a neutral policy and helped solve the problem.

   C. He made a terrible policy and helped solve the problem.

   D. He made no definite policy and helped solve no problem.

2. A. Confession, practice and courtesy.　　B. Conclusion, politics, and currency.

   C. Concession, politeness, and courtesy.　　D. Coordination, practice, and curiosity.

3. A. He did not want it to extend to more other states.

   B. He did not want it to be abolished in west states.

   C. He did not want it to exist in the southern states.

   D. He did not want it to exist in all the Unite states

4. A. A more serious worry.　　B. A more acceptable plan.

   C. A more honorable duty.　　D. A more peaceful offer.

Ex. 2　Listen to the last part of the passage and fill in the blanks with the missing information.

　　Clay said there was equal justice in his resolutions (1) _____
_____. He said the south, perhaps, would be helped more than the north by his proposals. But the north, he said, was richer and had more money and power.

　　To the north, slavery was a matter of feeling. But to the south, Clay said, it was a hard social and economic fact. He said the north could look on in safety while (2) _____
_____.

　　Then Clay attacked the south's claim that it had the right to leave the Union. He said the Union of states was (3) _____.

Ex. 3　Make dialogues on the following topics.

1. Talk about your view on the need of tolerance and understanding. Take a few subjects into consideration such as religion, feminism, generation gap, etc.

Communication Is the Key to Success

2. The story in the passage took place right before the American Civil War, which marked the emancipation of thousands of hundreds of Negro slaves. Do you think war is unavoidable in settling disputes in human history? Give your reasons.

Part Ⅳ Watch and Debate

In the following video clip, the world famous linguist Noam Chomsky from MIT (Massachusetts Institute of Technology) are being interviewed by Al Page on the program *Upon Reflection* of UWTV (a TV website of University of Washington) about his view on how variations of language exist and affect human life.

Glossary

is prone to 倾向于	cockney 伦敦腔
decode 解码	retune 调节
innovative 创新的	be in 时尚的
archaic 落伍的, 陈旧的	kinship 亲族关系
utility 效用	property right 财产权

Ex. 1 Watch the video clip three times and fill in the missing information with either the exact words from the interview or with your own words.

Al Page: *Why is pronunciation and intonation so important to language? Why aren't words themselves sufficient to convey meaning?*

Noam Chomsky: You have to understand somebody else's words. I mean if you go to central London and somebody is prone to speaking cockney, and the words happen to match ours at some abstract level, you still may not understand them. ...part of your knowledge of language is a way of _____**1**_____. Sometimes not only have our decoding systems to work, the systems have to be close enough. Actually if you listen to us closely we are speaking different languages. But they are close enough so that _____**2**_____ _____. But again that's a little artificial. That's because of the artificial unity of the English language spoken in the United States. I happened to _____**3**_____. I mean if I listen to them for a while we can establish communication. But you have to kind of "retune your system" and some manner that's not understood so you can begin to decode what you're hearing.

Al Page: *We've all the slang habit of language. Why does slang exist?*

Noam Chomsky: People are innovative. They like to do things differently, and especially ____**4**____. Why do teenagers ____**5**____? Well, you know, whatever the reason is, they want to be different. They like to be innovative. They are creative.

Al Page: *To these fast fashions in language?*

Noam Chomsky: Oh, sure. And then in fact there are styles of different groups and they change… Some of them change very rapidly—the words that are in and then one year are archaic, and then in another year… that can be three years or something like that. And people are playing with their languages often. Again this is not too common in our societies. _____6_____. Our intelligence and creativity and so on goes into other things. But if you go to, say, central Australia, where _____7_____. A lot of the culture wealth _____8_____. It's just the creative mind of work, you know. So you get very complex language games… special language system to us as a property right that only a particular group of people speak…

Ex. 2 Watch the video again and express your opinions on the following questions.

1. Do you think you can adapt yourself to the local variation of language very well when you visit somewhere? Does it have anything to do with your capacities of "decoding" the language systems? Which part of your language ability may develop faster, listening or speaking? Try to analyze the reasons.
2. Slangs are also updating at an unprecedented speed in China, especially among youngsters by the convenience of the Internet. What is your attitude toward this innovation of language? Take notes of your view and list your reasons.

Part V   Extracurricular Listening

Listen to the following 10 short dialogues and choose the best answer to each of the questions you will hear.

1. A. $29.   B. $50.   C. $25.   D. $30.
2. A. Once.   B. Twice.   C. Three times.   D. None.
3. A. 163 pounds.   B. 148 pounds.   C. 104 pounds.   D. 113 pounds.
4. A. $60.   B. $174.   C. $140.   D. $170.
5. A. Fifteen minutes.   B. Twenty minutes.
   C. Ten minutes.   D. Twenty-five minutes.
6. A. Four years old. B. Five years old. C. Three years old. D. Six years old.
7. A. 80.   B. 160.   C. 40.   D. 18.
8. A. 65.   B. 50.   C. 100.   D. 30.
9. A. Five fifty-one. B. Five sixty-one. C. Four sixty-one. D. Six sixty-one.
10. A. $390.   B. $99.   C. $198.   D. $285.

Unit 2 Emotions Have Taught Mankind to Reason

Part I Door to Wisdom

Read, think and interpret your understanding of the following proverbs and well-known sayings.

1. Love looks through a telescope; envy through a microscope.
   —Josh Billings

2. A man is about as big as the things that make him angry.
   —Winston Churchill

3. Anger and intolerance are the enemies of correct understanding.
   —Mahatma Gandhi

4. There is only one happiness in this life, to love and be loved.
   —George Sand

5. Great anger is more destructive than the sword.
   —Indian Proverb

Part II Join in the Dialogue

Dialogue 1

Ex. 1 Listen to the dialogue and choose the best answers to the following questions.

1. A. He is in debt.
   B. He has to resign as Chairman of the Students' Union.
   C. He lags behind in his studies.

D. He has to sell his car.

2. A. The first year.   B. The fourth year.
  C. The second year.   D. The third year.

3. A. He can't get along with his schoolmate in the Union.
  B. He can't do the work well.
  C. He is in debt.
  D. He can't get through his studies.

4. A. Mathematics.   B. Physics.   C. Electronics.   D. Economics.

Ex. 2 Make dialogues on the following topics.

1. Talk about what makes you feel depressed in your life.
2. Talk about how to get rid of depression.

Dialogue 2

Ex. 1 Listen to the dialogue and decide whether the following statement is true or false.

1. Tonight is the last performance of *Fiddler on the Roof*.
2. The man called the theater.
3. There were tickets available a week ago.
4. The man would like to go to the theater tonight.
5. The man is probably alone in the city.
6. Maryann works at the Visitor Information Center.
7. There are many tickets available for tonight.
8. The man will pick up the ticket now.
9. The man lives in Phoenix.
10. The man thinks that people in the city are not usually helpful.

Ex. 2 Listen to the dialogue and answer the following questions.

1. Where does the conversation take place?
2. Where did the man get the information about the performance?
3. Who are the two speakers?
4. Why does the man feel sorry by the end of the conversation?
5. How do you describe the two speakers' attitude?

Ex. 3 Make dialogues on the following topics.

1. What do you do when you are angry? Talk about whether these means are helpful.
2. How to avoid being angry?

Emotions Have Taught Mankind to Reason

Part III Listen and Discuss

Passage 1

Glossary

disequilibrate 使失去平衡   homeostasis 体内平衡
cobweb 蜘蛛网,困惑

Ex. 1 Listen to the passage and choose the best answers to the following questions.

1. American men don't cry because they believe _____.
   A. crying is characteristic of the female
   B. crying is a mark of weakness
   C. crying is impermissible
   D. crying is inexcusable

2. American men are unable to cry because _____.
   A. they are trained not to cry whenever they feel like doing so
   B. their biological time clock causes them to lose the ability as they grow older
   C. they have been discouraged from crying since they were child
   D. they think it unnecessary to cry when they want to

3. Being unable to cry is bad because _____.
   A. it interferes with the damage to the organism.
   B. it prevents the human being from understanding the natural need of crying
   C. it deprives the human being of his ability to restore his emotional balance
   D. it lessens one's ability to be human

4. What can be learned from the passage?
   A. Inability to cry is unhealthy and makes one less human.
   B. Women and children are allowed to cry in all circumstances.
   C. The trained incapacity to cry is slightly damaging to health.
   D. American parents are ignorant of the natural necessity of crying.

Ex. 2 Make dialogues on the following topics.

1. What's your opinion on man's crying?
2. What are some of the things that will make you cry?
3. Share with your partner one thing that moves you into tears.

Passage 2

Ex. 1 Listen to the passage and fill in the blanks with the word(s) you've heard

What makes people happier: money or having happy friends and neighbors? Researchers from

Harvard University and the University of California, San Diego, have found an answer as part of a study.

Nicholas Christakis and James Fowler based the study on the ___1___ of almost five thousand people. They used information ___2___ over a period of twenty years, until two thousand three, in the Framingham Heart Study. That study began sixty years ago in Framingham, Massachusetts, to learn more about the risks of heart attack and ___3___.

The new study found that friends of happy people had a greater chance of being happy themselves. And the smaller the ___4___ between friends, the larger the effect they had on each other's happiness.

For example, a person was twenty percent more likely to feel happy if a friend living within one and a half kilometers was also happy. Having a happy neighbor who lived next door increased an individual's chance of being happy by thirty-four percent. The effects of friends' happiness ___5___ for up to a year.

The researchers found that happiness really is ___6___. Sadness also spread among friends, but not as much as happiness.

The study showed that having an extra five thousand dollars increased a person's chances of becoming ___7___ by about two percent. Another finding is that people who are ___8___ or work together do not have as much of an effect on happiness as friends do.

The study is described as the first to demonstrate the indirect ___9___ of happiness. In other words, that _____10_____.

Earlier studies by the two researchers described _____11_____.
The new study shows that _____12_____
—a virus people would be happy to catch.

Ex. 2   Make dialogues on the following topics.

1. How do you understand happiness?
2. Do you agree that unhappiness originates from men's greed?
3. What can graduate students do to acquire utmost happiness?

Part IV   Watch and Debate

Ex. 1   Watch the video about self-esteem, and answer the following questions.

1. Why did the speaker say self-esteem is a paradox?

2. How could we break down self-esteem to its components according to the speaker?

3. What are the three kinds of self-esteem mentioned by the speaker?

4. What will an author with independence self-esteem do about the book he publishes?

5. Which is the highest level of self-esteem?

_____

Ex. 2 Watch the video again and express your opinions on the following questions.
1. What role does self-esteem play in your research work?
2. What role does self-esteem play in making you a happy person?

Part V Extracurricular Listening

Listen to the following 10 short dialogues and choose the best answer to each of the questions you will hear.

1. A. At 4 pm.　　　　B. At 6 pm.　　　　C. At 3 pm.　　　　D. At 2 pm.
2. A. In October.　　　B. In December.　　C. In February.　　D. In January.
3. A. At 2 pm.　　　　B. At 12 pm.　　　　C. At 5 pm.　　　　D. At 7 pm.
4. A. In 15 minutes.　 B. In 10 minutes.　 C. In 20 minutes.　D. In 5 minutes.
5. A. 6:45.　　　　　　B. 6:55.　　　　　　C. 7:00.　　　　　　D. 6:50.
6. A. At 7:00.　　　　 B. At 7:45.　　　　 C. At 8:00.　　　　 D. At 9:00.
7. A. Tuesday.　　　　B. Thursday.　　　　C. Wednesday.　　 D. Friday.
8. A. 9:15.　　　　　　B. 9:35.　　　　　　C. 9:30.　　　　　　D. 9:00.
9. A. After a practice.　　　　　　　　　　B. After a class.
　　C. After an examination.　　　　　　 D. After a sports meet.
10. A. At 4:30.　　　　B. At 5 o'clock.　　C. At 5:30.　　　　D. At 4 o'clock.

Unit 3 Education Is the Transmission of Civilization

Part I Door to Wisdom

Read, think and interpret your understanding of the following proverbs and well-known sayings.

1. It is a miracle that curiosity survives formal education.

   —Albert Einstein

2. Education is not preparation for life; education is life itself.

   —John Dewey

3. Education is not the filling of a pail, but the lighting of a fire.

   —William Butler Yeats

4. The roots of education are bitter, but the fruit is sweet.

   —Aristotle

5. The direction in which education starts a man will determine his future.

   —Plato

Unit 3 Education Is the Transmission of Civilization

Part II Join in the Dialogue

China's Education Reform on Gaokao

Gaokao (College Entrance Exam) is an annual exam in China. It takes place in early June each year, when people are expressing their best wishes to students. However, there are always debates as to when and how to reform China's education. Will Gaokao produce and cultivate talents rather than just taking exams? Or is it a good method? To answer those questions, we are joined in the studio by Dr. Wu from Arizona State University and Evans Carl from New Yorkers.

Dialogue 1

Glossary

horn 喇叭   overstretch 过分紧张
legitimacy 合法性   extra-curricular 课外的

Ex. 1 Listen to the following dialogue and choose the best answer to each of the questions you will hear.

1. What is the interview mainly about?
   A. Students should be given more opportunities for admission and be well-rounded socially.
   B. Parents are trying hard to help their children with their college entrance exams.
   C. Schools should cancel exam systems.
   D. The government is launching educational reform in China.
2. The whole society is paying huge attention to the students, _____.
   A. only to put too much pressure on them
   B. only to put too much care for them
   C. both A and B
   D. in order to show love for the next generation
3. 30 years ago, _____ of students could get the entrance.
   A. only 15%   B. only 5%   C. about 80%   D. about 18%
4. Going to college is thought of as a _____ by families and society.
   A. pressure   B. success
   C. pride   D. measure of students' abilities
5. Many parents and their children go to Confucius temples in order to _____.
   A. ask for their fates   B. relax themselves
   C. pray for their exams   D. relieve their pressure
6. The exam-oriented system can be changed by _____.
   A. adding more admission criteria   B. measuring extra-curricular activities
   C. praying for the best school   D. both A and B

Ex. 2 Make dialogues on the following topics.

1. When did you go in for Gaokao? Please tell your story and experience during your Gaokao.
2. Why do you think our parents, teachers and even society attach so much importance to Gaokao? Do you think Gaokao is the best way to create a bright future?
3. What disadvantages does exam-oriented or exam-driven education bring to us? Why does our education need to be reformed?
4. What can we learn from the United States in terms of evaluation criteria?

Dialogue 2

Glossary

token 标志,标记   as the same token 由于同样的原因
recruit 招收   counterpart（在职位、地位等方面）相对等的
preserve 保护,保存人,对手方

Ex. 1 Listen to the following dialogue and fill in each blank with the word(s) you've heard.

A: Just now we've been talking about the general picture of Gaokao in relation to China's education reform. Now let's go to some of very interesting questions ___1___ Gaokao. One of the things is 50,000 Chinese students went to universities in the United States in 2008. Those are high school students, of course. But this year, I mean 2009, it's 4 times more, ___2___. And this year, 2010, we do not know the ___3___ yet. How shall we see this trend: Chinese students are all going abroad at very young age?

B: Ah, I, I wouldn't say all of them, but some of them are up to facing the pressure of trying to see the world using their own eyes. I think it's a good kind of trend. Two years ago, I led one group of American students to have an exchange program with Tsinghua University and also Fudan University. When I see the ___4___ discussions and debates, I see the difference ___5___ people's self-confidence and how they kind of express their ideas. For the foreigners, especially under the American education system, they're more kind of ___6___ and self-confident, but as the same token, the Chinese students, they have very solid background and knowledge in terms of history or geography, a lot of things. So, when we put them together, we can see this kind of difference.

A: What quality is more important, Evans?

C: Well, the truth is there're a lot of things I've seen when I go to Chinese universities that I admire. I mean, frankly, the level the students give their professors is very ___7___. That is the element we want very much to celebrate and preserve. I think there are also obviously elements of western education system Chinese students are seeking, such as a more ___8___ study plan. In a sense, if you major in economics, you can decide to pursue something in history, something in completely far fields.

A: We see so many Chinese young students going abroad. Some of them are the best students here in China. So, the thing is, will China be able to _____9_____

· 14 ·

Education Is the Transmission of Civilization

from this country? Do you think Chinese universities in that way can compete against international counterparts?

C: I think they can compete. I mean, for one thing, simply the number is on their side. They have a huge number of very qualified students every year who are going to seek Tsinghua and Beida. The other thing is competition is very healthy. I mean, for a long time, Chinese universities existed in a vacuum. They've only been competing against each other. Now they are facing competition worldwide. That's going to help them. I think, at some level it's going to help universities in the United States. What we've seen is the huge increased number of students going to the U.S. and the West to study. That's positive, because I think _____**10**_____.

A: But we have Dr. Wu already teaching at Arizona State University instead in Beijing.

B: Yeah. Actually there is another angle to look at this issue. On the one hand, there are more and more middle school students going abroad to get their college degrees. But at the same time, there is more and more interest from foreigners. Especially _____**11**_____. So I think this is a very healthy kind of exchange.

Ex. 2 Make dialogues on the following topics.

1. How much do you know about the major differences between Chinese students and American students? What have caused these differences as far as you think?
2. Why are more and more young Chinese students going abroad to study? Do you think it is good or bad for both Chinese students and universities?
3. In what way do you think "competition is very healthy"?

Part III Listen and Discuss

Amy Chua(蔡美儿) is Professor of Law at Yale Law School. She is the author of *Battle Hymn of the Tiger Mother* and a noted expert in the fields of international business, ethnic conflict, and

globalization. She lives in New Haven, Connecticut, with her husband and two daughters.

Battle Hymn of the Tiger Mother is published in 2011. The complete subtitle of the book is: "This is a story about a mother, two daughters, and two dogs. This was supposed to be a story of how Chinese parents are better at raising kids than Western ones. But instead, it's about a bitter clash of cultures, a fleeting taste of glory, and how I was humbled by a thirteen-year-old."

Passage 1

Ex. 1   Listen to the following passage and choose the best answer to each of the questions you will hear.

1. Chua's way of treating her children _____.
   A. came from her husband   B. caused her husband's strong criticism
   C. was taught by the monster   D. came from her own family education
2. If Chua and her sisters spoke any _____ at home, they would be punished by their father.
   A. Chinese   B. English   C. Cantonese   D. Spanish
3. When Chua received second prize at school, her _____.
   A. father was very angry   B. mother was very angry
   C. father was very happy   D. mother was very happy
4. From tiger mother's approach, practice means _____, which is crucial for excellence.
   A. more testing   B. more homework C. repetition   D. more writing
5. Chua's book caused _____.
   A. worldwide attention   B. anger from some people
   C. gratitude from many people   D. A, B, and C
6. Many parents and educators in China _____.
   A. agree with what Chua is doing   B. partly agree with what Chua is doing
   C. mostly agree with what Chua is doing   D. disagree with what Chua is doing

Ex. 2   Discuss with your partner(s) and express your opinions on the following topics.

1. What is free-range parenting? What is helicopter parenting? Which one do you prefer? Why?
2. In 2008, there appeared a website named "Anti-parents(父母皆祸害)". Are parents evil? What should parents be like from your point of view?

Passage 2

Ex. 1   Listen to the following passage and fill in each blank with the word(s) you've heard.

Chua's reports from the trenches of authoritarian parenthood are indeed __1__ in their candid admission of maternal ruthlessness. But there's something else behind the intense reaction to Tiger Mother, which has shot to the top of __2__ lists even as it's been denounced on the Internet. Though Chua was born and raised in the U.S., what she __3__ as traditional "Chinese parenting" has hit hard at a national sore spot: our fears about losing ground to China and other rising powers and about adequately preparing our children to __4__ in the global economy. Her stories of never accepting a

· 16 ·

Education Is the Transmission of Civilization

grade lower than an A, of __5__ on hours of math and spelling drills and piano and violin practice each day (weekends and vacations included), of not allowing playdates or sleepovers or television or computer games or even school plays, for goodness' sake, have left many readers outraged but also __6__. The tiger mother's cubs are being raised to rule the world, the book clearly implies, while the offspring of "weak-willed," "indulgent" Westerners are growing up __7__ to compete in a fierce global __8__.

For though Chua hails the virtues of "the Chinese way," the story she tells is quintessentially American. It's the tale of an immigrant striver, determined to make a better life for himself and his family __9__. "I remember my father working every night until 3 in the morning; I remember him wearing the same pair of shoes for eight years," Chua says. "__10__."

Hard work, persistence, no patience for excuses: whether Chinese or American, __11__.

Ex. 2 Make dialogues on the following topics.

1. What do you think of Chua's family education?
2. Why is Chua so strict with her daughters?
3. Are Chinese parents and authorities in favor of her way of education? Why?

Part Ⅳ Watch and Debate

Glossary

mellifluous 甜美的,流畅的	mash 用力压
scratchy 发刮擦声的	floppy 松软的
edgy 紧张不安的	longevity 长寿
earlobe 耳垂	snipe 斗嘴
caviar 鱼子酱	juvenile delinquent 少年犯
hiss (用嘘声)责骂	shard 碎片
spurn 蔑视,摒弃	sprint 疾跑
sandal 凉鞋	mausoleum 陵墓

Ex. 1 Watch the video and choose the best answer to each of the following questions.

1. Tiger Mother Chua screamed "relax", when _____.
   A. her daughter Lulu was teaching the violin
   B. her daughter Lulu was learning to play the violin
   C. she was teaching Lulu to play the violin
   D. Mr. Shugart was teaching Lulu to play the piano

2. Lulu felt annoyed at playing music _____.
   A. when Mr. Shugart criticized her
   B. when she failed to produce the right tone
   C. when she had no time for her homework
   D. even when Chua was present and didn't say anything

3. Chua stopped arguing with her daughter Lulu, because _____.
   A. she thought she was wrong
   B. she hoped Lulu could continue playing music
   C. she had to leave
   D. Lulu was right

4. Chua is often asked a question _____.
   A. whether everything she did is for her daughter or herself
   B. why she forced her daughter to learn music
   C. why she wanted Lulu to learn to play the piano rather than the violin
   D. how she taught Lulu to play music so well

5. "You're both lucky that I have enormous longevity" means that _____.
   A. Chua can take off her own youth to work for the two daughters
   B. Chua can spend more time making money
   C. Chua can do housework while her daughters have enough time to play music
   D. Chua can see her daughters graduate from university

6. Chua thinks _____.
   A. western way of education is better than the Chinese one
   B. western way of education is as good as the Chinese one
   C. Chinese way of education is better than the western one
   D. Chinese way of education is as good as the western one

Ex. 2 Watch the video again and complete each blank with what you've heard in the video clip.

1. I tried to be goofy and easygoing, the mood my girls most like me in, _____ _____ about what they were wearing or how many times they said "like". But there was something ill-fated about that day.

2. We decided to go to Red Square. Lulu and Sophia kept sniping at each other, which irritated me. Actually, _____—teenagers my size (in Sophia's case, three inches taller), instead of cute little girls. "It goes so fast," older friends had always said wistfully.

3. After roaming around for a bit, we sat down at an outdoor café. It was attached to the famous GUM shopping mall, which is housed in a palatial, arcade-lined nineteenth-century building _____ _____ Red Square, directly across from the fortresslike Kremlin.

4. "Why?" Lulu asked defiantly. "Why do you care so much? You can't force me to eat something." _____. Could I not get Lulu to do even one tiny thing? "You're behaving like a juvenile delinquent. Try one egg now."

5. "Amy," Jed began diplomatically, "everyone's tired. Why don't we just—" I broke in, "Do you know _____ if they saw this, Lulu—you publicly disobeying me? With that look on your face? You're only hurting yourself…"

6. A lump rose in my throat. Lulu saw it, but she went on. "You're a terrible mother. You're

selfish. _____. What—you can't believe how ungrateful I am? After all you've done for me? Everything you say you do for me is actually for yourself."

7. I'd made a career out of spurning the kind of Western parents who can't control their kids. Now I had _____ of all.

Ex. 3 Express your opinions on the following questions after watching the video.

1. What do you think of the sharp conflict between Tiger Mother Chua and her daughter Lulu? Who do you think is right?
2. How do you think children should behave in a traditional Chinese family or a Western family? Which do you prefer?
3. What is the popular way of education in ordinary Chinese families in your eyes? What is family education in your family?

Part V Extracurricular Listening

Listen to the following 10 short dialogues and choose the best answer to each of the questions you will hear.

1. A. In a hotel.   B. At home.
   C. In a hospital.   D. In his own office.
2. A. In a park.   B. In a museum.
   C. In a zoo.   D. In a pet shop.
3. A. Near a railway station. B. Near an airport.
   C. Near a super highway.   D. Near a bus station.
4. A. In a supermarket.   B. In a hotel.
   C. In a department store.   D. In a Customs.
5. A. In an art museum.   B. In a library.
   C. In a newspaper office.   D. In a bookstore.
6. A. Near an art gallery.   B. In front of a library.
   C. Outside a reading-room. D. Outside a bookstore.
7. A. Gas station.   B. Police station.
   C. Lost and found office.   D. Bar.
8. A. In a classroom.   B. In the post office.
   C. In a courtroom.   D. In a lawyer's office.
9. A. In a machine repair shop. B. In an art gallery.
   C. In a hardware store.   D. In a warehouse.
10. A. In a pet shop.   B. In a medical laboratory.
    C. In a veterinary.   D. In a pediatrician's office.

Unit 4 Work to Become, Not to Acquire

Part I Door to Wisdom

Read, think and interpret your understanding of the following proverbs and well-known sayings.

1. Be more dedicated to making solid achievements than in running after swift but synthetic happiness.
   —Abdul Kalam
2. Defeat is not the worst of failures. Not to have tried is the true failure.
   —George Edward Woodberry
3. All lasting business is built on friendship.
   —Alfred A. Montapert
4. Choose a job you love, and you will never have to work a day in your life.
   —Confucius
5. Recession is when a neighbor loses his job. Depression is when you lose yours.
   —Ronald Reagan

Part II Join in the Dialogue

Dialogue 1

Ex. 1 Listen to the dialogue and choose the best answer to the following questions.

1. What impresses the man about the girl at the beginning of the conversation?
   A. The girl arrives promptly on time.
   B. The girl carries her own business cards.

Work to Become, Not to Acquire Unit 4

C. The girl comes prepared to cook for the kids.

D. The girl can work on a Friday evening.

2. How often has Kelly babysat for Mr. Adams in the past?

   A. Never. B. One or two times.

   C. On a regular basis. D. Not mentioned.

3. According to the girl's financial consultant, why should she charge more for babysitting?

   A. She does some housework while the parents are out.

   B. She purchases groceries for evening meals.

   C. She provides special educational entertainment.

   D. She has received certificate in babysitting.

4. What specialized training has the girl received to become a babysitter?

   A. Educational. B. Emotional. C. Medical. D. Dietary.

5. How much is the girl's rate increase?

   A. One dollar per child per hour. B. Two dollars per child per hour.

   C. One dollar per night. D. Two dollars per night.

Ex. 2 Make a dialogue on the following topics.

1. Talk with your partner about whether it is necessary for college and graduate students to have a part-time job.

2. Share with your partner about the part-time job you once had.

Dialogue 2

Ex. 1 Listen to the dialogue and choose the best answer to the following questions.

1. In which field is the man looking for a job?

   A. Education. B. Medicine.

   C. Technology. D. Service.

2. Which statement best describes the pay for the job?

   A. Employees can receive periodic pay increases based on their work.

   B. The salary for the position is above the industry average.

   C. Workers are paid on a commission basis depending on their sales.

   D. The payment is fixed.

3. What are some of the benefits that the company provides?

   A. Insurance, paid vacation, and a company vehicle.

   B. Paid vacation, opportunities for promotion, and insurance.

   C. Opportunities for advancement, insurance, and a free bus pass.

   D. Paid vacation, insurance, and a free bus pass.

4. What does the future hold for the industry that he is considering?

   A. Growing, yet uncertain. B. Expanding and secure.

   C. Contracting, yet stable. D. Not mentioned.

5. From the conversation, what do we know about the man's educational background?

   A. He dropped out of high school. B. He dropped out of junior middle school.

   C. He has a college degree. D. He dropped out of college.

Ex. 2 Make a conversation based on each of the following topics.

1. Your classmate just had a job interview, and you asked him/her about the job interview.
2. You and your friend are both graduate students. You interview your friend about his/her reason to choose to continue the study.

Part III Listen and Discuss

Passage 1

Ex. 1 Listen to the passage and correct errors in each of the following statements.

1. The company was founded in 1996.
2. They have a turnover of 800,000 euros a year.
3. Malcolm helped in the marketing department in Paris.
4. Malcolm had to secure the advertising deals.
5. He spoke French on the phone every day.
6. He observed the marketing team brainstorm ideas for advertising new products.
7. He ate lunch in the office canteen.
8. The main disadvantage was that he didn't meet people from other departments.

Ex. 2 Have a discussion with your partner about the following topics.

1. Discuss with your partner about the other dos and don'ts about job interviews.
2. Share with your partner about your experience as an intern.

Passage 2

Ex. 1 Listen to the passage and choose the best answer to the following questions.

1. Why do angry customers yell at you?

   A. Because they are angry with you.

   B. Because they are angry with your organization.

   C. Because you don't listen to them.

   D. Because you are the source of their anger.

2. What does an angry customer want most?

   A. To solve the problem.

   B. To complain about the product or people.

   C. To be heard, and acknowledged.

   D. To humiliate people.

Work to Become, Not to Acquire   Unit 4

3. What if you just try your best to solve the problem when angry customers yell at you about problems?
   A. They may become even more angry.
   B. They will feel satisfied.
   C. They will calm down.
   D. They will apologize for being angry at you.
4. What should you do to prevent a potential hostile situation from escalating into a major conflict?
   A. Prepare yourself for the possible hostile behavior.
   B. Smile and remember never to get angry at them.
   C. Try to solve the problem.
   D. Ask the customer to talk to the supervisor.
5. When in contact with an angry customer, which of the following should be done?
   A. Solve the problem in a cold way.
   B. Try to show understanding.
   C. Prevent the customer mentioning the problem.
   D. Encourage the customer to calm down.

Ex. 2　Have a discussion with your partner about the following topics.
1. Talk with your partner about your experiences of complaining about problematic goods or service and how you liked their way of making things done.
2. Imagine you buy a laptop, but the battery can be used for half an hour only instead of two hours as it promises. You complain to the seller about it.

Part IV　Watch and Debate

Ex. 1　Watch the video and complete each sentence with the exact word you've heard in the video.
1. Never assume the interviewers have read your CV. So feel free to talk about things in the CV. _____ on them, _____ them, use some examples there.
2. Prepare at least three _____ questions that they may ask you. Think about what you really want to know. Do you want to know the _____, the culture of the company, what is important for you to know, and may it _____.
3. Do you research. Make sure you've done your research before the interview. So you know all the things that are _____ about the company. And make sure throughout the interview, you bring about little slippys about their _____, their _____ to show them you know what they are about.

Ex. 2　Watch the video again and express your opinions on the following questions.
1. Do you think we should listen more or talk more when we are in an interview?
2. Among the things mentioned, which do you think is the most important? Debate with your partners on that.

Part V Extracurricular Listening

Listen to the following 10 short dialogues and choose the best answer to each of the questions you will hear.

1. A. A plumber. B. An electrician.
   C. A telephone repairman. D. A salesman.

2. A. Parents. B. Friends.
   C. Colleagues. D. Neighbors.

3. A. His advisor. B. His teacher.
   C. His partner. D. His boss.

4. A. A house repairman. B. A paperhanger.
   C. A house painter. D. A carpenter.

5. A. The woman herself. B. Her neighbor.
   C. A professional hairstylist. D. Her friend.

6. A. A traffic guard. B. A garage mechanic.
   C. A taxi driver. D. A car salesclerk.

7. A. A pharmacist. B. A salesman.
   C. A doctor. D. A librarian.

8. A. An electrician. B. A porter.
   C. A plumber. D. A bellboy.

9. A. Her neighbor. B. A tourist agent.
   C. A housekeeper. D. A real estate agent.

10. A. George. B. George's father.
    C. George's father-in-law. D. George's wife.

· 24 ·

Unit 5 While There's Life, There's Hope

Part I Door to Wisdom

Read, think and interpret your understanding of the following proverbs and well-known sayings.

1. People who live in glass houses shouldn't throw stones.

   —George Herbert

2. When life hands you lemons, make lemonade.
3. Life is like a box of chocolate; it's full of surprises.

   —Forest Gump

4. Don't be picky about what you wear and eat, be it square or round.

   —Chinese proverb

5. Life consists not in holding good cards, but in playing well those you hold.

   —J. Billings

Part II Join in the Dialogue

People all around the world like to live in cities, because of convenience and comfort. Some people prefer traveling to staying just in one place during their lives. They travel by car, boat, train or plane.

Dialogue 1

Glossary

plummet 骤然跌落   fleece 敲竹杠
prestige 威望   get stuck 受骗

Ex. 1 Listen to the following dialogue and choose the best answer to each of the questions you will hear.

1. The possible title for the interview would be?
   A. Buying a new car.
   B. Buying a car or leasing a car.
   C. Buying a used car.
   D. Leasing a car.

2. What can we conclude from the interview?
   A. The adviser, Dave, suggests buying a new car.
   B. The adviser, Dave, suggests buying a used car.
   C. The adviser, Dave, suggests leasing a car.
   D. The adviser, Dave, suggests not getting involved with car.

3. According to the adviser Dave, new cars go down in value like a rock in the first 4 years, losing _____.
   A. 13% of the value
   B. 16% of the value
   C. 30% of the value
   D. 60% of the value

4. How does the adviser Dave think of leasing a car?
   A. Leasing a car is the most cool way to operate a vehicle.
   B. Leasing a car is the most economical way to operate a vehicle.
   C. Leasing a car is the most expensive way to operate a vehicle.
   D. Leasing a car is the most wonderful way to operate a vehicle.

5. The adviser Dave suggests that it is good to buy a used car of _____.
   A. 1 year old
   B. 2 years old
   C. 5 years old
   D. 10 years old

6. According the adviser Dave, when we buy cars, we should _____.
   A. make a loan
   B. pay in cash
   C. pay in credit
   D. pay half in cash and the rest in credit

Ex. 2 Make dialogues on the following topics.

1. If you have enough money after your graduation, which do you prefer, buying a car or leasing a car? Give your reasons.
2. If you want to buy a car, which one is your best choice, a brand-new car or a used car? Give your reasons.

While There's Life, There's Hope

Unit 5

Dialogue 2

Glossary

tab 跳格键   credit 赞同
handicap 障碍   fantasy 幻想

Ex. 1 Listen to the following dialogue and choose the best answer to each of the questions you will hear.

1. What does it mean by saying "South Korea is one of the most wired countries"?
    A. It means South Korea's main product is wires.
    B. It means South Korea's networked system is widespread.
    C. It means South Korea is closely connected to other countries.
    D. It means South Korea is in urgent need of telegram.
2. What does the report mainly talk about?
    A. Accessible science and technology.
    B. Shopping online at home.
    C. Networked homes in South Korea.
    D. Comfortable living in South Korea.
3. What's the "web pad" that Chung Sung-young uses?
    A. It is a computer located in her kitchen.
    B. It is a radio she always listens to.
    C. It is a book on cooking recipe.
    D. It is a portable Internet appliance.
4. Which of the following is NOT mentioned in the interview?
    A. Chung Sung-young's son exchanges email with others.
    B. Chung Sung-young uses Internet device to order groceries online.
    C. Chung Sung-young's husband gets news from the web pad.
    D. Chung Sung-young's daughter plays games on the Internet.
5. What results in Korea's super-connected environment according to the industry officials?
    A. Low house prices.   B. Korea's dense population.
    C. Low-cost construction.   D. Wise Korean people.
6. What are the regulations the Korean government issued aimed to?
    A. To speed up the Internet.
    B. To construct more apartments.
    C. To encourage apartments' access to speedy Internet.
    D. To spread its Internet system to other countries.

Ex. 2 Make dialogues on the following topics.

1. Tell your classmates about the convenience and inconvenience of Internet at home.

2. Do you want your house be "wired"? Why? Give your reasons.

Part III Listen and Discuss

Passage 1

Ex. 1 Listen to the following passage and choose the best answer to each of the questions you will hear.

1. A. Far away from the city.   B. Inside the city.
   C. Near the city.   D. In the city center.
2. A. Traveling by bus or car.   B. Living in an expensive way.
   C. Enjoying city life.   D. Convenient transportation.
3. A. The local newspaper.   B. The TV programme on Saturday.
   C. The Sunday magazine.   D. The radio programme on Saturday.
4. A. When they are on holidays.   B. On Sunday morning.
   C. On Saturday night.   D. As soon as they have information.

Ex. 2 Make dialogues on the following topics.

1. Where do you prefer to be accommodated in your future work, near or far away from your working place? Give your reasons.
2. When you look for sources of houses and apartments, what do you usually do? Why?

Passage 2

Ex. 1 Listen to the following passage and fill in each blank with the word(s) you've heard.

　　Few Americans remain in one position or one place for a lifetime. We move from town to city to __1__, from a job in one region to a better job elsewhere, from the home where we __2__ our children to the home where we plan to live in __3__. With each move we are forever making new friends, who become part of our life at that time. Today millions of Americans __4__ abroad, not only to see new sights but also to make friends. No one really expects a holiday trip to produce a close friend. But surely the beginning of a friendship is possible, isn't it? The answer is of course __5__. The difficulty when strangers from two countries meet is not a lack of __6__ of friendship, but of different expectations about what __7__ friendship and how it comes into being. In those European countries that Americans are most likely to visit, friendship is quite sharply distinguished from other more __8__ relations, and is differently related to family life. _____9_____.

　　But as we use the word, "friend" can be applied to a wide range of relationships—_____10_____, to a man or woman, to a trusted confidant. There are real differences among these relations for Americans—a friendship may be superficial, casual, situational or deep and enduring. _____11_____.

Ex. 2 Make dialogues on the following topics.

1. Do you like American way of living and surviving? Why?
2. Which place in China, do you think, is the best place for you to live in? Give your reasons.

Part IV Watch and Debate

  City is often defined as tall buildings and heavy traffic while countryside as resorted places. The Empire State Building is a 102-story landmark Art Deco skyscraper in New York City, the United States, at the intersection of Fifth Avenue and West 34th Street. It is 1,250 ft (381 meters) tall. Its name is derived from the nickname for New York, the Empire State. It stood as the world's tallest building for more than 40 years, from its completion in 1931 until construction of the World Trade Center's North Tower was completed in 1972. Following the destruction of the World Trade Center in 2001, the Empire State Building once again became the tallest building in New York City.

Glossary

skycraper 摩天大楼   jostle 撞，挤
streetscape 街景   archetypal 原型的
premium 质优价高的   majestically 雄伟地
reign 占优势

Ex. 1 Watch the video and choose the best answer to each of the following questions.

1. Why is the Empire State Building so famous and unique?
   A. Because of its elegant, simple, subtle and powerful design.
   B. Because of its long history as the tallest building in the world.
   C. Because it symbolizes the very idea of skyscrapers all over the world.
   D. All of the above.
2. What makes New York different from any other city in the world according to the video clip?
   A. The endless tall buildings.   B. The noticeable open space.
   C. The modern style of the buildings.   D. Its history and location.
3. According to this video, which is the tallest building in New York now?
   A. The World Trade Center.   B. The Walter Chrysler Building.
   C. The Empire State Building.   D. The United Nations Building.
4. What was the main reason for the existence of the skyscrapers in Manhattan?
   A. Tall buildings could beautify the city.
   B. There wasn't enough office space on the crowded island.
   C. Famous architects liked taller buildings.
   D. The Government encouraged businessmen to invest.
5. When was the Empire State Building completed?
   A. On May 1st, 1931.   B. In April, 1931.
   C. In 1929.   D. In the 1920s.

6. Which of the following statements is true about the Empire State Building?
   A. It was built faster than any other skyscrapers.
   B. It brought profits to its owner immediately.
   C. It was taller than the World Trade Center.
   D. It is always fully rented.

Ex. 2 Watch the video and complete each blank with what you've heard in the video clip.

New York, more than any other city __1__ skyscrapers. They are not towers standing alone __2__. They are big buildings that come together to fill streets, to make streets, to make a whole urban environment of total skycraperdom, of a sort that you see in Manhattan but almost __3__ in America. The buildings are built right out to the street. They kind of jostle each other for position, and together form a whole complete streetscape of towers. In these New York towers, of course, the view from a lot of windows, is only of somebody else's windows.

Getting those windows up __4__ fast enough was one of the problems for the revolutionary Empire State Building.

The Empire State Building is more than 70 years old. It's still the most famous skyscraper in the world. It's a long time since it's been the __5__ building in the world. But it's still the archetypal skyscraper, the building that symbolizes the New York skyline, and symbolizes the very idea of skyscrapers __6__.

The 1920s were boom years. Pressure for office space on the crowded island of Manhattan was __7__ taller and taller buildings. Building the biggest brought the prestige and also profits.

For a time, it seemed that the prize would go to the car-maker Walter Chrysler, with his magnificent Lexington Avenue office block, at a __8__ feet the tallest building in the world, and still one of __9__. But even as the Chrysler building opened its doors in 1929, architects would work on an even taller skyscraper. Legend has it that William Lamb __10__ a humble pencil, and decided that was how his new building should look.

Ex. 3 Watch the video again and express your opinions on the following questions.

1. Please describe the city you live in and tell your classmates about the most wonderful building in the city.
2. Do you like city life? Give your reasons.
3. What is the most serious problem existing in your city? Give your suggestions on the solution of the problem.

Part V Extracurricular Listening

Listen to the following 10 short dialogues and choose the best answer to each of the questions you will hear.

1. A. She's an apartment manager.   B. She's a shopkeeper.
   C. She's a real estate agent.   D. She's a maid.

Unit 5
While There's Life, There's Hope

2. A. He's a publisher.   B. He's an author.
   C. He's an automobile collector.   D. He's bookseller.
3. A. Telephone operator.   B. Waitress.
   C. Secretary.   D. Maid.
4. A. A thief.   B. A locker.
   C. A patrolman.   D. A doorkeeper.
5. A. A building inspector.   B. A window cleaner.
   C. An acrobat.   D. A builder.
6. A. He's a typewriter repairman.   B. He's a typist.
   C. He's a carpenter.   D. He's a gardener.
7. A. He's a mailman.   B. He's a writer.
   C. He's a telephone repairman.   D. He's a waiter.
8. A. A telephone operator.   B. A travel agent.
   C. A bus conductor.   D. A flight attendant.
9. A. He's a professor.   B. He's a reporter.
   C. He's a librarian.   D. He's an accountant.
10. A. Dentist.   B. Physician.
    C. Pharmacist.   D. Surgeon.

Unit 6 Life Well Spent Is Long

Part I Door to Wisdom

Read, think and interpret your understanding of the following proverbs and well-known sayings.

1. One of the symptoms of an approaching nervous breakdown is the belief that one's work is terribly important.

   —Bertrand Russell

2. And in the end it's not the years in your life that count. It's the life in your years.

   —Abraham Lincoln

3. Change is not merely necessary to life, it is life.

   —Alvin Toffler

4. He who controls others may be powerful, but he who has mastered himself is mightier still.

   —Lao Tzu

5. Life isn't about finding yourself. Life is about creating yourself.

   —George Bernard Shaw

Part II Join in the Dialogue

Public health is the science and art of preventing disease, prolonging life and promoting health

Life Well Spent Is Long

Unit 6

through the organized efforts and informed choices of society, organizations, public and private, communities and individuals. It is concerned with threats to health based on population health analysis. Public health incorporates the interdisciplinary(跨学科的) approaches of epidemiology(流行病学), biostatistics(生物统计学) and health services. Environmental health, community health, behavioral health, and occupational health are other important subfields.

The focus of public health intervention is to improve health and quality of life through the prevention and treatment of disease and other physical and mental health conditions, through surveillance of cases and the promotion of healthy behaviors. Promotion of hand washing and breastfeeding, delivery of vaccinations, and distribution of condoms to control the spread of sexually transmitted diseases are examples of common public health measures.

Dialogue 1

Glossary

cooperative 合作的   fine 罚款
lawsuit 诉讼,打官司

Ex. 1 Listen to the following dialogue and choose the best answer to each of the questions you will hear.

1. A. She wanted to study health but politics and environment also appeal to her.
   B. She wanted to study health but she was worried about politics and environment.
   C. She wanted to study politics and environment but her parents wanted her to be a doctor.
   D. She wanted to study politics and environment but her health was not good enough.
2. A. Protests or riots against pollution from the public.
   B. Strikes and unemployment for office workers.
   C. Pollution or insecure working conditions.
   D. Economic crisis or insufficient funds.
3. A. They may fire workers for their threatening complaints about the insurance policy.
   B. They may fire workers for their poor cooperation with the public health department.
   C. They may fire workers for their bad health caused by the polluted environment.
   D. They may fire workers for improving working environment would be costly.
4. A. They are a good way to replace traditional resources and keep healthy.
   B. They are a good way to reduce the costs of improving working conditions.
   C. They are a good way to regain their positions in the public health lawsuits.
   D. They are a good way to recycle the wastes emerging in the production.
5. A. Companies may be bankrupt and sold to the public.
   B. Companies may be attacked by the rude workers.
   C. Companies may be punished by the government.
   D. Companies may be punished and fined by law.

Ex. 2 Make dialogues on the following topics.

1. In some colleges in China, condom vending machines have been installed. What do you think of this phenomenon? Discuss with your classmates in groups and make a survey of their views either for or against the installation.

2. In modern society, sleep disorders could disturb people of different backgrounds. What do you think might be the major causes? Refer to the following checklist and talk to your friends to see if you can make any analysis or conclusion. You may add other necessary items for the discussion.

Dialogue 2

Glossary

Gettysburg 葛底斯堡(美国城镇) final 期末考试
reinforce 巩固,增强 stuff 材料,东西(多用于口语)

Ex. 1 Listen to the following dialogue and choose the best answer to each of the questions you will hear.

1. A. Places the man has visited.
   B. A paper the woman is writing for a class.
   C. School activities they enjoy.
   D. The woman's plans for the summer.

2. A. She has never been to Gettysburg.
   B. She took a political science course.
   C. Her family still goes on vacation together.
   D. She's interested in the United States Civil War.

3. A. Why her parents wanted to go to Gettysburg.
   B. Why her family's vacation plans changed ten years ago.
   C. Where her family went for a vacation ten years ago.
   D. When her family went on their last vacation.

4. A. It's far from where she lives.
   B. Her family went there without her.
   C. She doesn't know a lot about it.
   D. She's excited about going there.

Ex. 2 Make dialogues on the following topics.

1. Do you like visiting places with historical significance? Make a survey of any historical site you know and talk about the reasons it attracts you.

2. Do you think making on-the-spot investigation and practice are still necessary for observing life and work? Discuss and give your reasons.

Part III Listen and Discuss

Passage 1

Ex. 1 Listen to the following passage and choose the best answer to each of the questions you will hear.

1. A. Factors that affect the ability to remember.
   B. The influence of childhood memories on adulthood.
   C. A proposal for future psychological research.
   D. Benefits of a busy lifestyle.
2. A. The need to exercise the memory.
   B. How the brain differs from other body tissues.
   C. The unconscious learning of a physical activity.
   D. How nerves control body movement.
3. A. Repeat it aloud.   B. Write it down.
   C. Make a mental picture of it.   D. Practice recalling it.
4. A. Ask questions about the assigned reading.
   B. Give an example of active learning.
   C. Explain recent research on recalling childhood memories.
   D. Make an assignment for the next class session.

Ex. 2 Make dialogues on the following topics.

1. While at school, attending classes and taking tests, we sometimes dream of "escaping the ivory tower" and going to work as soon as possible. However, after we get a job and become a member of a working place, say, a company or an organization, we may feel like returning to and reliving our old school years. Why is that? In what way do you think the concept "learning throughout one's life" is suggestive for an individual as part of a society? Discuss in pairs and list your views in an organized way.

2. Do you believe that innovative thinking is more important for the study of a graduate student than for that of an undergraduate student? What do you think are the major differences between their studies?

Passage 2

Glossary

verify 证实   undergrad(undergraduate 的口语体)
get one's bronze on 皮肤晒成古铜色
a tanning salon 人造日光浴室   fake'n'bake 做人造日光浴

addictive 上瘾的
dermatology 皮肤病学
hook 诱惑

criteria 标准
peer pressure 攀比心态
intervention 干预

Ex. 1 Listen to the following radio report and fill in the blanks with the missing information, using the exact words you have just heard or your own words.

This is *Scientific Americans-60-Second Science*. I'm Christopher Intagliata. Got a minute?

Scientists have finally verified something that Jersey Shore stars Snooki and Pauly D. have probably known all along—that _____1_____. And the more often you tan, the more likely you are to get hooked, according to a study in the *Archives of Dermatology*. The researchers started with two questionnaires _____2_____. But they modified the questions to _____3_____. For example: "Do you try to cut down on the time you spend in tanning beds or booths but find yourself still tanning?" Then they gave those surveys to a couple hundred undergrads who fake'n'bake, on average, 23 times a year. The result? Fifty students, or about a fifth of those surveyed, met the authors' criteria for addiction to indoor tanning. This group also reported _____4_____. The investigators say _____5_____, including peer pressure. As for Snooki, it may be time for an intervention. When asked how she would change the world if she could, she said, "Ah...! I would put tanning beds in everybody's homes!"

Thanks for the minute. For *Scientific Americans-60-Second Science*. I'm Christopher Intagliata.

Ex. 2 Make dialogues on the following topics.

1. There have always been the trends of keeping healthy. We are bombed by information on nutrition or fitness every day from a variety of media. In response to this, what do you think is the most rational attitude? Discuss with your partners and list your views.
2. How do you view peer pressure in college graduates' job hunting? Try to design a consultation course on students' preparation for future careers. Work in pairs and exchange ideas with your partner.

Part IV Watch and Debate

In the following video clip, you will see James Hansen, the NASA climatologist, director of NASA Goddard Institute for Space Studies outlining how and when the accumulation of greenhouse gases will make Earth uninhabitable for our species—and why human life cannot be transferred to a different planet.

James Hansen is the director of NASA's Goddard Institute for Space Studies and adjunct professor in the Department of Earth and Environmental Sciences at Columbia University. Since 1988, he has warned about the threats of heat-trapping emissions, including carbon dioxide, that result from burning fossil fuels. A member of the National Academy of Sciences, he received the Heinz Environment Award in 2001 for his climate research. In 2006, he was named one of *Time* magazine's

Unit 6 Life Well Spent Is Long

100 Most Influential People.

Glossary

disintegrate 分解　　　　　　　　　　　weathering 风化
gradient 倾斜, 不均衡的　　　　　　　　methane 甲烷, 沼气
latitudes 纬度　　　　　　　　　　　　clathrate 包合物 (化学)
chaotic 混乱　　　　　　　　　　　　　hydrates 氢氧化合物
analogous 类似的　　　　　　　　　　　tundra 苔原, 冻土地带
runaway greenhouse effect 失控的温室效应　continental shelves 大陆架
monarch butterfly 黑脉金斑蝶 (美洲, 形体大)

Ex. 1 Watch the video clip three times and fill in the missing information with either the exact words from the interview or with your own words.

Question: *What will life be like if carbon emissions continue to grow?*

James Hansen: Well, if we allow emissions to continue at a high rate, in this century _____ _____ **1** _____. And one of the things I write about in my book is the effect that will have on storms, because as Greenland begins to release more fresh water, cold fresh water, and Antarctica does, what it does is cool the North Atlantic Ocean and the southern ocean, and that _____ **2** _____. And that will increase the strength of storms that are driven by horizontal temperature gradients. So our children can look forward to increasing storms. And with a rising sea level that is going to lead potentially to a very chaotic situation, because once you have hundreds of cities in the situation analogous to what happened in New Orleans, then we've got an economic situation that's just out of control globally.

In the long run, if that really happened, as I point out in the book, over centuries, we could actually get a runaway greenhouse effect, and then that's it for all the species on this planet. And as I try to point out, _____ **3** _____; we can't even transfer one species to another planet. I discuss the monarch butterfly and just how complex it is. And for us to hope that _____ **4** _____ _____ is really unrealistic.

Question: *What is the runaway greenhouse effect?*

James Hansen: A runaway greenhouse effect means _____ **5** _____. And water vapor is a very strong greenhouse gas, even more powerful than carbon dioxide. So you can get to a situation where it just— _____ **6** _____. And that happened to Venus. That's why Venus no longer has carbon in its surface. Its atmosphere is made up basically of carbon dioxide because it had a runaway greenhouse effect. Now the earth, it can _____ **7** _____. And the earth has had a runaway snowball earth situation. This happened most recently about 700 million years ago. The earth froze all the way to the equator.

So these runaway situations can occur. We've never had a runaway greenhouse effect, because if we did, that would have been the end. Once—that's a permanent situation. In the case of a snowball earth, when the earth becomes ice-covered, then the planet can escape from that situation because volcanoes continue to go off, but the weathering process is greatly reduced. So _____ 8 _____. But we can't push the planet off of the runaway greenhouse end. That's the end for everybody if we do that.

Question: *How long would this take to occur if we stay on this path?*

James Hansen: Well, you would have to—first of all, you'd have to melt the ice sheets, and that takes a while. The Antarctic ice sheet is a couple miles thick. But _____ 9 _____. And then things start to get hotter and hotter. So over a period of several centuries it would be conceivable to have a runaway greenhouse. That would also require bringing into play what we call the methane clathrates or methane hydrates. We already observe in the tundra region in Canada and Siberia that as the tundra is melting, methane, frozen methane, begins to be released. And methane is another powerful greenhouse gas. And there have been times in the earth's history when _____ 10 _____ of six to nine degrees Celsius, which is 10 to 18 degrees Fahrenheit. So if you add that on to the carbon dioxide warming and the water vapor warming, you could begin to push the planet into a very different state.

Ex. 2 Watch the video again and express your opinions on the following questions.

1. Make a list of the global catastrophic scenes illustrated here by Doctor James Hansen. Discuss in pairs the possibility of such disastrous consequences. Give your reasons.
2. There are the negative sides of life and work in today's world that can cause the high emission of carbon dioxide, therefore seriously leading to a worsening environment. Discuss with your partner (s) and list as many as you know and consider your possible efforts to improve the situation.

Part V Extracurricular Listening

Listen to the following 10 short dialogues and choose the best answer to each of the questions you will hear.

1. A. Husband and wife.   B. Boss and secretary.
   C. Telephone repairman and customer.   D. Telephone operator and customer.
2. A. Customer and waiter.   B. Customer and tailor.
   C. Customer and salesman.   D. Customer and cashier.
3. A. Professor and student.   B. Doctor and patient.
   C. Merchant and customer.   D. Lawyer and client.
4. A. Manager and candidate.   B. Boss and secretary.
   C. Manager and customer.   D. Father and daughter.

Life Well Spent Is Long — Unit 6

5. A. Daughter and father. B. Patient and doctor.
   C. Athlete and coach. D. Client and lawyer.
6. A. Aunt and nephew. B. Mother and son.
   C. Niece and uncle. D. Patient and doctor.
7. A. Brother and sister. B. Friends.
   C. Father and daughter. D. Son and mother.
8. A. Athlete and coach. B. Patient and doctor.
   C. Employee and boss. D. Son and mother.
9. A. Cousins. B. Mother and son.
   C. Niece and uncle. D. Daughter and father.
10. A. Guide and tourist. B. Waiter and customer.
    C. Conductor and passenger. D. Host and guest.

Unit 7 All Holidays Can Be Good Times

Part I Door to Wisdom

Read, think and interpret your understanding of the following proverbs and well-known sayings.

1. When in Rome, do as the Romans do.
2. A picture is worth a thousand words.
3. Politeness costs nothing and gains everything.

—M. W. Montagu

4. Different strokes for different folks.

—From the chorus of *Everyday People*

5. Man lives by the soil for a whole life and the soil buries him only one time.

—Shanxi Proverb

Part II Join in the Dialogue

Travel tips and advice can be obtained from the websites of your destination of your trip. You must plan your journey before you get started. You should also learn about precautions to take when you are travelling in your destination.

Before you leave you should:
Make sure that your travel documents have ample validity.

All Holidays Can Be Good Times

Obtain necessary visas for the places you will visit.

Take suitable travel insurance to cater for unforeseen circumstances.

While travelling, remember to:

Bring along your travel documents/ identification documents, in case verification of identity is required.

Keep travel documents, identification documents and cash separate and secure, and beware of pickpockets.

Take care of your personal safety and situation in destinations, and avoid staying in crowded areas.

Contact the Chinese diplomatic or consular missions in that state in case of emergency.

Dialogue 1

Glossary

unconventional 非传统的　　　　bassinette 婴儿车
reconfirm 再次确认

Ex. 1　Listen to the following dialogue and choose the best answer to each of the questions you will hear.

1. What is the unconventional way Christina chooses to confirm her flight?
   A. She calls the airline company directly.
   B. She turns to the reporters for help.
   C. She asks an online personal assistant for help.
   D. She makes a special request to the local airline company.

2. What's this program on BBC's World Service about?
   A. New fashion.　　　　　　　　B. Airline service.
   C. Special help.　　　　　　　　D. Interpersonal communication.

3. Why doesn't Christina want to call an airline?
   A. Because she must hold the phone for twelve minutes.
   B. Because she is required to mail first.
   C. Because she does not want to wait.
   D. Because she is bothered by someone.

4. Which of the following is NOT the request Christina makes in the program?
   A. Confirming one flight.　　　　B. Ordering warm milk for her baby.
   C. Booking a front row seat.　　　D. Ordering a bassinette for her baby.

5. What is Alex's nationality?
   A. America.　　B. The Philippines.　　C. India.　　D. Not known.

6. Which of the following statements is NOT true according to the interview?
   A. Christina dialed a local number.
   B. A foreign operator answers Christina's call.
   C. The operator is usually in the United States.

D. One may connect with an operator in another country.

Ex. 2 Make dialogues on the following topics.

1. How do you manage your tickets when you travel? Why do you do it in that way?
2. What would you do during your journey when you happen to lose everything, including your pocket money?

Dialogue 2

Glossary

tot 小孩   shambles 大混战
time frame 时限   the marine corps 海军陆战队
crate 板条箱

Ex. 1 Listen to the following dialogue and choose the best answer to each of the questions you will hear.

1. What is the purpose of Toys for Tots?
    A. Selling toys.
    B. Gathering and handing out Christmas gifts.
    C. Making toys for children.
    D. Earning profits from dealing with toys.
2. What is the problem for Toys for Tots this year according to the hostess Barbara Starr?
    A. The money needed is unavailable.   B. Workers do not work hard.
    C. The management is poor.   D. There are not enough toys.
3. When did the program of Toys for Tots start?
    A. 61 years ago.   B. 16 years ago.
    C. 60 years ago.   D. 6 years ago.
4. Why did Ebony come to the Marine Corps Toys for Tots center?
    A. She came to borrow some money to buy Christmas gifts.
    B. She came to get a letter from the Marines.
    C. She came for toys for her children as Christmas gifts.
    D. She complained about the service of the center.
5. Which statement is NOT true about Marine Corps Toys for Tots center?
    A. It is an organization receiving donations for Christmas gifts.
    B. It is anxious about how to deliver the toys to the needy family.
    C. The center needs tens of thousands toys this year.
    D. Last year it received $13,000 as donation at Union Train Station.
6. How many children in Washington D.C. should the Marine Corps find toys for?
    A. 80,000.   B. 18,000.   C. 82,000.   D. 12,000.

Unit 7 All Holidays Can Be Good Times

Ex. 2 Make dialogues on the following topics.

1. Tell a story of your own about gifts given by your relatives during Spring Festival.
2. Do you have a plan to donate some gifts to those who do not have any gifts during Spring Festival or Christmas? Why do you want to do it that way?

Part III Listen and Discuss

Passage 1

Ex. 1 Listen to the following passage and choose the best answer to each of the questions you will hear.

1. A. Eating some salad.   B. Having a sandwich.
   C. Reading a book.   D. Drinking coffee.
2. A. By asking the waiter for advice.   B. By asking the speaker for advice.
   C. By pointing at some pictures in the menu.   D. By point at the speaker's food.
3. A. Because it was on a special plate.
   B. Because they thought it was a kind of soup.
   C. Because they liked to drink chilly sauce.
   D. Because they thought it was vinegar.

Ex. 2 Make dialogues on the following topics.

1. When you are in a remote area and have difficulty in communicating with the locals, what would you do then in order to make things simple?
2. Please make a dish, say noodles or dumplings, through a dialogue with your desk-mates.

Passage 2

Ex. 1 Listen to the following passage and fill in each blank with the word(s) you've heard.

If you're planning to travel overseas, the most common form of transportation is by airplane. Knowing the entire __1__ from purchasing plane tickets to coping with in-flight emergencies can __2__ that you have a pleasurable trip.

Now, once you've __3__ your ticket, you still need to make the long journey through the airport. Once you arrive, you usually check your bags at the main ticket __4__. Then, you have to pass through the __5__ checkpoint, where you will have to walk through an X-ray machine, and they will check your carry-on bags for any __6__ items, including firearms, explosives, and knives. Of course, this is for __7__ safety. You might also be asked to open your bags to be __8__ checked.

Once you pass through this checkpoint, then _____ __9__ _____
_____. Just wait there until they announce your night.

Of course, once aboard the plane, no one ever wants to experience any emergencies. But

There are also life jackets under the seats, and oxygen masks in case the plane's cabin unexpectedly loses pressure. _____11_____.

Airplane travel can be exciting, and knowing what to expect before you go can make this experience even better.

Ex. 2 Make dialogues on the following topics.

1. Tell about one of your experiences during your journey back home from school.
2. By which means do you go back home? By bus, train or plane? Give your reasons.

Part IV Watch and Debate

As soon as you land in an international airport, you will notice the advertisement for accommodation service: Comfortable, Inexpensive, Clean, Warm and Helpful. We speak English and French. All rooms have TV and central heating.

Glossary

superlative 最佳品质   lava 熔岩
magma 岩浆   sulfur dioxide 二氧化硫
asphyxiate 使窒息

Ex. 1 Watch the video and choose the best answer to each of the following questions.

1. What is disappearing in the Island of Tahiti?
   A. The land of the island.   B. The fresh air and clean water.
   C. The Tahitian culture.   D. All of the above.
2. What kind of town does Tahiti's capital look like?
   A. A French town.   B. A British town.
   C. A Polynesian town.   D. A unique town.
3. Which is NOT one of the factors that give Tahiti the atmosphere of a French town?
   A. The language.   B. The merchandise.
   C. The culture.   D. The beautiful women.
4. What still attracts modern people's attention when it comes to Tahiti?
   A. The philosophical ideal of "noble savage".   B. The French tradition.
   C. The unparalleled beautiful nature.   D. The enthusiastic Tahitian dancing.
5. Why do the young Tahitians practice their traditional dance?
   A. To attract more visitors.   B. To preserve their unique culture.
   C. To show they have become adults.   D. To exercise physically.
6. In addition to teaching Tahitian, the language itself, what is another more important purpose for the Tahitian classes?
   A. To educate the students in morality.
   B. To teach the students how to be a civilized person.

All Holidays Can Be Good Times

C. To give the students the love for their own culture.

D. To compare the differences between French and Tahitian.

Ex. 2 Watch the video and complete each blank with what you've heard in the video clip.

On the fable island of Tahiti, it is not the land which is __1__ disappearing but the __2__. The outside world has refused to leave this place alone. Since __3__, Tahiti and its neighboring islands have been the colony of France. __4__ you look at the capital Papeete, the French language, French culture and French merchandise give it the atmosphere and the appearance of a provincial town __5__ in France itself.

It was a very __6__ which greeted the old European mariners when they first dropped anchor in Matavai Bay. Here is __7__ life completely at odds with their own. It is the description the glorious brought back to Europe that inspired the artists and writers with the philosophical ideal of the "noble savage" which still maintain its appeal in our modem over-regulated world. They painted the pictures of feasting and dancing, and above all, the beauty of the women, so __8__ their favors. These young Tahitians of today have just one purpose to preserve the rich __9__ their own unique culture, so mighty with their expressing dance before it is too late. Each one of these carefully rehearsed movements reflects the traditional pattern of Polynesian life and all has its root in the ancient legend. Dance is the very language of the soul, passed from one generation __10__.

Ex. 3 Watch the video again and express your opinions on the following questions.

1. Tell your experience of staying away from city busy life.
2. If you get a chance or a free ticket to a resorted place, where would you like to go? Give your reasons.
3. Which do you prefer, climbing high mountains or swimming in an open sea?

Part V   Extracurricular Listening

Listen to the following 10 short dialogues and choose the best answer to each of the questions you will hear.

1. A. By bus.   B. By plane.   C. By car.   D. By train.
2. A. By bus.   B. By train.   C. By car.   D. By taxi.
3. A. By car.   B. By bus.   C. On foot. D. By bike.
4. A. By eating grapefruit.   B. By going on diet.
   C. By having a balanced diet.   D. By running.
5. A. She was understanding.   B. She was apologetic.
   C. She was annoyed.   D. She was careless.
6. A. They have two children already.
   B. Mrs. Taylor wishes to have children, but her husband doesn't.
   C. They will start a family as soon as they get married.
   D. They don't want children for the time being.

7. A. He read the newspaper. B. One of his students told him.
   C. He listened to a radio report. D. He attended a Cabinet meeting.

8. A. He went directly to the boss with his problem.
   B. He decided to keep the problem to himself.
   C. He let his mother speak to the boss about the problem.
   D. He told his boss's mother about the problem.

9. A. It's larger. B. It's nicer.
   C. It's closer to the campus. D. It's quieter.

10. A. He is satisfied. B. He is impatient.
    C. He is exhausted. D. He is bored.

Unit 8 Travel Is More Than the Seeing of Sights

Part I Door to Wisdom

Read, think and interpret your understanding of the following proverbs and well-known sayings.

1. The world is a book and those who do not travel read only one page.

—St. Augustine

2. A traveler without observation is a bird without wings.

—Moslih Eddin Saadi

3. A journey of a thousand miles must begin with a single step.

—Lao Tzu

4. To travel is to discover that everyone is wrong about other countries.

—Aldous Huxley

5. Tourists don't know where they've been, travelers don't know where they're going.

—Paul Theroux

Part II Join in the Dialogue

Dialogue 1

Ex. 1 Listen to the dialogue and choose the best answer to the following questions.

1. What is Robert concerned about regarding his suitcase?
   A. Whether it contains prohibited items.   B. Whether it will be overweight.
   C. Whether it is strong enough to hold the items.   D. Whether it will be safe.
2. Where did Robert want to send the package?
   A. London.   B. Mexico.
   C. China.   D. Not mentioned.
3. Where did Robert prefer to sit?
   A. Near the window.   B. Near the washroom.
   C. Near the emergency room.   D. Near the isle.
4. Why did the security agent recommend going through the security immediately?
   A. There are a lot of people waiting.
   B. There is a lot to see in the departure areas.
   C. It will be boarding soon.
   D. The scanning machine may be out of work any time.
5. When should Robert be at the boarding gate at least?
   A. 11 o'clock.   B. 10:30.   C. 10 o'clock.   D. 9 o'clock.

Ex. 2 Make dialogues on the following topics.

1. How do you like traveling by air? Why?
2. Suppose your partner has never travelled by air, have a dialogue with him/her about the necessary procedure about air travel.

Dialogue 2

Ex. 1 Listen to the dialogue and choose the best answer to the following questions.

1. What is the current time in the conversation?
   A. 3:40 PM   B. 4:15 PM   C. 4:30 PM   D. 4:45 PM
2. How does the driver figure out that the passenger is a first-time visitor to the city?
   A. The passenger catches a taxi for a short one-mile trip.
   B. The passenger does not understand the rules for tipping drivers.
   C. The driver finds the passenger lost on the street before picking him up.
   D. The driver notices the passenger gazing upward at the tall buildings.
3. What sort of restaurant is the man looking for?
   A. One that is relatively inexpensive.

Travel Is More Than the Seeing of Sights

B. One that is not very crowded.

C. One that offers large servings.

D. One that is situated close to his hotel.

4. What is one item the driver did not mention about the restaurant?

   A. The price.   B. The service.
   C. The interior design.   D. The serving size.

5. The driver suggests that the passenger go _____ to the restaurant.

   A. by taxi   B. by bus   C. by subway   D. on foot

Ex. 2 Make dialogues on the following topics.

1. Recommend your favorite restaurant in the city to your partner and the reasons for recommendation.
2. What do you prefer, bus or taxi, when you are in a strange city for travelling? Why?

Part Ⅲ Listen and Discuss

Passage 1

Ex. 1 Listen to the passage again and fill in the blanks with the exact words you hear.

Carl has been working as a __1__ for about 10 years. One thing that he likes about his job is that he gets __2__ and holidays. His main task is to sell holidays. He advises people on the holiday options __3__ to them, different __4__, types of holiday, ways to get there, and so on. When customers have decided what they want, he __5__ it for them and makes any other __6__ they might need, such as car hire or tours. He also has to __7__ customers have all the information they need—if any __8__ are necessary, if they will need __9__ and how to get them, when they have to __10__ and when they will be arriving, what the __11__ is likely to be, etc. He loves organizing tailor-made holidays— __12__ an itinerary, book flights, ferries, trains, __13__ and everything. He loves providing a __14__, especially if it's to places he knows. Sometimes he gets __15__ customers. Sometimes I get difficult customers. One man came in wanting a flight to Venice the next day. I checked out __16__ on the computer, and found a very __17__ flight at a __18__ time, so we booked it there and then. A week later he came in and he was absolutely __19__. He wanted to know why I had __20__ him to Venice, in Italy, when he had had an important meeting in Vienna, which is in Austria. I didn't know what to say, but since then I've always been careful to check that people really know where they want to go.

Ex. 2 Make dialogues on the following topics.

1. Talk about your dissatisfactions with some of your travelling experiences.
2. Briefly describe one tourist guide, and how you like him/her.

· 49 ·

Passage 2

Ex. 1   Listen to the passage and choose the best answer to the following questions.

1. A. His travel.   B. His short stories.   C. His finances.   D. His family.
2. A. Florida.   B. California.   C. Nevada.   D. Hannibal.
3. A. Typesetter.   B. River pilot.   C. Soldier.   D. Prospector.
4. A. He wanted to be a journalist.   B. He liked the climate there.
   C. He wanted to get away from the army.   D. He was sent there by his father.
5. A. His stories were inspired by his travels.
   B. His travels prevent him from the writing.
   C. He traveled in order to relax from the pressure of writing.
   D. He traveled around to publicize his writings.

Ex. 2   Make dialogues on the following topics.

1. Talk about one of your most exciting travelling experience with your partner.
2. Discuss about the benefits of travelling.
3. Talk with your partner about your favorite ways of travelling.

Part IV   Watch and Debate

Ex. 1   Watch the video and answer the following questions.

1. The advantages of home exchange over staying in the hotel are _____ and they can take the pet with them.
2. The usual concern about home exchange is _____ living in the home.
3. Generally speaking, _____ people tend to exchange home with others.
4. The movie *The Holiday* relates with home exchange in that _____.
5. Home exchange resembles internet dating in that they both _____.

Ex. 2   Watch the video again and express your opinions on the following questions.

1. Do you think home exchange is a good way of travelling? Why or why not?
2. What should be made clear of before home exchanging?
3. What kind of people do you want to home change with?

Part V   Extracurricular Listening

Listen to the following 10 short dialogues and choose the best answer to each of the questions you will hear.

1. A. Spain.   B. Switzerland.   C. Scotland.   D. Denmark.
2. A. New York.   B. Chicago.   C. Philadelphia.   D. Washington.

Travel Is More Than the Seeing of Sights

Unit 8

3. A. A movie. B. A soccer game.
   C. A documentary. D. A soap opera.
4. A. The first hot dogs came from Germany.
   B. Hot dogs originated in the United States.
   C. Some hot dogs are made from reindeer meat.
   D. Even countries like Finland have a kind of food similar to hot dog.
5. A. Packaging one's own groceries. B. The indifference of the employees.
   C. The narrow choice of meats. D. The higher prices.
6. A. She spends too much money. B. She works in a factory.
   C. She prefers to go shopping. D. She likes to argue.
7. A. The fifth. B. The sixth. C. The seventh. D. The ninth.
8. A. Do filing. B. Type. C. Clean the office. D. Write letters.
9. A. History. B. Psychology. C. Anthropology. D. Sociology.
10. A. Coffee. B. Tea. C. Water. D. Coca-cola.

Unit 9 Sports Are a Microcosm of Society

Part I Door to Wisdom

Read, think and interpret your understanding of the following proverbs and well-known sayings.

1. Olympism is the marriage of sport and culture.

—Juan Antonio Samaranch

2. Our greatest glory is not in never falling but in rising every time we fall.

—Confucius

3. Life is like riding a bicycle. To keep your balance you must keep moving.

—Albert Einstein

4. A horse with two heads wins no races.

—American proverb

5. If you risk nothing, then you risk everything.

—Afghanistan proverb

Part II Join in the Dialogue

The Olympic Games, first held in 776BC, has a history of more than one thousand years. The Games is held every four years.

The colours of the interlinked Olympic rings were chosen by the International Olympic Committee (IOC), to represent the union of the 5 continents—Australia, Africa, America, Asia and Europe—and further signify the meeting of the world athletes at the Olympic Games.

The Olympic motto is "Swifter, higher, stronger." The Games can promote the understanding and friendship among different peoples and different nations.

Unit 9 Sports Are a Microcosm of Society

Dialogue 1

Glossary

resilience 愉快的心情　　fence 击剑者
description 描述　　　　seasoned 经验丰富的
backstroke 仰泳　　　　primal 最初的

Ex. 1 Listen to the following dialogue and choose the best answer to each of the questions you will hear.

1. What is the interview mainly about?
   A. China, a good host.
   B. Beijing Summer Olympics Closed.
   C. The first-ever Olympic medals of some countries.
   D. The excellent athletes at Beijing Summer Olympics.

2. The closing ceremony was _____.
   A. a simple reflection of the joy of competition
   B. a simple reflection of the Olympic spirit
   C. both A and B
   D. a simple reflection of the star performances

3. The Olympic Games are _____.
   A. also a political event
   B. not about winning gold
   C. not about competition
   D. also about athletes' efforts to achieve their limits

4. Usain Bolt of Jamaica won 3 gold medals because of his _____.
   A. unparalleled speed on the track　　B. team spirit
   C. star quality　　　　　　　　　　　D. strong desire to win

5. Why was American swimmer Michael Phelps so impressive?
   A. Because he never gave up.
   B. Because he is a very handsome swimmer.
   C. Because he overcame backache to take part in the Olympic Games.
   D. Because he is the first athlete to win 8 gold medals at a single Olympics.

6. By saying "I feel like I have gone full circle", the American 25-year-old athlete means that _____.
   A. she finally found the primal joy from sports again
   B. she always enjoys competition
   C. she is under great pressure
   D. she loved the sport only as a beginner

Ex. 2 Make dialogues on the following topics.

1. How do you understand the Olympic Spirit? Give an example to illustrate your point of view.
2. Do you like sports or not? Give your reasons.

Dialogue 2

Glossary

congenital 天生的,先天的   affiliate 分公司
feat 壮举   prosthetic arm 臂假肢
yoke 方向盘   solo 单独(驾驶)

Ex. 1 Listen to the following dialogue and choose the best answer to each of the questions you will hear.

1. In which way is the pilot exceptional?
   A. She is a woman.
   B. She is only 25 years old.
   C. She is a patient who suffers from incurable disease.
   D. She has no arms.

2. Why does Jessica Cox want to be a pilot?
   A. Because she can earn a lot.
   B. Because she wants to really have her life in her own hands.
   C. Because she has no other choices.
   D. Because she is interested in flying.

3. Which of the following is NOT used when Cox checks the oil in her pre-flight inspection?
   A. Her shoulder.   B. Her foot.
   C. Her head.   D. A screwdriver.

4. What is the first challenge for Cox in her flight training?
   A. How to get rid of airsickness.   B. How to buckle the seat belt.
   C. How to get along with other crews. D. How to seat herself in the pilot's seat.

5. How many years had Cox been using prosthetic arms?
   A. Eleven years.   B. Three years.
   C. Eight years.   D. Twenty years.

6. Why did Parrish Traweek, the flight instructor, have confidence in Cox's learning to be a pilot?
   A. Because Cox is rich enough to pay for the training.
   B. Because Cox has no arms.
   C. Because Cox is strong enough to be trained as a pilot.
   D. Because Cox has firm drive.

Ex. 2 Make dialogues on the following topics.

1. Please retell the heroic story of the heroine. Give your comments on the importance of her practice.

2. As a student, what can you learn from the heroine? Give an example like the heroine in China or someone around you.

Sports Are a Microcosm of Society Unit 9

Part III   Listen and Discuss

Passage 1

Ex. 1   Listen to the following passage and choose the best answer to each of the questions you will hear.

1. A. As soon as she realized that something was wrong.
   B. Only after her husband advised her to.
   C. A long time after the trouble began.
   D. When John asked what was wrong with her.
2. A. Get an expert to treat John's mother.
   B. Send John's mother to hospital.
   C. Advise John's mother to come into his hospital at once.
   D. Advise John's mother to wait for a few weeks.
3. A. He became bad tempered, too.   B. He spent less and less time at home.
   C. He became more and more patient.   D. He became more and more quiet.
4. A. John and his father would live at Aunt Daisy's house.
   B. John's aunt was coming to look after him.
   C. John would go to his aunt while his father would stay on at home.
   D. John and his father were to look after themselves.

Ex. 2   Make dialogues on the following topics.

1. What are the causes of being sick, in your opinion? Give your reasons.
2. What is the possible relationship between health and sports? Give some examples.

Passage 2

Ex. 1   Listen to the following passage and fill in each blank with the word(s) you've heard.

The International Olympic Committee awarded Salt Lake City the 2002 Winter Olympics by a big majority. It seemed that its persistent __1__ had paid off.

But because of a __2__ by a dissatisfied employee of the local organizing committee to a Salt Lake City TV station, the Salt Lake City Olympic organizers are __3__ of bribing the I. O. C. members. It is the I. O. C. members who __4__ where the next Olympics will take place. So far, four groups—the I. O. C, the U. S. Olympic Committee, the Justice Department and the Utah Ethics Committee have begun to __5__ into the mess.

Some members of the local organizing committee do not intend to make __6__, but are expressing their regrets instead. "Obviously, we did break the rules," says Ken Bullock, an ashamed organizer. He points out that the __7__ on a bidding city to be friendly and generous can be __8__, and Salt Lake City was hardly the first to bribe the I. O. C. "The I. O. C. allowed this," says

Bullock. _____9_____, but the facts seem beyond doubt. I. O. C executive Marc Hodler announced last month that _____10_____. Hodler then accused the previous winning cities of Atlanta, Nagano and Sydney of corruption, but officials in all three cities deny this charge. _____11_____.

Ex. 2 Make dialogues on the following topics.

1. What is the real story behind the message? What really causes the "mess"?
2. Why are there so many countries eager to be the holder of Olympic Games? Give your reasons.

Part Ⅳ Watch and Debate

Some of the winter sports played at the Olympics are internationally known, such as ice hockey. Others, like curling, are less widely known. Curling is a team sport played on ice. Two teams take turns pushing stones weighing almost twenty kilograms towards a circular target drawn on the ice.

Olympic athletes spend many hours training for the games. This can be very costly. In many countries, the government provides athletes with special trainers, equipment and economic support.

Glossary

    luge 单人平底雪橇   thrill 刺激
    alpine 高山上的,极高的 course 赛场,跑道

Ex. 1 Watch the video and choose the best answer to each of the following questions.

1. The title for the video clip could possibly be _____.
   A. the Winter Olympics and Danger B. the Winter Olympics and History
   C. the Winter Olympics and Speed   D. the Winter Olympics and Thrill

2. What can we conclude from the interview?
   A. The Winter Olympics should add more speedy items.
   B. The Winter Olympics should be cancelled.
   C. The Winter Olympics should be more attractive to young people.
   D. The Winter Olympics should be regulated.

3. How do speakers feel about the Winter Olympics?
   A. Athletes are gaining more money for their performance.
   B. Athletes are pushing the limits of human performance.
   C. Athletes are showing their beautifully human performance.
   D. Athletes are showing their talent in sports performance.

4. What does the International Luge Federation think of the crash accident?
   A. It is the athlete's fault to blame. B. It is the audience's fault to blame.
   C. It is coach's fault to blame.   D. It is the course's fault to blame.

Sports Are a Microcosm of Society

Unit 9

5. What was the situation in the Winter Olympics 20 years ago?
   A. The Winter Olympics was losing crazy audience.
   B. The Winter Olympics was losing old audience.
   C. The Winter Olympics was losing professional audience.
   D. The Winter Olympics was losing young audience.

6. When was the luge item added to the Olympics?
   A. In 1940.   B. In 1946.   C. In 1964.   D. In 1965.

Ex. 2   Watch the video and complete each blank with what you've heard in the video clip.

Jeffery brown: Well, to the degree that there is this line between the thrill and—and real danger, who is supposed to—how is it supposed to __1__? Who is supposed to be finding that line?

David wallechinsky: The International Olympic Committee is the umbrella organization that runs the Olympics. But, __2__, the competition themselves are run by the international sports federation in charge of each sport.

So, the Ski Federation is __3__ everything about skiing, the Skating Federation, skating, and, in this case, the Winter Olympics and Risk was supposed to make sure that the course was safe and that everything was going well.

Of course, the International Olympic Committee can criticize the sports federations, but, in the end, it is the sports federation that takes __4__.

Jeffrey brown: And, when you look at what's to come here in terms of audiences, __5__ governing bodies, do you expect any change, or does it all fade away over time?

David wallechinsky: I'm a little __6__ what is going to happen in the luge situation, primarily __7__ the initial way that the Luge Federation dealt with it.

I can see __8__ a full investigation until after the Games are over. But when they just quickly came out and said, "OK, we have done an investigation, there is __9__ with the course, it was all the athlete's fault, but, by the way, since you mentioned it, we're going to change the course," I think there is something wrong here.

And, at this point, I'm __10__ that the International Luge Federation realizes that they have to make some changes, or at least they have to __11__ themselves.

Jeffrey brown: And is there any way of bringing those concerns to the federation?

David wallechinsky: I would say that, other than __12__ and the media calling attention to them, it is the International Olympic Committee who is going to talk to them, I'm sure, __13__ after the Games are over and go, this was outrageous. You got us __14__. You need to—we're going to have to put you under stricter controls if you want to keep your sport in the Olympics.

Keep in mind that luge was added to the Olympics in 1964, and, two weeks before the opening of those Games, a luge athlete was killed on the Olympics course. Now, it was two weeks before the Games. We didn't have so much television, so it wasn't a __15__.

But, here, you would have thought that they would have learned after 26 years. And here we had it on the opening day.

Jeffrey brown: All right, David Wallechinsky in Vancouver, thank you very much.
David wallechinsky: Thank you.

Ex. 3 Watch the video again and express your opinions on the following questions.
1. Please retell the history of the Winter Olympics. What has happened to the Winter Olympics nowadays?
2. What is most important thing in the competition of the Winter Olympics, from your point of view?

Part V Extracurricular Listening

Listen to the following 10 short dialogues and choose the best answer to each of the questions you will hear.

1. A. A surprise party.   B. A picnic.   C. A meeting.   D. An appointment.
2. A. A movie.   B. A lecture.   C. A play.   D. A speech.
3. A. A pair of glasses.   B. A flashlight.   C. A camera.   D. A telescope.
4. A. A new restaurant.   B. A new hotel.   C. A new hospital.   D. A new airport.
5. A. Setting the table.   B. Polishing silverware.
   C. Sewing napkins.   D. Stocking a pantry.
6. A. A driving test.   B. A traffic accident.
   C. A police movie.   D. When to make signals.
7. A. An armed robbery.   B. A hold-up.
   C. An attempted murder.   D. A burglary.
8. A. Thick socks.   B. Too much walking.
   C. New shoes.   D. Not enough exercise.
9. A. A correspondence course.   B. Summer vacation plans.
   C. Job hunting.   D. Correspondence between them.
10. A. The cost of fixing the window.
    B. The difficulty of cleaning up the broken glass.
    C. How to punish Tommy.
    D. The possible harm to the people involved.

Unit 10 Character Is Long-Standing Habit

Part I Door to Wisdom

Read, think and interpret your understanding of the following proverbs and well-known sayings.

1. Personality is to a man what perfume is to a flower.

—Charles M. Schwab

2. Men's natures are alike; it is their habits that separate them.

—*Confucius*, *Analects*

3. Habit is a cable; we weave a thread each day, and at last we cannot break it.

—Horace Mann

4. Character building begins in our infancy, and continues until death.

—Eleanor Roosevelt

5. Humility is no substitute for a good personality.

—Fran Lebowitz

Part II Join in the Dialogue

Dialogue 1

Ex. 1   Listen to the dialogue and choose the best answer to the following questions.

1. What is the most important aspect of a manager's job according to Professor Bevan?
   A. Assigning the right task to the right people.
   B. Demanding cooperating spirit among his employees.
   C. Motivating people to work well.
   D. Helping the employees get as many benefits as possible.

2. Which of the following is NOT the tool for the managers to get things done?
   A. Praise approval.   B. Trust and expectation.
   C. Money.   D. Promotion.

3. Which of the following is done by managers from Western Electric?
   A. Getting workers involved in decision making.
   B. Raising the salary of the workers.
   C. Stopping giving workers orders.
   D. Persuading workers to accept new things.

4. What's the effect of the motivation practice on the Swedish company, Kochums?
   A. In just 10 years, they paid off the debts, and got a profit of 100 million dollars.
   B. In just 5 years they managed to get a profit of 10 million dollars a year.
   C. In just 10 years, they managed to pay off all the debts.
   D. In just 10 years, they paid off the debts, and got a profit of 15 million dollars.

5. What is illustrated with the two examples cited by Professor Bevan?
   A. Workers are not interested in money.
   B. Workers are very interested in money.
   C. Motivation can be turned into productivity.
   D. Communication can be turned into productivity.

Ex. 2   Make dialogues on the following topics.

1. Talk with your partner about how your parents or teachers motivated you to study harder.
2. Share with your partner about one story where motivation plays a key role.

Dialogue 2

Ex. 1   Listen to the dialogue and choose the best answer to the following questions.

1. What was Rocky doing at the beginning of the conversation?
   A. Eating and drinking.   B. Dancing to the music.
   C. Standing around at the party.   D. Talking with his girlfriend.

· 60 ·

Unit 10 Character Is Long-Standing Habit

2. Rocky likes women who _____.
   A. serve him hand and foot
   B. stimulate his intellect
   C. pursue their own careers
   D. enjoy reading novels
3. In addition to eating, Rocky feels his household chores include _____.
   A. fixing the appliances like the TV and throwing out the trash
   B. washing the car and collecting the trash
   C. watching television and taking out the garbage
   D. fixing things around the house
4. What's Ed's ideal woman like?
   A. Outgoing and judgmental.
   B. Optimistic and non-judgmental.
   C. Outgoing and caring.
   D. Caring and optimistic.
5. From the conversation, what is the most likely scenario of events for the rest of the evening for Rocky?
   A. He returns home alone and spends the night with his dog.
   B. He remains at the party to try to make new friends.
   C. He decides to visit his friend, Rusty, and they have TV dinners.
   D. He meets a woman who shares his interest in archeology.

Ex. 2 Make dialogues on the following topics.
1. What's your idea about the ideal woman/man?
2. To succeed in your career, what are the important qualities that one should possess?

Part III Listen and Discuss

Passage 1

Ex. 1 Listen to the passage and choose the best answer to the following questions.
1. What does "you are responsible for your successes and also your failures" entail?
   A. We shouldn't let others decide what we should say and should do.
   B. We should not complain to others when we are frustrated.
   C. We should solve our own problems all by ourselves.
   D. We should face the successes and failures in life bravely.
2. After we know we should be responsible for our study, what comes next?
   A. Setting the priorities.
   B. Establishing the goal of study.
   C. Understanding the motivation.
   D. Understanding the time schedule.
3. When deciding where to study, which of the following is not the factor to consider according to the passage?
   A. Whether it is full of attraction.
   B. Whether the climate is suitable.
   C. Whether the room has necessary facilities for study.

D. Whether it is safe.

4. How can you communicate well with the instructor?

A. Put yourself in the instructor's position and understand what's appropriate.

B. Always keep good distance with the instructor.

C. Speak with the greatest courtesy.

D. Never disagree with the instructor.

5. What's the old adage about study?

A. Practice makes perfect.

B. A good beginning is half done.

C. If you don't succeed, try and try again.

D. Where there is a will, there is a way.

Ex. 2 Make conversations about the following topics.

1. Talk with your partner about your study habits.

2. What are the most important personality traits in achieving good academic performance in your understanding?

Passage 2

Ex. 1 Listen to the passage and choose the best answer to the following questions.

1. It can be known from the passage that who's who _____.

A. is a very useful book telling us how to succeed

B. is a book providing us with the information about the family life of some famous people

C. is a book providing us with the names and brief biographies of the top successful people

D. is a book from which we can find out the names of different people in the world

2. According to the author, common sense _____.

A. is something that common people like best

B. is a popular quality a person is born with

C. is something that enables one to form correct opinions

D. is a quality that is possessed by common people

3. It can be inferred from the passage that a successful businessman _____.

A. tries to get experience through practice

B. pays attention to the essence of a problem when he tries to solve it

C. keeps on learning in order to be successful

D. has strong willpower, extensive interest and intelligence

4. The passage is mainly concerned with _____.

A. organizational ability and good work habits

B. the way to obtain big profits and achieve fame and success

C. knowledge and interest which are primary to success

D. what successful people have in common

· 62 ·

5. According to the author, how to develop one's common sense?
   A. To become a businessman.
   B. To learn how to debate and learn from mistakes.
   C. To become famous.
   D. To be simplifying.

Ex. 2 Make conversations about the following topics.
1. Discuss with your partner the importance of the following factors, and rearrange them according to their importance to success.
   —Luck, personality, connections, professional knowledge, relationship with others, creativity, leadership, intelligence.
2. Give some facts both real and unreal about you, and ask your partner to judge which are true and which are not. Remember to ask your partner the reasons for their judgments.

Part Ⅳ Watch and Debate

Ex. 1 Watch the video and complete each sentence with the exact word you've heard in the video.

   In order to find out more about how our __1__ of people are __2__ by what we know about them, Ranhanson, a __3__ at New York University, conducted an interesting experiment with his colleagues. In this experiment, they __4__ different __5__ descriptions to the same face. For one group, they give the description of a very mean-heated person, while for the other group, they give the description of the same picture as a __6__ person. They found the personality of the person changed the __7__ of the person. Although the face was the same, the mean hearted person was __8__ as being less attractive. So, the perception of people really changes as the result of the information about the person's personality. We may be __9__ of appearance, but we are not always __10__ by looks.

Ex. 2 Watch the video again and express your opinions on the following questions.
1. What in your opinion can affect a person's personality? Discuss them with your partner.
2. How important is personality in your understanding? What do you say on your personality?
3. Debate with your partner on whether personality is born or is subject to change.

Part Ⅴ Extracurricular Listening

Listen to the following 10 short dialogues and choose the best answer to each of the questions you will hear.

1. A. Life is less expensive in the city.   B. Jobs are easier to find in the city.
   C. Her job is in the city.   D. Living in the suburbs is expensive.

2. A. To keep his feet warm. B. To protect his carpet.
   C. To avoid tripping on the carpet. D. To keep his shoes from wearing out.
3. A. He went through a stop sign. B. He ran a red light.
   C. He turned a corner too fast. D. He was speeding.
4. A. He got angry with his boss. B. He always got to work late.
   C. He was often sick and absent from work. D. He prepared a financial report incorrectly.
5. A. To mail a letter. B. To buy stamps.
   C. To get a package. D. To deliver a check.
6. A. His homework is difficult. B. He doesn't like his professor.
   C. He's having trouble learning Spanish. D. He has to decide which professor he wants.
7. A. He forgot his phone number. B. He hasn't seen him recently.
   C. He never invites him to dinner. D. He doesn't phone ahead before visiting.
8. A. He was late. B. He's a new employee.
   C. He's hoping for a promotion. D. The boss usually leaves messages for him.
9. A. She must read lots of books. B. She doesn't like history.
   C. She can't get books she needs. D. She hasn't finished her history course.
10. A. She's a little tired. B. She's going to study.
    C. She wants to listen to music. D. She's going to make a reservation.

Unit 11 Love Is the Fruit of Marriage

Part I Door to Wisdom

Read, think and interpret your understanding of the following proverbs and well-known sayings.

1. I love you not because of who you are, but because of who I am when I am with you.

—Roy Croft

2. You can give without loving, but you cannot love without giving.

—Amy Carmichael

3. Life without love is like a tree without blossom and fruit.

—Khalil Gibra

4. Love is an act of endless forgiveness, a tender look which becomes a habit.

—Peter Ustinov

5. Love is the master key that opens the gates of happiness.

—Oliver Wendell Holmes

Part II Join in the Dialogue

Dialogue 1

Ex. 1   Listen to the dialogue and fill in each blank with lonly ONE word you've heard.

Interviewer: How long have you been a _____ _____ counselor, Mr. Thurber?

Mr. Thurber: _____ _____ years.

I: You must have _____ a deep _____ into the problems of _____ _____.

T: I think I have, yes.

I: What do you _____ to be the _____ _____ problem?

T: Well, many people become _____ with their partners, their _____, or with _____ itself, especially in the _____ _____.

I: What _____ do you mean by " _____ "?

T: They start off with _____ _____ of their partners and of _____ _____. Gradually these _____ _____ give way to _____ _____ as they find out their partner's _____ _____ and start to _____ their own _____ _____ with those of their _____ _____. They become _____ to make _____.

I: _____?

T: Yes. Marriage _____ a great deal of _____ and _____. For the _____, this may mean _____ an important _____ in order to spend _____ with his _____; for the _____, it may take the form of _____ the tedious, soul-destroying life of a _____. In many marriages, one or both partners find themselves _____ to make these _____ and begin to _____ _____ _____.

I: Is it possible to _____ a marriage when it has reached that _____?

T: _____ _____, yes.

I: One _____ question, Mr. Thurber. Are you _____?

T: No, not _____ _____. My _____ wife _____ me last month.

Ex. 2   Make dialogues on the following topics.

1. How to solve the conflicts between man and wife.
2. How to maintain a marriage.

Dialogue 2

Ex. 1   Listen to the dialogue and choose the best answer to the following questions.

1. What can we assume about the death of Tim's father?

   A. He fell ill and passed away unexpectedly.

   B. His father died in a traffic accident.

   C. Tim's dad had a lingering illness.

Love Is the Fruit of Marriage   Unit 11

    D. He died quietly.
2. How is his mother taking the passing of her husband?
    A. She feels very depressed.
    B. She remains optimistic about the future.
    C. She senses no purpose to her own life.
    D. She thinks the death relived her husband of the pain.
3. How is his mother going to support herself now that her husband is gone?
    A. She will be able to live off her government pension.
    B. She is planning to work.
    C. Proceeds from life insurance will sustain her.
    D. She will depend on her children.
4. When is the public viewing for Tim's father?
    A. In the morning.   B. In the afternoon.   C. In the evening.   D. Not mentioned.
5. What does Tim ask Heather to do at the funeral?
    A. Offer a prayer.   B. Sing a song.   C. Give a speech.   D. Be a host.

Ex. 2 Make dialogues on the following topics.
1. How to get over the pain of losing a beloved one.
2. Talk about some common strategies for comforting someone in pain.

Part III   Listen and Discuss

Passage 1

Ex. 1 Listen to the following passage and choose the best answer to each of the questions you will hear.

1. A. Family violence.   B. The Great Depression.
   C. Her father's disloyalty.   D. Her mother's bad temper.
2. A. His advanced age.   B. His children's efforts.
   C. His improved financial condition.   D. His second wife's positive influence.
3. A. Love is blind.
   B. Love breeds love.
   C. Divorce often has disastrous consequences.
   D. Happiness is hard to find in blended families.

Ex. 2 Make dialogues on the following topics.
1. Talk about your opinions on the role of stepmother.
2. Talk about your opinions on lightning marriage.
3. Why a lot of people hide the truth about their marital status and the ways to prevent it.

Passage 2

Ex. 1 Listen to the passage and fill in the blanks with the words you've heard.

On May 15, 2008, the California Supreme Court __1__ same-sex marriages in the state of California. By a vote of 4 to 3, the court declared that __2__ a marriage to a union between a man and a woman __3__ the state constitution.

The court's decision was a huge victory for gays and __4__ throughout the state. Hundreds waited outside the courthouse in Sacramento for the __5__, which they greeted with __6__, hugs, and kisses. TV crews interviewed joyful couples.

However, conservative __7__ have vowed to fight the decision. They plan to gather over a million __8__ for a constitutional amendment in November to __9__ this decision. If California voters approve the amendment, lawyer Gloria Allred said, "I will take this case to the US Supreme Court. Gays must be free to marry."

It was only 60 years ago that most states banned __10__ marriages. However, in 1967 the US Supreme Court __11__ those bans. Now the conflict is about sex instead of race. At present, only two states legally __12__ same-sex marriages—Massachusetts and California. Worldwide, only five countries legally recognize such marriages.

"California has joined the 21st __13__," said Elton John. "Now Cole Porter and I can finally get married in our favorite city, San Francisco."

"If we normal people don't vote for the __14__," said conservative George Smith, "God will surely __15__ this entire state."

Ex. 2 Make dialogues on the following topics.

1. Talk about what you have known about same-sex marriage.
2. Do you agree with the legalization of same-sex marriage?

Part IV   Watch and Debate

Ex. 1 Watch the video and choose the right answer to the following questions.

1. What holiday is the interviewed for?
    A. New Year's Day.   B. Valentine's Day.
    C. Chinese New Year.   D. Women's Day.
2. What did the man prefer to be called?
    A. Fengshui master.   B. Fengshui expert.
    C. Fengshui practioner.   D. Fengshui follower.
3. Which of the following is not the most important area in the home according to the man?
    A. Entrance.   B. Kitchen.   C. Toilet.   D. Bedroom.
4. What's the ideal size for a bed?
    A. The bigger, the better.   B. The smaller, the better.

Love Is the Fruit of Marriage — Unit 11

    C. Queen size.　　　　　　　　　　D. King size.

5. Where is the best position of the bed?
   A. A view of the door, but not in line with the door.
   B. On the same bed as the door.
   C. Directly facing the door.
   D. Not mentioned in the video.

Ex. 2　Watch the video again and express your opinions on the following questions.
1. Do you think Fengshui is very important? Why or why not?
2. Do you know any stories or any practices related to Fengshui?

Part V　Extracurricular Listening

Listen to the following 10 short dialogues and choose the best answer to each of the questions you will hear.

1. A. Attend a later performance.　　　B. Read in a well-lit place.
   C. Go immediately to the seats.　　D. Buy a program.
2. A. See the dentist.　　　　　　　　B. Give a speech.
   C. Attend the board meeting.　　　D. Travel to a business conference.
3. A. Mow the lawn.　　　　　　　　B. Pay $50 a month for a gardener.
   C. Work in the flowerbeds.　　　　D. Weed the yard.
4. A. Attend a party.　　　　　　　　B. Appoint them.
   C. Have dinner.　　　　　　　　　D. Go home.
5. A. Talking about their house.　　　B. Walking near the campus.
   C. Looking for a place to live in.　　D. Reading a newspaper.
6. A. Pay a visit to their neighbor.　　B. Go on a two-week trip.
   C. Take care of their neighbor's house.　D. Make an ad for their house.
7. A. Talk to the landlord.　　　　　　B. Go to the doctor.
   C. Give a speech.　　　　　　　　D. Find a new apartment.
8. A. Listening to the radio news.　　　B. Watching television.
   C. Listening to the weather forecast.　D. Making preparations for the coming storm.
9. A. He played football.　　　　　　B. He read the sports magazines.
   C. He kept track of the players and games.　D. He busied himself with golf games.
10. A. Fixing their car.　　　　　　　B. Watching a movie.
    C. Making a call.　　　　　　　　D. Listening to radio.

Unit 12 Money Isn't Everything

Part I Door to Wisdom

Read, think and interpret your understanding of the following proverbs and well-known sayings.

1. Time is money.

—Benjamin Franklin

2. The first wealth is health.

—Ralph Waldo Emerson

3. It is at our mother's knee that we acquire our noblest and truest and highest, but there is seldom any money in them.

—Mark Twain

4. No country, however rich, can afford the waste of its human resources.

—Franklin Roosevelt

5. Sometimes one pays most for the things one gets for nothing.

—Albert Einstein

Part II Join in the Dialogue

Money is a powerful force. From the notes and coins in our pockets to the billions that flow around the world each day—it drives business and the economy. Money and financial activity are essential to our world.

No marriage is immune to the effects of money. Financial stress can quickly tear apart already

Unit 12 Money Isn't Everything

fractured marriages and break apart even the strongest relationships.

Dialogue 1

Glossary

groceries 食品，杂货	recession 不景气
thrill 强烈的兴奋	coupon 优惠券
verify 核实	tip 提示
deli 熟食店	grind 磨碎

Ex. 1 Listen to the following dialogue and choose the best answer to each of the questions you will hear.

1. What are the speakers mainly talking about?
   A. How to deposit money.
   B. How to do shopping.
   C. How to cut down living expenses.
   D. How to make a loan.

2. In the program, the Economides gave some tips for listeners, indicating _____.
   A. a good way to cherish your dollars
   B. a good way to eliminate your dollars
   C. a good way to save your dollars
   D. a good way to stretch your dollars

3. What is the story of the family mentioned in the interview?
   A. The family is an example of all the families who are paying less for groceries.
   B. The family is an example of all the families who are paying more for groceries.
   C. The family is an exception to all the families who are paying less for groceries.
   D. The family is an exception to all the families who are paying more for groceries.

4. For the family of six, how much does the family spend on feeding in a month?
   A. $53.　　　B. $140.　　　C. $350.　　　D. $530.

5. What is the suggestion mentioned in Tip One?
   A. Don't go to the grocery store often.
   B. Go to the grocery store every afternoon.
   C. Go to the grocery store often.
   D. Never go to the grocery store.

6. Tip Two indicates that _____.
   A. Don't leave the kids at home and do the shopping by yourself, because baby-sitter cost is expensive
   B. Don't leave the kids at home and do the shopping by yourself, because your kids can help you to get the cheapest thing in the shop
   C. Leave the kids at home and do the shopping by yourself, because shopping means serious calculation
   D. Leave the kids at home and do the shopping by yourself, because it is expensive to have a baby-sitter around

Ex. 2 Make dialogues on the following topics.

1. What is the theme of the dialogue? What can we learn form the dialogue?
2. Tell your budget plan for your school life. With your greatest imagination, how can you survive in

big cities, like Shanghai and Beijing, as soon as you graduate from school? Give examples to illustrate.

Dialogue 2

Glossary

nest egg 存款,储备金　　　　　　precarious 不安全的,不稳固的
spouse 配偶,夫或妻　　　　　　　marriage penalty 婚姻惩罚税
real estate 房地产所有权　　　　　wishy-washy 缺乏特点或决心的
alimony（诉讼期间男给女）生活费　prenup 婚前协议

Ex. 1 Listen to the following dialogue and choose the best answer to each of the questions you will hear.

1. What are speakers talking about?
   A. Divorce and its expenses.　　　　B. Marriage and its expenses.
   C. Divorce and law.　　　　　　　　D. Marriage and law.
2. According to the speakers, getting married will _____.
   A. illegalize one's income　　　　　B. legalize one's income
   C. lower one's income　　　　　　　D. raise one's income
3. For what reason are people now getting married later than before?
   A. Running into a risky position of losing assets.
   B. Running into a risky position of losing income.
   C. Running into a risky position of losing social status.
   D. Running into a risky position of losing true love.
4. The money talk makes the interviewee _____.
   A. disappointed　　B. happy　　　　C. painful　　　　D. sexy
5. According to the interviewee, getting married means saving money on taxes, doesn't it?
   A. Absolutely.　　B. Absolutely not.　C. Necessarily.　　D. Not necessarily.
6. According to the passage, getting a prenup means that _____.
   A. the spouses to be married should sit and talk until an oral agreement is reached
   B. all the family members of the spouses should sit and talk until an oral agreement is reached
   C. lawyers on behalf of both spouses to be married should go to court for a written agreement
   D. lawyers on behalf of both spouses to be married should reach a written agreement

Ex. 2 Make dialogues on the following topics.

1. Do you agree with the saying of "When poverty knocks at your door, love flies out of window"? Give your reasons.
2. When you are going to get married, do you think it is necessary to make clear your wealth or real estate in documents before your marriage? Give your reasons.

Money Isn't Everything Unit 12

Part III   Listen and Discuss

Passage 1

Ex. 1   Listen to the following passage and choose the best answer to each of the questions you will hear.

1. A. Between the age of 20 to 30.   B. Between the age of 30 to 40.
   C. Between the age of 40 to 50.   D. Between the age of 50 to 60.
2. A. To sell computers directly to the consumers.
   B. To sell computers to the consumers through retailers.
   C. To sell computers to Apple Computer Corporation.
   D. To sell computers to the other countries.
3. A. Start a business when you need money.
   B. Start a business when others do so.
   C. Start a business when you really love it.
   D. Start a business when you want to be famous.
4. A. The reason why Michael Dell starts his business.
   B. The reason why Michael Dell sells computers.
   C. The reason why Michael Dell takes apart an Apple computer.
   D. The reason why Michael Dell is successful at such a young age.

Ex. 2   Make dialogues on the following topics.

1. Do you want to start a business of your own soon after your graduation? Why? Give your reasons.
2. What is the most important thing in starting a business of your own? Money? Confidence? Family support? Knowledge and skills? Interest?

Passage 2

Ex. 1   Listen to the following passage and fill in each blank with the word(s) you've heard.

More and more Americans are reading their own credit report. Credit reports are __1__ by lenders to decide how risky it would be to offer a loan or credit to an individual.

The report holds information about a person's __2__ loans and credit-card debt. It records late __3__ of bills and any unpaid loans. It all adds up to a credit history. These days, though, lenders often __4__ people with bad credit histories. They are __5__ higher interest rates and other loan costs.

Some Americans want to read their credit report to know if they have a __6__ of identity theft. They can see if any loans or credit cards have been __7__ in their name with stolen person information.

Another reason is that __8__ reports are not always correct. They might contain wrong information or old information. One change, in 2001, permits people to see their FICO score. FICO

· 73 ·

is short for the Fair Isaac Corporation. _____9_____.

Fair Isaac says many lenders not just in the United States but around the world use its technology to create credit scores. _____10_____.

As of May, the company says it sold ten million credit scores to individuals. _____11_____.

Paying bills on time and paying off credit-card debt improve credit scores.

Ex. 2 Make dialogues on the following topics.

1. Do you have a credit card? Do you know how to make better use (or take advantage) of your credit card?
2. What are advantages and disadvantages of having a credit card? Give an example to illustrate.

Part Ⅳ Watch and Debate

Financial problems triggered by the U. S. subprime mortgage crisis years ago led to a global financial and economic crunch that's now rigorously testing the world's economic development.

This experience is unlike previous crises in several ways. First, the crisis started in developed economies with sound financial infrastructures, while past crises occurred in developing countries.

Second, although this crisis on the surface appeared to be triggered by the burst of an assets bubble, the more profound reason was unbalanced world economic development. Thus, structural barriers are at the core of the crisis.

Glossary

foreclosure 丧失赎取权	default 违约, 拖欠债务
pent-up 被压抑的	discretionary 任意的
momentum 势头	pothole 坑洼
deleverage 减债	mortgage 抵押借款
delinquent 到期未付的	robust 强壮的

Ex. 1 Watch the video and choose the best answer to each of the following questions.

1. What does the video clip mainly tell us about?
   A. Falling retail sales for February.   B. Rising retail sales for February.
   C. Rising retail sales for January.   D. Falling retail sales for January.
2. From the speakers, we can conclude that _____.
   A. consumer electronic sales were down   B. consumer electronic sales were up
   C. real-estate sales on mortgage were down   D. real-estate sales on mortgage were up
3. What happened to consumers according to a monthly survey?
   A. Consumer confidence raised.   B. Consumer confidence slipped.
   C. Consumer number increased.   D. Consumer number decreased.
4. As far as spending was concerned, most of the money was spent on _____.
   A. discretionary   B. education   C. luxuries   D. necessities

Money Isn't Everything — Unit 12

5. Why do Americans still feel terrible about their economy?
   A. They are still suffering from 5 percent or more real unemployment in their economy.
   B. They are still suffering from 10 percent or more real unemployment in their economy.
   C. They are still suffering from 15 percent or more real unemployment in their economy.
   D. They are still suffering from 20 percent or more real unemployment in their economy.

6. How many banks are on the troubled bank list now by the FDIC?
   A. Around 400.   B. Just 400.   C. Less than 400.   D. More than 400.

Ex. 2 Watch the video and complete each blank with what you've heard in the video clip.

Judy Woodruff: In fact, a monthly survey showed consumer __1__ slipped. And while a private report this week found new home foreclosures are slowing, more than __2__ households were put on notice last month, and three million homes are expected to face foreclosure this year.

Meanwhile, the Federal Reserve reported that total U. S. household debt fell last year for the first time since __3__. Much of that was due to a wave of defaults, people walking __4__ their obligations.

Well, to help us unravel these varied economic signals, we __5__ Diane Swonk, chief economist and senior managing director at Mesirow Financial, a diversified financial services firm __6__ Chicago.

Diane Swonk, good to see you again.

We seem to have arrows pointing in a lot of different directions. Let's start with these retail sales number—number—up better than people expected, but—so, is this something—does this say the economy is __7__ we thought?

Diane Swonk: Well, it's nothing to pop champagne corks over. That's for sure. I think we are still cracking beers, __8__, out there.

What we seeing is the level of consumer spending fell to such a low level, there is almost nowhere to go but __9__. We are seeing a lot of pent-up demand. And, in fact, a lot of the spending we're seeing is coming from transferred income, which is everything from Social Security to unemployment insurance __10__, a lot of spending on—not the spending on discretionary, but on necessities out there.

And we are seeing repair and __11__ of things that we have just postponed for __12__. There is just nothing else we can do. So, the level of spending is still extremely low, but the momentum in the __13__.

That said, the data for January will revise down. And so, even though we are moving up, it is sort of two steps forward, __14__. And we could still see this data get revised down as well. So, it really is that level vs. momentum. It kind of feels like we're moving __15__ in a traffic jam.

Ex. 3 Watch the video again and Express your opinions on the following questions.

1. What is the real cause of financial crisis across the world, from your point of view? Give your

reasons. What is the story of the video clip?

2. What is the contribution from China to the world for the economic development in the past few years?

Part V Extracurricular Listening

Listen to the following 10 short dialogues and choose the best answer to each of the questions you will hear.

1. A. Play the piano. B. Learn to sing.
   C. Keep her company. D. Teach her to sing.
2. A. Have her heart checked. B. Buy bread.
   C. Try hard. D. Laugh at her problems.
3. A. Open a gallery. B. Lose weight before getting any new clothes.
   C. Add up the cost before going shopping. D. Buy some new clothes immediately.
4. A. Make his own arrangements. B. Take a spring vacation.
   C. Go to the places she's visited. D. See a travel agent.
5. A. Apologize to Donna. B. Confront Donna directly.
   C. Excuses Donna's behaviour. D. Write Donna a letter of apology.
6. A. Change places with her. B. Postpone buying towels.
   C. Hold up the towel. D. Go sailing next month.
7. A. Earn more money. B. Save more money.
   C. Find a different job. D. Accept unsatisfactory working conditions.
8. A. Run around the town. B. Look more carefully.
   C. Buy shoes from a catalog. D. Find a better place for exercise.
9. A. Look in a different place. B. Stand on something.
   C. Move the cupboard aside. D. Not have tea.
10. A. Keep all the volumes of books together.
    B. Bring the problem to his roommate's attention.
    C. Find a quieter place to study in.
    D. Listen to the music together with his roommate.

Unit 13 Success Is Sweet

Part I Door to Wisdom

Read, think and interpret your understanding of the following proverbs and well-known sayings.

1. Achievement provides the only real pleasure in life.

   —Thomas Edison

2. I succeeded because I willed it; I never hesitated.

   —Bonaparte Napoleon

3. Success covers a multitude of blunders.

   —George Bernard Shaw

4. Happiness is from courage.

   —H. Jackson

5. Most folks are about as happy as they make up their minds to be.

   —Abraham Lincoln

Part II Join in the Dialogue

Most countries have been using GDP to measure its economic development. But some countries have decided to use gross national happiness (GNH), which is supposed to make people's welfare the real goal of a country. GDP measures a country's economic status, whereas GNH measures a society from different aspects such as health standards, social welfare, economic output and the quality of its environment, giving government departments a real view of people's lives.

Happiness is a great thing and a request of all the people around the world but it is not easy to get it because it is found in one thing while many people look for it in a wrong way. They think that they will be happy if they achieve their desires and that is the basic cause for many problems in the unbelieving society such as marriage problems and the problems between the neighbors.

Dialogue 1

Glossary

brag 自吹自擂　　humble 谦逊的,谦虚的
anthem 圣歌,颂歌　　herring 鲱鱼
Fiji 斐济　　Caribbean 加勒比海

Ex. 1 Listen to the following dialogue and choose the best answer to each of the questions you will hear.

1. What are the speakers talking about?
   A. The richest country in the world.　　B. The poorest country in the world.
   C. The happiest country in the world.　　D. The most beautiful country in the world.
2. On what aspects do the speakers talk about happiness?
   A. Health, wealth, and education.　　B. Size, landscape, and beauty.
   C. Longevity, peace and environment.　　D. Nationality, race and religion.
3. What do we learn from one of the speakers about Fiji?
   A. A country in large size.
   B. A country with modern living-quarters.
   C. A country with a long history.
   D. A country with happy cultural environment.
4. Why does the Danish Embassy say that its people are happy?
   A. The people there have an optimistic attitude towards their work and their private life.
   B. The people there have a pessimistic attitude towards their work and their private life.
   C. The people there have a balance between their work and their private life.
   D. The people there have a promise for their work and their private life.
5. How does U. S. rank among 178 countries according to the report from researchers at the University of Leicester in England?
   A. 5th.　　B. 6th.　　C. 23rd.　　D. 32nd.
6. When asked if she would like to live in Fiji instead of U. S., she answers _____.
   A. she would live in Fiji forever
   B. she would not live in Fiji forever
   C. she would live in Fiji for a while
   D. she would not live in Fiji for a while

Success Is Sweet

Unit 13

Ex. 2 Make dialogues on the following topics.

1. Where is the paradise from your point of view? Why? Give your reasons.
2. Some people say we are born in lucky and happy times, do you agree with that? Give examples to illustrate.

Dialogue 2

Glossary

stride 进步	cut to the chase 说话直接
freak 变得极度焦躁	masculine 男子气的
feminine 女子气的	deprive 剥夺

Ex. 1 Listen to the following dialogue and choose the best answer to each of the questions you will hear.

1. What are speakers mainly talking about?
    A. Husband listens to wife when she is rich.
    B. Marriage means money when house is expensive.
    C. Problems emerge when husband earns more than wife does.
    D. Problems emerge when wife earns more than husband does.

2. From the interview, we can conclude that _____.
    A. out-earned wife types of marriages are stable
    B. out-earned wife types of marriages tend to end in divorce
    C. traditional types of marriages are more stable
    D. traditional types of marriages tend to collapse

3. What is percentage of marriages which shows that fact that woman earns more than man does?
    A. 20 percent.   B. 25 percent.   C. 30 percent.   D. 35 percent.

4. According to the interview, man feels uncomfortable because money means _____.
    A. career   B. masculinity   C. nothing   D. something

5. Why man gets freaked out when his wife out-earns?
    A. He feels annoyed that he is left home.
    B. He feels frustrated that he has to take care of household chores.
    C. He feels that he has no bright future in his career.
    D. He feels that he is deprived of his masculinity.

6. What would a clever wife do when she out-earns her husband?
    A. She often talks about the fact she makes a lot of money.
    B. She openly talks about the fact she makes a lot of money.
    C. She rarely talks about the fact she makes a lot of money.
    D. She secretly talks about the fact she makes a lot of money.

Ex. 2　Make dialogues on the following topics.

1. In a family, who should play the most important role, in your opinion? Give your reasons.
2. How to make yourself a successful husband or wife? In what way? Give an example to illustrate.

Part Ⅲ　Listen and Discuss

Passage 1

Ex. 1　Listen to the following passage and choose the best answer to each of the questions you will hear.

1. A. The history of Benjamin Franklin.　　B. The history of the U.S. mail.
   C. The changes of writing letters.　　D. The history of U.S.
2. A. To deliver the mail from Boston on horseback to its destination.
   B. To take charge of the mail for all the colonies in North America.
   C. To introduce the use of stagecoaches to carry mail.
   D. To deliver mail to the communities from railways by horse and wagon.
3. A. The British government.　　B. The American government.
   C. Benjamin Franklin.　　D. George Washington.
4. A. He established a government service.　　B. He developed a system called "star routes".
   C. He built a lot of postal offices.　　D. He established the postal system.

Ex. 2　Make dialogues on the following topics.

1. What is the most successful progress or development for mankind in the last centuries? Give an example to illustrate.
2. How do you understand a successful man or woman? Give your reasons.

Passage 2

Ex. 1　Listen to the following passage and fill in each blank with the word(s) you've heard.

　　Jeffrey Zaslow, the advice columnist for the Chicago Sun-Times, grew up in suburban Philadelphia. His biggest __1__ in life was to be a writer. "I never wanted to be anything else," he says, "I was ten or eleven when I saw *Gone with the Wind* and I wrote my own __2__ War story," After earning a degree in __3__ writing at Carnegie Mellon University, he got a job at a newspaper in Orlando, Florida. He made his mark with his article on the __4__ working conditions endured by the people inside the Mickey and Minnie costumes at Walt Disney World. Later he became a __5__, writer for the Wall Street Journal.

　　In 1988, when the famous advice columnist, Ann Landers, __6__ her job at the Chicago Sun-Times, the paper __7__ a nationwide contest to find her replacement. Jeffrey Zaslow __8__. Among the 12,000 contestants, women outnumbered men nine to one,

Success Is Sweet — Unit 13

_____ 9 _____. When he reached the semifinals, his editors at the Journal ran a headline: "Why He'll Never Make it". But Jeffrey did make it in the finals. Today, eighteen years later, his column, "All that Jazz" is read by thousands of readers in the Chicago area.

_____ 10 _____. He is also greatly moved by the generosity, sincerity and good nature of his readers. "Wonderful people," he says, "do outnumber terrible people in this world. _____ 11 _____."

Ex. 2 Make dialogues on the following topics.

1. What is your dream to be realized from your childhood? Any measures taken to manage your goal?
2. What are your beliefs? Do you think dreams and beliefs are the support for your survival? Give your reasons.

Part IV Watch and Debate

In 2009 when receiving Nobel Peace Prize, United States President Barack Obama said that the ideals of Mahatma Gandhi and Martin Luther King "must always be the North Star that guides us on our journey."

Ex. 1 Watch the video and choose the best answer to each of the following questions.

1. The two wealthiest men in the world went back to the university _____.
   A. to visit the students
   B. to discuss how to study finance effectively
   C. to communicate with the students
   D. to make a speech on success

2. While Bill Gates becomes rich with innovation, Warren Buffett is extremely successful _____.
   A. by investing in high-tech industries
   B. by investing in traditional industries
   C. by selling insurance
   D. by producing soft drinks

3. According to Buffett, most of his money will _____.
   A. be used in philanthropy
   B. be inherited by his children
   C. go to some funds
   D. be given to the Government

4. What is Bill Gates' goal for success outside of work?
   A. Adopting and raising some poor children.
   B. Dealing with some unique challenges.
   C. Instructing American students to succeed.
   D. Raising a family and educating his children.

5. Buffet's answer to the second question shows that a person is successful if he _____.
   A. can win the respect and love from the people around him
   B. is on the Forbes 400
   C. is enormously wealthy
   D. is close to his age

6. Which is NOT right about Buffet and Bill Gates according to the video?
   A. Both of them will donate a big portion of their wealth to help others.
   B. Both of them have grandchildren.

C. Both of them are rich and successful.

D. They share the passion interacting with American students.

Ex. 2   Watch the video and complete each blank with what you've heard in the video clip.

Q2: Hello, my name is Paul Ternes. I'm a Senior of Business Administration and a __1__ from North Dakota, originally. I was wondering what is your definition of success and what has been your largest __2__ in life?

Gates: In my case, my goal for success outside of work is definitely raising a family. I'm just getting __3__ that, and I think there are some unique challenges when a parent is very __4__ and has money and things like that. It's not easy in any case to raise kids the right way, but I'd say, you know, I hope to be successful at that. So far, I haven't caused them any damage. They __5__ be doing Okay.

Buffet: We get a lot of people that want to adopt them. He's __6__ his children, and I'm working on my great grandchildren, but otherwise I guess with __7__. I would say that in terms of success. This will surprise you. But I would say, I've never known anybody that __8__, close to my age, that had lots of people that loved them, that felt anything __9__. I mean that you have lived a successful life if as you get older, the people that you hope love you do. That includes your family, your business associates— __10__. And I... the converse of that is that I know people enormously wealthy, and they get schools __11__ them, and they get, uh, you know, they get dinners in their honor, uh, all that sort of thing, and the truth is that nobody __12__ of them, and I got, I have to believe they know that and that everything __13__ in their life at that point. And they've got all these markers and there're people on the Forbes 400, you know that are __14__, and I won't name names. But they... but it's... I really... I can't think of anyone I've known, and I've known some, you know, a lot of people at this point in my life. I've seen them in very ordinary jobs, all kinds of situations, if the people __15__ love them. They feel very successful.

Ex. 3   Watch the video again and express your opinions on the following questions.

1. What is most important in pursuit for success in the opinions of Gates and Buffet? What is your opinion?

2. If you become rich and successful in the future, what would you like to do most? Give example to illustrate.

Part V   Extracurricular Listening

Listen to the following 10 short dialogues and choose the best answer to each of the questions you will hear.

1. A. John should not talk to Bill any more.

   B. John should tell Bill not to think negatively.

   C. John should take Bill's remarks seriously.

Success Is Sweet

Unit 13

D. John should pay little attention to what Bill says.

2. A. He hadn't finished his house.
   B. He had furnished his house.
   C. He could draw beautifully.
   D. He wasn't really dreaming.

3. A. It's one of their favorite places to eat in.
   B. Its decoration and food are the best around.
   C. They are both disappointed in its recent changes.
   D. It's the best restaurant in the town.

4. A. Susan can hear better when she sits alone.
   B. Susan is becoming a better student.
   C. Susan may be copying Marsha's exam paper.
   D. Susan will do better on the exam if she sits alone.

5. A. He works at the post office.
   B. He's wealthy.
   C. He has just gone bankrupt.
   D. He's unemployed.

6. A. She should be careful about her money.
   B. She should buy the brown suit immediately.
   C. She should try to earn money.
   D. She shouldn't have bought the brown suit.

7. A. He's been in the program for several days.
   B. He's working hard on the program.
   C. He works only during the day.
   D. He will probably never finish.

8. A. It was badly performed.
   B. He liked it very much.
   C. The actors were enthusiastic.
   D. It was funny.

9. A. She doesn't like John and Jim.
   B. Both John and Jim would do better.
   C. One copied from the other.
   D. John and Jim look alike.

10. A. It's big and difficult job.
    B. It's easier than she thought it would be.
    C. It's not as easy as she expected.
    D. It's not difficult for her to write.

Unit 14 No Environment = No Development

Part I Door to Wisdom

Read, think and interpret your understanding of the following proverbs and well-known sayings.

1. I'm not sure about automobiles. With all their speed forward they may be a step backward in civilization.

   —Booth Tarkington

2. What we do for ourselves dies with us. What we do for others and the world remains and is immortal.

   —Albert Pine

3. Almost all absurdity of conduct arises from the imitation of those whom we cannot resemble.

   —Samuel Johnson

4. Of all the animals, man is the only one that is cruel. He is the only one that inflicts pain for the pleasure of doing it.

   —Mark Twain

5. There can be no economy where there is no efficiency.

   —Disraeli

No Environment = No Development   Unit 14

Part II Join in the Dialogue

Although the "green" movement has been going on for years for cleaner and more efficient sources of energy, more than 80 percent of the world's energy supply today still comes from fossil fuels. Solar panels and wind turbines haven't been able to make much of a dent in coal and petroleum's dominance. But efforts never stop to find affordable and renewable new energy, and some scientists have recently claimed that it will be possible and affordable for the world to achieve 100 percent renewable energy by 2030. The renewable sources of energy within the researchers' calculations and focuses include wind power, solar power, waves and geothermal energy.

Dialogue 1

Glossary

impurities 杂质   methanol 甲醇
reactors 反应堆

Ex. 1 Listen to the following dialogue and choose the best answer to each of the questions you will hear.

1. A. An alternative use of fuel oil.
   B. A way to make fuel oil less polluting.
   C. A new method for locating underground oil.
   D. A new source of fuel oil.

2. A. She was doing research for a paper on it. B. She read a newspaper article about it.
   C. She was told about it by her roommate.   D. She heard about it in class.

3. A. To produce a gas containing carbon and hydrogen.
   B. To remove impurities from methanol.
   C. To heat the reactors.
   D. To prevent dangerous gases from forming.

4. A. It hasn't been fully tested.
   B. It's quite expensive.
   C. It uses up scarce minerals.
   D. The gas it produces is harmful to the environment.

Ex. 2 Make dialogues on the following topics.

1. Do you think it is time that we took a fresh look at the appropriateness of using the nuclear power, especially after the nuclear leak accident in Fukujima, Japan?
2. Private cars are very popular in China nowadays. They bring conveniences to human life, but they also bring bad consequences, esp. in the big cities. Discuss in groups to list the problems caused by the cars and suggest your solutions.

Dialogue 2

Glossary

PCBs (polychorinated biphenyls 多氯联苯,有害动物及环境的工业化合物)

pesticide 杀虫剂

Ex. 1 Listen to the following dialogue and choose the best answer to each of the questions.

1. What is Bob's survey about?
   A. How people's shopping preferences affect their environmental protection.
   B. How people's shopping manners affect their environmental protection.
   C. How people's environmental awareness affects their shopping decisions.
   D. How people's environmental preferences affect their shopping decisions.

2. What does the old woman mainly complain about?
   A. Big animals threatening her grandchildren.
   B. Surveys disturbing her business meetings.
   C. Markets damaging natural resources.
   D. Industries threatening environment.

3. What does the old man want to know about Bob?
   A. His consumers and products.
   B. His company and purpose.
   C. His research and future.
   D. His family and children.

4. What does the old woman imply about food in the end?
   A. Industrial pollution threatening humans and animals.
   B. Advertisements affecting people's shopping decisions.
   C. Restaurants changing people's eating inclinations.
   D. Factories showing gratitude to their customers.

Ex. 2 Make dialogues on the following topics.

1. Work in pairs or groups to reflect on our tradition of having wildlife as food. List the measures you think necessary to stop the illegal killing and trading wildlife, in regard to a healthy development of the national economy. Give your reasons to support your ideas.

2. Suppose you and your friends are going to form a volunteer group to promote training in a community on food safety knowledge. Design a plan for your lecture. Include as much necessary information as possible when you prepare.

No Environment = No Development   Unit 14

Part III Listen and Discuss

Passage 1

Ex. 1 Listen to the following passage and choose the best answer to each of the questions you will hear.

1. A. A rare species of algae.
   B. The treatment of wastewater.
   C. A threat to the aquatic environment.
   D. The increasing number of algae in rivers.
2. A. They are becoming more dangerous to the user.
   B. They are encouraging the growth of algae in streams.
   C. They are being made with fewer chemicals.
   D. They are being made to kill bacteria.
3. A. It does not remove all chemicals.
   B. It encourages the growth of some bacteria.
   C. It is not done on a regular basis.
   D. It has been improved by new technologies.
4. A. The role of algae in the food chain.
   B. The effect of household chemicals on algae.
   C. The detection of chemicals in wastewater.
   D. The creation of safer household products.

Ex. 2 Make dialogues on the following topics.

1. Work in groups and list the household products we regularly use that could carry disadvantageous substances such as the bacterial killing chemicals or other nondegradable(不可降解的) ingredients. Make some suggestions that may help reduce the use of them in our life in order to improve our environment.
2. Make a survey on people's awareness of proper water use and discuss with your partner(s) about how to use water properly in life and work.

Passage 2

Ex. 1 Listen to the following passage and choose the best answer to each of the multiple questions you will hear.

1. A. The increase in beachfront property value.
   B. An experimental engineering project.
   C. The erosion of coastal areas.
   D. How to build seawalls.
2. A. To protect beachfront property.
   B. To reduce the traffic on beach roads.
   C. To provide privacy for homeowners.
   D. To define property limits.
3. A. By sending water directly back to sea with great force.
   B. By reducing wave energy.
   C. By reducing beach width.
   D. By stabilizing beachfront construction.

4. A. Protect roads along the shore. B. Build on beaches with seawalls.
   C. Add sand to beaches with seawalls. D. Stop building seawalls.

Ex. 2 Make dialogues on the following topics.

1. Dams and hydropower stations have been globally constructed along the major rivers such as Rhine, Amazon, Nile, and Yangtze. They are controversial. Consult some references and discuss with your partner(s) to list the advantages and disadvantages of water conservancy projects.

2. Cultural sites and historical relics are important part of our national legacy. However, at times, we heard news about pursuing economic benefits at the cost of unscrupulously damaging and destroying such legacy. How are we supposed to protect them, especially when our objectives of development come in conflict with maintaining our ancestors' irretrievable treasures? Brainstorm and illustrate the possible measures to take in both personal and social senses.

Part Ⅳ Watch and Debate

In the following video clips, Carl Pope, Executive Director of the Sierra Club and Stephen Walt, Professor of International Affairs, Harvard University, are talking in their interviews with bigthink. com on the planet's carrying capacity in relation to the rapid development of global economy.

Glossary

Gandhi 甘地(印度独立运动领袖)	strains 压力
compatible 协调	simultaneously 同时地
piracy 海盗行为	tradeoff 权衡考虑
diminution 减少	ostentation 炫耀,卖弄
appropriate 盗用	McMansion 华而不实的豪宅
scenarios 戏剧性场景	carbon footprint 碳排放记录
advent 出现,到来	sit well with 让人心安理得

Ex. 1 Watch the video clips and fill in the missing information with either the exact words from the interview or with your own words.

Clip 1

Question: *Are development and environmentalism compatible?*

Carl Pope: Well I suppose that depends on what you mean by development. And I'm reminded of Gandhi's response when he was asked what he thought about western civilization. And he said it would be a good idea. I think development… human development would be a good idea. What we mostly call development is not actually development. It's piracy. It's just grabbing stuff. No, _____1_____. We cannot have an economy in which those who get there first and take everything off the table are rewarded. That's not _____2_____. So we need a new definition of development. But if development means learning how to grow 100 plants and feed a family off a smaller garden, yeah, that's definitely compatible. If it's the development that _____3_____

No Environment = No Development

Unit 14

_____ as opposed to the development that _____ 4 _____, it's not only compatible; it's essential.

Clip 2

Question: *What is the world's biggest challenges?*

Stephen Walt: I think there is a sense... a growing sense that there are going to be limits to _____ 5 _____. And I think the major constraint there is environmental. The most obvious symptom of that is growing concern with global warming and climate change of various kinds; and the sense that we may not be able to stop that particular train before it goes off the cliff, you know if you imagine some of the more catastrophic scenarios. Does that end all life on the planet? No. But does it have very severe consequences for different parts of the world? I think that's... that's there.

I think we are going to see over the next 40 or 50 years a fundamental shift in the balance of power between what has been the sort of transatlantic access—Europe and America—for the last several hundred years shifting more towards Asia. The United States will be a critical part of that too; but again India and China much more so.

I think, third, there is a... an issue of equality... an inequality on a global scale now, which is compounded by the fact that increasingly, people who are further down the inequality scales are more and more aware of what their relative positions are. And again, the advent of global communications and things like that is starting to make it much more obvious to people. So we have at least, I think, a potential train wreck of different trends happening where India and China are developing. Their development is going to _____ 6 _____. They're not going to _____ 7 _____, right? The advanced countries like the United States _____ 8 _____. And everyone is going to be more aware of all of this simultaneously. So I think the potential for real trouble down the road is... is considerable.

Question: *Is development at odds with environmentalism?*

Stephen Walt: I think there's an obvious tradeoff. We can't have, you know, _____ 9 _____. So one of the problems we're going to have to address as a society is how do you convince people in the most advanced societies who are consuming most of the resources to... to essentially... what I regard as not necessarily a diminution of their lifestyles, but a diminution of their ostentation. Or to put it in really crude terms, how do you get more Americans and Europeans to have a much, much smaller carbon footprint, right? Without thinking that that requires us all to live in tiny homes; that requires us all to ride bicycles to work or things like that; but rather can we be happy about a different lifestyle where maybe the 12,000 foot McMansion is not the American dream, and that _____ 10 _____. I actually regard that as a social and cultural problem that we are, again, just beginning to have to think about. And it's not one that's going to sit well with many Americans.

We tend to think, "We're Americans. We're entitled to whatever we can afford."

Ex. 2 Watch the video again and express your opinions on the following questions.

1. What do you think of the compatibility between development and environment? How do you understand "piracy" mentioned by Mr. Carl Pope in clip 1? Discuss in pairs and list suggestions about putting development in agreement with environmental protection.

2. In clip 2, Professor Stephen Walt refers more than once to India, China and the United States in his illustration. Analyze in groups his points on the roles to play for developing and advanced countries in sustainable global development. Make a list and find supporting clues from the clip.

Part V Extracurricular Listening

Listen to the following 10 short dialogues and choose the best answer to each of the questions you will hear.

1. A. He has a promising career. B. He can't sell books.
   C. He and his boss get along well. D. He prefers to be a salesman.

2. A. Both of them have overcome their fear.
   B. They are both afraid of high places.
   C. The woman is still afraid of high places, but the man isn't.
   D. Both of them prefer high places these days.

3. A. The woman will go home for dinner.
   B. The woman won't go to the concert.
   C. The man and the woman will eat together.
   D. The man and the woman will go home before going to the concert.

4. A. He'll buy a sports car as soon as he gets the money.
   B. He can't afford to buy a new sports car.
   C. He has already made a down payment on the car.
   D. He bought a sports car last week.

5. A. Their original plans were bad. B. They kept to their original plans.
   C. They failed to make a profit. D. They managed to make more money.

6. A. His project proved to be unsuccessful.
   B. He failed to get sufficient money.
   C. Lack of land prevented his success.
   D. He was successful with his project.

7. A. The man couldn't find a parking lot.
   B. It's hard to find a place to leave the car.
   C. The woman was upset due to his late arrival.
   D. The man apologized because of his negligence.

8. A. She likes going to bed early. B. She seldom feels sleepy.
   C. She likes going to bed late. D. She never gets up early.

No Environment = No Development

Unit 14

9. A. She has very few friends.
   B. She likes to telephone her friends.
   C. She likes to have long talks with her friends on the phone.
   D. She doesn't like to be disturbed by phone calls.

10. A. The exam was difficult for the woman.
    B. The test consisted of one page.
    C. The woman found the exam easy.
    D. The woman completed the exam in one hour.

Unit 15 Problems Are the Price of Progress

Part I Door to Wisdom

Read, think and interpret your understanding of the following proverbs and well-known sayings.

1. A man who has committed a mistake and doesn't correct it is committing another mistake.
   —Confucius

2. He who knows others is learned; he who knows himself is wise.
   —Lao-Tze

3. It is only because of problems that we grow mentally and spiritually.
   —M. Scott Peck

4. All difficult things have their origin in that which is easy, and great things in that which is small.
   —Lao-Tze

5. Give a man a fish, he'll eat for a day. Teach a man how to fish, he'll eat for a lifetime.
   —Chinese proverb

Problems Are the Price of Progress

Unit 15

Part II Join in the Dialogue

Dialogue 1

We live in a world of deep inequality, and the gap between the rich and the poor is widening. We generally agree that this is a problem we ought to help fix. For decades, Wilkinson has studied why some societies are healthier than others. He found that what the healthiest societies have in common is not that they have more—more income, more education, or more wealth—but that what they have is more equitably shared.

New research shows that the healthiest and happiest aren't those with the highest incomes but those with the most equality. In his latest book, *The Spirit Level*: *Why More Equal Societies Almost Always Do Better*, Richard Wilkinson discusses why.

Glossary

life expectancy 预期寿命	intuition 直觉
divisive 分裂的	corrosive 腐蚀的
illustrative 作为说明的	corrosion 腐蚀
trigger 扳机, 触发器	superiority 优势
inferiority 劣势	mediator 中介, 媒介

Ex. 1 Listen to the following dialogue and choose the best answer to each of the questions you will hear.

1. The impact of inequality on health is related to _____.
    A. income   B. violence   C. death rate   D. status divisions
2. According to the interview, social problems are more likely to be tied to _____.
    A. poverty in poor and developed countries
    B. level of income in poor and developed countries
    C. both A and B
    D. social gaps in developed countries
3. How do the media respond to these social problems?
    A. They blame parents or teachers or lack of religion.
    B. They blame teachers.
    C. They blame people for lack of belief.
    D. A, B, and C.
4. The author Richard's book focuses on _____ effect of inequality upon people.
    A. psychosocial   B. material
    C. economic   D. A, B, and C
5. In a more unequal society people are more likely to _____.
    A. spend more   B. work more
    C. both A and B   D. save more

6. In a more equal society, people are more likely to _____.
   A. establish trust   B. be in debt
   C. make statements about themselves   D. A, B, and C

Ex. 2 Make dialogues on the following topics.
1. In what ways do you think inequality does harm to society? Give an example to illustrate your point of view.
2. How do people behave in an unequal society? Why? Give your reasons.
3. What do you think of China in terms of? Why is it so? How can we create a harmonious society?

Dialogue 2

Experiencing Megacities in New Ways

Interview with Harald Mieg and Christian Hoffmann by Norbert Aschenbrenner.

Prof. Harald Mieg is the director of the Metropolitan Studies Center at Humboldt University in Berlin. Christian Hoffmann specializes in the psychology of innovation and urban-environment relationships.

Glossary

cohesion 内聚力   stigmatize 玷污
anonymous 匿名的   desolate 荒芜的
advent 出现   circumvent 绕过
pedestrian 行人

Ex. 1 Listen to the following dialogue and fill in each blank with the word(s) you've heard.

Aschenbrenner: *What makes a city worth living in?*

Hoffmann: Satisfaction with one's living situation depends on a lot more than a city's physical design. Also very important are soft factors such as social cohesion—in other words, the degree to which people are __1__ into personal networks. There are also __2__ criteria, of course, including noise levels, air pollution and crime, job opportunities, freedom of movement and good public transport.

Aschenbrenner: *Why do cities with a poor quality of life, from an objective standpoint, often have the most dynamic population growth?*

Mieg: People move to cities because they're the most attractive places in their countries. We may not find them __3__, but people go to them because they enable them to take control of, and improve, their lives. There's also a lot of psychology involved. The myths __4__ with city life exert a very powerful attraction.

Aschenbrenner: *How can crime be reduced?*

Hoffmann: According to the "Defensible Space" concept, urban construction should be carried out in a manner that leads residents to __5__ with their surroundings. Put simply, you have to build in a way that prompts people to say: "This is my neighborhood and I'm going to

Problems Are the Price of Progress

Unit 15

help take care of it." Spaces should be open and visible, and no areas should become stigmatized due to cheap forms of construction. The less __6__ a building doorway is, for example, the more likely you'll see a higher level of crime there.

Aschenbrenner: *What must an architect take into account to ensure that residents feel comfortable?*

Mieg: The most important factor is the design of semi-private areas—those between public places, such as streets and squares, and private spaces. This could be the area in front of a building, or an inner courtyard—places where people talk with their neighbors, which is why they're so __7__ for communication. The design of apartment building lobbies, for example, has a major __8__ on whether people talk to each other or remain anonymous.

Aschenbrenner: *And what about public places?*

Mieg: Outdoor spaces will be _____9_____. If a square is desolate, people won't treat it with respect—they won't feel responsible for it. Generally, people feel responsible for their private spaces and to some extent for semi-private areas.

Aschenbrenner: *What can technology accomplish here?*

Mieg: It can help to meet basic needs _____10_____. It can also have a more subtle impact in the form of lighting, which not only creates a sense of security but also can make a city more attractive. The typical urban atmosphere is in fact created with the advent of electric light. New types of traffic guidance systems are also greatly enhancing the quality of urban life by helping visitors to circumvent traffic jams. In the future, pedestrians will even _____11_____.

Ex. 2 Make dialogues on the following topics.

1. What do you think should be a livable city? Is Nanjing, Shanghai, Beijing, Canton, or your hometown a livable city?
2. What is your first consideration for a livable city? Why?
3. How to create a livable city in China?

Part III Listen and Discuss

Passage 1

What Are Social Problems?

Glossary

    sparsely 稀少地   hygiene 卫生
    inhibit 阻碍   tamper 损害

Ex. 1 Listen to the following passage and choose the best answer to each of the questions you will hear.

1. A. When people living together in a society have conflicts.

B. When people live in sparsely populated areas.
   C. When people live together close enough.
   D. When people live relatively isolated.

2. A. Because people are rich.
   B. Because people are poor.
   C. Because people are unemployed.
   D. Because people in different social groups disagree with each other.

3. A. In small countries.
   B. In developing countries.
   C. In developed countries.
   D. Both A and B.

4. A. It is a single problem.
   B. It is infectious.
   C. It is easy to solve.
   D. It is complex to understand.

5. A. There are many kinds of solutions.
   B. There are not enough solutions.
   C. There are easy solutions.
   D. Solutions are not effective.

6. A. Yes, there are always good solutions.
   B. Yes, but only some solutions are achievable.
   C. No, no solution is perfect.
   D. No, no one feels happy with solutions.

Ex. 2 Make dialogues on the following topics.

1. Do you think both developed countries and developing countries have social problems? What are their differences? Give your reasons.
2. What do you think about the social problems in China? Which social problem is the most serious? Give some examples.

Passage 2

Aiming to Reduce Fatal Traffic Accidents: Zero Vision, Zero Results?

   The zero vision has had its day. Ten years after the Norwegian authorities launched its zero casualties objective for road safety, statistics have not improved.

Glossary

fatality（死亡）事故	casualty 伤亡事故
stall 停止,停顿	implement 贯彻,履行
compulsory 强制的	breach 违反

Ex. 1 Listen to the following passage and fill in each blank with the word(s) you've heard.

   "The zero vision has drawn more attention to road safety, but it has not __1__ any significant short-term gains so far," says Langeland, staff engineer at the Norwegian Public Roads Administration. He based his thesis on interviews with 30 experts on road safety, and his conclusion is less than __2__.

   Since the mid-1990s, the number of people killed in road accidents has not decreased

Problems Are the Price of Progress

Unit 15

significantly. 560 people were killed in traffic accidents in 1970. Fifteen years on, it was less than 300. The National Transport Plan 2002-2011 was __3__ in 1999, and the zero vision with it. Since then, the number of fatalities has remained largely unchanged.

There may be a number of reasons why the casualty and severely __4__ has stalled since the mid-1990s. It could be attributed to a series of preventive measures implemented since the 1970s, which—in spite of the traffic boom—have had a __5__ effect. Compulsory use of safety belts and more secure vehicles are among them. Until 1990, the casualty shrunk by roughly 100 during each decade. This should imply a number of __6__ 150 road casualties today—not 250, he explains.

The zero vision stemmed from a desire to further reduce the number of fatalities and severe injuries from road accidents. According to Langeland, it is to be regarded more as a vision than an actual target. __7__, road users and infrastructure are interrelated. This interrelatedness is best exemplified by speed limits being set on the basis of the human body's __8__ at the moment of collision.

"_____9_____.
Implementing preventive measures to ensure lower speed levels, such as speed caps in cars, will reduce the annual number of people killed in road accidents significantly," Langeland says.

Although Langeland believes the zero vision to be an unobtainable goal, he still thinks it has something going for it. Even though the vision does not permeate traffic authorities and the police on a daily basis, it has raised awareness among the public and the safety sector. It may serve as a guiding light on the way to achieving lower casualty than 250, Langeland believes.

Langeland _____10_____.
The same should apply to not using a safety belt and driving above speed limits, which are the two main causes of road deaths today.

Future measures should concentrate on preventing head-on collisions, off-the-road accidents and accidents involving non-motorists. Physical obstacles are effective at preventing accidents, The traffic researcher offers a final word of advice: "_____11_____."

Ex. 2 Make dialogues on the following topics.
1. What are the main causes of increasing number of traffic accidents? Whose faults are they?
2. What can our government do to reduce traffic accidents? What measures can we take to achieve our goals?
3. Are you optimistic or pessimistic about the traffic situation in China/Nanjing/your hometown?

Part IV Watch and Debate

A Global Problem——Smoking Pollution

In the face of complex global problems, it's easy to feel overwhelmed and powerless, and to find ourselves asking, "What difference can one person make?" So adopt a greener lifestyle while encouraging others to change. Living a more eco-friendly life is a lot like starting an exercise program. As an added bonus, many green lifestyle choices even come with health and financial benefits.

Ex. 1 Watch the video and answer the following questions.

1. What crisis is China's smoking population facing according to BBC World News?
   _____.
2. What is the prediction on next 25 years if nothing is done to reduce smoking rate?
   _____.
3. Is it easy to give up smoking, especially for men?
   _____.
4. What changes has Beijing Olympic Games brought about?
   _____.
5. What is the situation to quit smoking? Why?
   _____.
6. What should we do as a whole society?
   _____.

Ex. 2 Express your opinions on the following questions after watching the video.

1. How does smoking function in China's human relationships? What is smoking culture in China?
2. Is there anyone you know smoking around you or in your family? Are they ready to quit smoking? Why?
3. Do you smoke or do you hate smoking? Why?

Part V   Extracurricular Listening

Listen to the following 10 short dialogues and choose the best answer to each of the questions you will hear.

1. A. The man shouldn't expect her to go along.
   B. She doesn't think she's in the mood for seeing the movie.
   C. She'll go even though the movie isn't good.
   D. The man should count the number of people going.
2. A. He doubts David's reliability.
   B. He's willing to trust David.
   C. He's confided some of his doubts to David.
   D. He thinks David will benefit form his experience.
3. A. She wants someone to talk to.
   B. She doesn't want to be disturbed either.
   C. She doesn't mind talking to Alan.
   D. She'll sit next to Alan through the whole movie.
4. A. Not everyone from England likes to read all the time.
   B. People who teach English like things besides books.
   C. The English like to read a lot and listen to music.
   D. English teachers usually like to read a lot.

Problems Are the Price of Progress

Unit 15

5. A. They shouldn't make too many requests.
   B. They should ask for more days to do the work.
   C. They shouldn't reject the professor's good wishes.
   D. They should wish themselves good luck.
6. A. It's not good.   B. It's crowded.
   C. It's expensive.   D. It's far away.
7. A. She has tried to avoid talking to the artists.
   B. She has made the decision to study art.
   C. She has decided to take a painting to her art class.
   D. She has made the punch for the artists' party.
8. A. She has temporarily forgotten the name.
   B. The record is very popular.
   C. She's been singing along with the music all day.
   D. The name is difficult for her to pronounce.
9. A. He couldn't get through to the woman.
   B. He was held up by traffic.
   C. He would be punctual next time.
   D. He wouldn't keep the woman waiting any longer.
10. A. The apartments are too small for the students to share.
    B. The apartments are not quite near enough to the campus.
    C. Most students can be reached at their campus address.
    D. Very few students could afford to live there.

 Cultural Diversity Shapes National Character

Part I Door to Wisdom

Read, think and interpret your understanding of the following proverbs and well-known sayings.

1. Real knowledge is to know the extent of one's ignorance.

—Confucius

2. Study without thought is vain; thought without study is dangerous.

—Confucius

3. Virtue is never left to stand alone. He who has it will have neighbors.

—Confucius

4. Everything has its beauty, but not everyone sees it.

—Confucius

5. Look for an occupation that you like, and you will not need to labor for a single day in your life.

—Confucius

Part II Join in the Dialogue

Culture is a term that has various meanings. However, the word "culture" is most commonly used in three basic senses:

Cultural Diversity Shapes National Character

Unit 16

- Excellence of taste in the fine arts and humanities, also known as high culture
- An integrated pattern of human knowledge, belief, and behavior that depends upon the capacity for symbolic thought and social learning
- The set of shared attitudes, values, goals, and practices that characterizes an institution, organization or group

Dialogue 1

People of the World—Interview with a Couple

Glossary

conspire 想法,图谋　　　cuisine 烹饪
ingredients 配料,成分　　flavor 风味
dart 镖

Ex. 1 Listen to the following dialogue and choose the best answer to each of the questions you will hear.

1. What language does Liz speak with her husband Uwe?
   A. Liz speaks English at home with her husband Uwe.
   B. Liz speaks German with Uwe's friends and family.
   C. Liz speaks German when they are back to Germany.
   D. A, B, and C.

2. How do they cook?
   A. They do not cook at home, but dine out.
   B. Uwe works outside while Liz cooks at home.
   C. Liz cooks international food except European one.
   D. Uwe cooks international food except European one.

3. What part of culture of her partner surprises Liz?
   A. Social.　　B. Political.　　C. Economic.　　D. A and B.

4. What is the best thing in their cross-cultural relationship?
   A. It can expand their world view.　　B. It can bring their love closer.
   C. It can improve her German.　　　 D. It can help her learn more experience.

5. What is the hardest thing in their cross-cultural relationship?
   A. It is how to adapt one way of communication to the other to relieve stress.
   B. It is how to change from an indirect style to a direct style.
   C. It is how to adjust personal feelings.
   D. It is how to adjust a separate discussion.

6. What is the advice for other cross-cultural couples?
   A. Be patient and respect other values.
   B. Analyze different frameworks of cultures and languages.
   C. Communication as well as compromise.
   D. A and C.

Ex. 2　Make dialogues on the following topics.

1. What is your attitude to different cultures? What is the trend for the development of cultures in the globalized world? Give your reasons.
2. What are the differences between Chinese culture and Western culture? Give examples.
3. How can we develop Chinese culture? Give an example to illustrate your point of view.

Dialogue 2

On the Different Cultures and Symbols of China

Happy Chinese New Year! As we launch a new lunar calendar year, we have the good fortune to reconnect with a master of Chinese culture, Martin Yan. He will share with us his profound knowledge of all things Chinese, particularly about the New Year symbols, food, and yin and yang. Join us, then, as we explore the world of Chinese culture through the eyes and words of Martin Yan.

Glossary

multi-ethnic 多民族的	snapshot 快照
staple 主食	steaming 蒸
ingredients 配料	metropolitan 大都市的
stew 炖,煨	braising (用文火)燉,蒸
embroidery 刺绣	recipe 烹饪

Ex. 1　Listen to the following dialogue and fill in each blank with the word(s) you've heard.

Kate: Chinese culture includes many symbolic foods, especially at Chinese New Year. Gifts of grapefruit and oranges, for instance, __1__ good fortune. Did you discover any new symbols on your journey through China?

Martin: Even in China, a lot of people don't realize that China is a multi-ethnic country and has very __2__ history, culture and food habits. So you see a lot of these kinds of things and because of that, when you look at Chinese foods, they are not really __3__ Chinese foods. And because of different cultures you see different __4__ meanings. In general, most of the traditional symbols are common for Chinese throughout the world.

Kate: In your latest book and TV series, you lead us through the heartland and even most __5__ areas of this vast nation. Would you walk us through China and give us a snapshot of what each area is all about? Let's start with Beijing…

Martin: The main staple of Beijing is wheat flour and noodles, and the most famous food is Peking Duck. In Northern China, you cannot grow rice because the weather is too cold. So because of the weather, __6__ and soil, they can grow wheat, and the wheat ends up on the table, as the main staple. So that's why you have a lot of noodles, dumplings, all kinds of buns, all wheat based. Canton is in the southern tip of China, __7__ to a lot of rivers and lakes as well as the ocean. So you see a variety of seafood, and there's a lot of steaming, stir-frying, seasonal ingredients. Shanghai is a port city and also an international city and a center of

· 102 ·

Cultural Diversity Shapes National Character

Unit 16

___8___. You know, you see a lot of food from different parts of China in Shanghai because it is metropolitan—I mean, the best of Beijing, the best of Canton, the best of Sichuan, you find them all in Shanghai. And also, Shanghai being a coastal city, you have a lot of seafood. They are very famous for red-cooked dishes, which means that meat, chicken, or seafood is cooked in a rich, brown, sweet sauce and they are cooked to a point that end up like stews, and braising. So they are very famous for that.

Kate: So Shanghai sounds a lot like Venice, which as a port town, had all of the different spices and flavors there because of the trading ships.

Martin: Yes, and also because of Hangzhou and Suzhou being the center of silk and embroidery. During the famous silk road, a lot of those spices and foods and cultures were introduced to this area.

Kate: So much of Chinese cooking is based on a yin yang balance of flavors—how can you really teach that? In that it's not just a recipe.

Martin: Actually, yin and yang philosophy is one _____9_____. For instance, if you love certain things, you learn always to watch out that you do not have too much of one thing—even exercise, even making money, even success. If somebody is too successful, making too much money, then they have lost sight of who they are, of the family values. They don't have time to spend with the parent or with the children. So the idea of yin and yang is _____10_____. And food is the same. When you go to a Chinese restaurant, when you order and prepare Chinese food, you got to watch out. You don't want to have too many deep fried dishes. You don't want too many dishes all with meat. You want to balance the meat with the vegetable dish, and you want to balance the sweet and sour with some lighter fare. You want to balance deep fried dishes with steamed dishes. It's all about balance. _____11_____.

Ex. 2 Make dialogues on the following topics.

1. What is Chinese food culture? How different is it from Western culture?
2. What are Chinese famous cuisines? How much do you know about them? Please say something about the food and cuisine in your hometown.
3. What is the theory of yin and yang in traditional Chinese culture? Give examples to support its truth.

Part III Listen and Discuss

Passage 1

10 Steps for Dealing with Different Cultures

Different national cultures may view the same thing in very different ways. Thus, communication can engender or distance you from potential clients or partners. Here are 10 ways that will help you

create strong sustainable relationships with peers, partners, team members or clients from other cultures or nationalities.

Glossary

stereotype 陈规　　　　　　　masculine 男性的,阳性的
feminine 女性的,阴性的　　　assertive 断定的
commitment 义务　　　　　　empathy 移情作用
protocol 礼仪　　　　　　　　patronize 庇护

Ex. 1　Listen to the following passage and choose the best answer to each of the questions you will hear.

1. In Step 1 we can learn that _____.

   A. your communication style may be refused by someone from another culture

   B. your values, attitudes, or behaviors may not be perceived by another culture the same way

   C. they may take your humor seriously in another culture

   D. feedback from another culture is likely to be friendly

2. In Step 2 we can learn that _____.

   A. an individual may not mean a stereotype in the same culture

   B. values, expectations and beliefs drive behaviors in different cultures

   C. culture is shaped by everything

   D. culture doesn't differ from anything

3. In Step 3 we can learn that _____.

   A. status is less important in the UK or the U.S. than in Greece and France

   B. in some cultures status is of more importance than decision making

   C. status is as important in Spain/Italy as in Sweden/Norway

   D. lower level decisions are made in Japan

4. In Step 4 we can learn that _____.

   A. the U.S is a masculine culture while Sweden is a feminine culture

   B. different masculine or feminine style may affect the type of relationship

   C. what is perceived positively in Sweden may be perceived negatively in the U.S.

   D. A, B, and C

5. In Step 5 we can infer that _____.

   A. Asian cultures take as a long view as Western cultures

   B. both Asian cultures and Western cultures have a short-term or long-term view

   C. Chinese culture takes a long-term view

   D. projects are assessed, justified and made by decisions

6. In Step 7 we can learn that _____.

   A. empathy is a skill to show people's feelings

   B. empathy is a skill to make effort to see and feel things

   C. empathy skills help people see positively

   D. we should look at things from their own language, knowledge or customs

Cultural Diversity Shapes National Character

Unit 16

7. In Step 8 we can learn that _____.
    A. it is appropriate to have explicit communication
    B. not everyone preferred Japanese style
    C. everyone preferred Japanese style
    D. the Japanese have as much implicit communication style as the British
8. In Step 10 we can learn that _____.
    A. positive behaviors may not mean agreement
    B. a smile and handshake may mean agreement
    C. unsmiling and silence may mean disagreement
    D. if you change your own behaviors, you can influence someone else

Ex. 2   Make dialogues on the following topics.

1. What is Chinese culture/Western culture? What are their advantages and disadvantages? Give examples.
2. What can we learn from Western culture? Why?
3. Some people think Chinese culture is backward and Western culture is modern? Do you agree? Why?

Passage 2

Misunderstandings Based upon Diversity

Cultural diversity exists everywhere, when people speak different languages, or when they come from different areas. Even when they speak the same language, communication problems, however, can still exist. What is cultural diversity?

Glossary

rapidity 迅速　　　defiance 蔑视
ethnicity 民族　　　kinship 亲族

Ex. 1   Listen to the following passage and fill in each blank with the word(s) you've heard.

1. Communication style.

    Even when the same language is used, people __1__ information differently. Therefore, the message sent is not always the message received. Differences in communication styles can make the sender of the message appear to be pushy, rude, __2__, passive, etc. Factors involved in this are __3__ and rapidity of speech, tone of voice, and emphasis on key words.

2. Nonverbal communication.

    Nonverbal communication is the sum total of our body's communication. It is how our body communicates or sends a message. Nonverbal communication has different meanings for different people or groups. Studies show that 50 percent of a message's __4__ comes from body movements or nonverbal communication. For example, crossing your arms may __5__ defiance. Putting your hand on your chin may show thought.

3. Trust.

Trust plays an important role in   6 , interracial, and inter-gender communication. A lack of trust can result not only in miscommunications, but even in no communication taking place.

4. Accents.

Some people react negatively to accents. They may even be rude when someone does not speak "proper" English. People have accents either because of ethnicity or region of country from which they come or because English is their second language. Some people consider them to be less intelligent, less   7 , and even less   8 . Leaders need to judge if accent interferes with the ability to communicate or perform. If accents do not interfere, then our focus needs to be on listening to what is being said, not on how it is said.

5. Stereotyres.

A stereotype is _____   9   _____.
Stereotyping is very common. _____   10   _____.
Stereotypes can either be positive or negative, for example, "Asians are intelligent" or "Hispanics are emotional." Positive stereotyping can be just as dangerous for a leader to use as negative stereotyping.

6. Values and beliefs.

Values are beliefs which regulate how we should or should not behave. Our values often reflect a larger, social value system. _____   11   _____.
When people hold different values or have different beliefs, communication may be very difficult. For example, some people value extended families and have close kinship ties.

Ex. 2 Make dialogues on the following topics.

1. What is cultural diversity? What problems are caused by cultural diversity? Do you accept it?
2. What is diversity between Chinese culture and Western culture? Give examples.
3. How do people between different cultures live in harmony with each other?

Part IV Watch and Debate

What Is Happiness?

Tal D. Ben-Shahar, a non-tenured lecturer in the Psychology Department of Harvard University, teaches a course at Harvard entitled "Positive Psychology". His course focuses on the psychological aspects of a fulfilling and flourishing life. Topics include happiness, self-esteem, empathy, friendship, love, achievement, creativity, music, spirituality, and humor. Tal D. Ben-Shahar discusses current research on the science of happiness and introduces ideas and tools that can actually make a difference in one's life.

Glossary

debilitate 使衰弱   enervate 软弱
obscure 掩盖

Unit 16 Cultural Diversity Shapes National Character

Ex. 1 Watch the video and answer the following questions.

1. Why is information not enough for education? What is more important? Why?
   _____
   _____.

2. What can you learn from Shahar's three examples?
   _____
   _____.

3. What is Shahar's statement of happiness?
   _____
   _____.

4. What does "Soul grows more by subtraction than by addition" mean in terms of our potential?
   _____
   _____.

5. How is Shahar's "Knowledge is about information, wisdom is about transformation" related to Laozi's teaching?
   _____
   _____.

6. How do you understand Voltaire's "Common sense is not that common"?
   _____
   _____.

7. What are John Carter's two findings?
   _____
   _____.

8. In what way can we better understand human nature?
   _____
   _____.

Ex. 2 Express your opinions on the following questions after watching the video.

1. How do you understand Shahar's sense of happiness: How to be happier, not happy? Do you agree with him? Why? Give examples in your life experience.

2. What is your sense of happiness? How do you achieve your happiness?

Part V Extracurricular Listening

Listen to the following 10 short dialogues and choose the best answer to each of the questions you will hear.

1. A. At a movie theatre.   B. At a supermarket.
   C. At a cafeteria.   D. At a laundry.

2. A. No one can find the manager's apartment.
   B. His family lives in the apartment building.

C. He has no idea where to find the manager.

D. He only helps people rent apartments here.

3. A. He likes to keep his car looking beautiful.

B. He wonders who their next neighbor will be.

C. He admires the neighbor's car.

D. He hasn't met the new neighbor yet.

4. A. He should be more careful with his books.

B. She will give him something to write on.

C. She thinks she knows who took his notebook paper.

D. She doesn't mind if he borrows her notes.

5. A. The red wallet cost two dollars.   B. He has been to the church.

C. The wallet was on the bottom.   D. He has looked there carefully.

6. A. The garden hasn't been planned.

B. The ground is too wet to plant vegetables.

C. The man wants to quit.

D. The man doesn't like to wait.

7. A. Buy a ticket for the ten o'clock flight.

B. Ask the man to change the ticket for her.

C. Go to the airport immediately.

D. Switch to a different flight.

8. A. She should be preparing for the track season.

B. She has an excuse for everything.

C. She has good reason for going jogging.

D. She's always willing to take good advice.

9. A. No one knows why the coach quit.

B. He missed the coach's retirement party.

C. The coach is trying to solve the mystery.

D. He doesn't know why the coach wants to see him.

10. A. No one expects him to move.   B. He decided not to go to New York.

C. He won an award recently.   D. He felt surprised.

Unit 17  Calamity Is Man's True Touch-Stone

Part I Door to Wisdom

Read, think and interpret your understanding of the following proverbs and well-known sayings.

1. When one door of happiness closes, another opens.

   —Helen Keller

2. I have not failed. I've just found 10,000 ways that won't work.

   —Thomas Edison

3. The only man who makes no mistakes is the man who never does anything.

   —Theodore Roosevelt

4. Little minds are tamed and subdued by misfortune; but great minds rise above them.

   —Washington Irving

5. The measure of a man is the way he bears up under misfortune.

   —Peter Nivio Zarlenga

Part II Join in the Dialogue

Dialogue 1

The earthquake off the coast of Japan on March 11, 2011 was one of the biggest recorded, measuring 9 on the Richter scale. It was the resulting tsunami, however, that caused the most destruction. It devastated the northeast of Japan, leaving many thousands dead or missing, and hundreds of thousands homeless or evacuated from the area.

Glossary

chronic 慢性的 acute 急性的
erratic 不稳定的 envisage 设想
deployment 部署，调度 contemplate 仔细考虑

Ex. 1 Listen to the following dialogue and choose the best answer to each of the questions you will hear.

1. What is the response to the earthquake and tsunamis?
   A. A response comes from 80,000 to 250,000 people in Japan.
   B. A response comes from 80,000 Self Defense Forces.
   C. A response comes from 250 emergency medical organisations.
   D. A response comes from some foreign and government aid groups.

2. What is the situation in the places that MSF has visited?
   A. It is getting better, but the situation is still serious.
   B. It is getting better because of nice weather.
   C. It is getting worse because of difficult communication and transportation.
   D. It is getting worse because of lack of food and water.

3. What is the long-term situation?
   A. It is too early for us to expand the team.
   B. It is too early for us to respond to the needs and strategy.
   C. We are expecting more teams, but not too many international personnel.
   D. We are looking at hundreds of international personnel coming from all over the world.

4. Why is it unnecessary for a massive intervention from all over the world?
   A. Because of aid from both the Japanese government and foreign governments.
   B. Because urgent needs are covered.
   C. Because hospitals, doctors, and drugs are available.
   D. A, B and C.

5. How is MSF dealing with the situation in the nuclear crisis?
   A. We'll evacuate when government and non-government agencies come.
   B. We'll evacuate when it becomes unhealthy or dangerous.
   C. We're evacuating quite rapidly because other agencies are monitoring the situation.

· 110 ·

D. We're evacuating because that's what we will do.
6. What can MSF do in treating illnesses caused by radiation?
   A. We can not treat any but are investigating to try and see if we can help.
   B. We can not treat any because nuclear radiation is dangerous to us.
   C. We're treating illnesses caused by radiation together with 25,000 or 30,000 people in this field.
   D. This is not our job but more the duty of the Japanese government.

Ex. 2 Make dialogues on the following topics.
1. What will happen to us when an earthquake breaks out? How should we deal with it?
2. What are natural disasters and man-made disasters when an earthquake breaks out? Give an example to illustrate your point of view.

Dialogue 2

Strategies for Disaster Reduction and Recovery

Interview with Salvano Briceno, Director, Secretariat of the International Strategy for Disaster Reduction (UN/ISDR)

Glossary

vulnerability 脆弱性　　　　hazard 危险

Ex. 1 Listen to the following dialogue and fill in each blank with the word(s) you've heard. How do you assess the international community's commitment to efforts that reduce the risks from natural disasters and improve chances for recovery?

For some time there has been specialized attention given to the study of natural hazards and their __1__ on societies. Until recently, these issues only drew wider public and official attention at the time of a crisis, and most often only following great loss and __2__ from a disaster. The international community now is becoming more __3__ and prepared to invest in protective and recovery measures, creating a __4__ "culture of prevention" throughout a society and across generations.

These events have shone a global __5__ on the need for better planned and professionally __6__ recovery strategies after a disaster. There is now emerging a __7__ of committing multiple resources to disaster risk reduction as an ongoing task of society before a disaster occurs. In many respects, we are at a __8__ beginning and that must be both encouraged and sustained.

To what extent are disaster reduction measures a matter of funding and how much are they a matter of awareness raising and longer-range planning?

Resource commitments, whether human, material, or financial, are needed to promote the issue and raise awareness among educators, media, and policy-makers. These investments will be productive in reducing disaster risks _____9_____.

What are the three key actions required to ensure recovery from natural disasters?

- First and foremost, each person needs to be risk aware, i.e. understand natural hazards and vulnerabilities at their homes, school, work place, and community. Therefore, educational

systems must incorporate disaster risk reduction as an essential topic in their curricula, training and community activities.
- We must _____ **10** _____.
Recognizing that most communities are exposed to some form of natural and related risks, we must embody that knowledge throughout the local cultures.
- We need to _____ **11** _____ that become part of daily life and work.

Ex. 2 Make dialogues on the following topics.

1. What is the value of "culture of prevention"?
2. What strategies can we take for disaster reduction and recovery?

Part Ⅲ   Listen and Discuss

Passage 1

Glossary

scapegoat 替罪羊   drainage 排水

Ex. 1 Listen to the following passage and choose the best answer to each of the questions you will hear.

1. The best title for this passage is _____.
   A. "Natural Disaster" Is a Poor Planning
   B. Why Most Natural Disasters Aren't Natural at All
   C. "Natural Disaster" Is Human Destruction
   D. Natural Disasters Are Human Disasters

2. When a natural disaster comes, people are likely to _____.
   A. blame nature   B. cry for their losses
   C. move their homes   D. ask God for help

3. Why are humans hit by a natural disaster?
   A. Because they allow rain to soak into floods.
   B. Because they build their homes right on the grasslands.
   C. Because they attempt to alter the natural cycles of nature.
   D. Both A and B.

4. People curse Mother Nature because _____.
   A. they have a poor planning
   B. they are short-sighted
   C. God has actually sent them an important message
   D. it is an easy scapegoat

5. According to the author, the way to avoid these "natural disasters" is _____.

Calamity Is Man's True Touch-Stone — Unit 17

A. not so difficult as you think B. more difficult than you think
C. a common task for all the nations on earth D. is destroyed by poor human planning

6. According to the author, to live in greater harmony with the nature world _____.
   A. is hard to accomplish
   B. needs a creative mind
   C. needs respect for the natural cycles of "destruction"
   D. needs the best way to be aware of your impact on the world around you

Ex. 2 Make dialogues on the following topics.

1. What do you think of natural disasters and man-made disasters? What are their connections?
2. Why are there increasing human activities on earth? What can we do with them? Give examples.
3. What is the environmental situation in China? Is it getting worse or better? What are we doing?

Passage 2

Glossary

hurricane 飓风	simultaneously 同时
antibiotics 抗生素	weirdness 命运
coral reef 珊瑚礁	freak 反常的
contagious 传染的	unleash 解开,释放

Ex. 1 Listen to the following passage and fill in each blank with the word(s) you've heard.

In recent years, the Earth has experienced one after another large natural disasters——earthquakes in Haiti, Chile, and in Japan together with tsunami, hurricanes off the coast of Florida and across the South Atlantic. Simultaneously, we're dealing with superbugs in our nation's hospitals that are __1__ to all known antibiotics. On the other side of the globe, we're __2__ a frightening spread of the H1N1 bird flu virus. And that's not the end of the weirdness. Twenty percent of the world's coral reefs have been destroyed. The fish in the open ocean are poisoned with mercury to such levels that some fish contain twenty times the acceptable limit of mercury standards. While all this is going on, we still have infectious diseases coming out of Africa, Ebola, for example, __3__ humanity. Freak weather and natural disasters suddenly seem to be the norm.

What's going on here? What's happening to our planet? The answer is that humanity has not yet learned how to live in harmony with nature. And much that we're seeing today in terms of natural disasters, outbreaks, superbugs, and the destruction of ecosystems is a direct result of mankind's inability or __4__ to respect nature.

Some people __5__ this as "Nature's Revenge." They say nature is getting back at man and is planning to wipe out humanity to return to its own natural balance. This is a simple __6__ : if we continue to destroy the environment and terrorize the ecosystems of this planet, there are going to be consequences. Those consequences will, one way or another, ultimately bring the planet back into balance. It is humanity's decision whether that balance will include the human race.

Among all the ___7___ side effects, the worst effect is probably going to be the ___8___ of deadly contagious diseases. They exist already, of course: we have SARS, AIDS, Ebola, malaria, smallpox and influenza in all its various strains. _____9_____. But now, as we are wounding the planet, we are directly encouraging a situation in which these agents could be unleashed upon the human population by nature itself. Unless we learn from our lessons and find a way to honor and respect the very planet that has given us life, this planet will take it away from us.

_____10_____ than the largest volcanoes in history. It doesn't even count how we're poisoning rivers and streams, obliterating the rainforest, destroying ocean ecosystems, and now we're even poisoning our own water supplies. How stupid is that? We even poison ourselves. So much for "advanced civilization."

We've done it to ourselves. We are headed down a path of certain self-destruction. Our behavior is simply not sustainable. _____11_____. Without the impact of humanity, the planet would heal itself. And that's the blink of an eye in the lifetime of our planet. Earth can shrug off humanity without breaking a sweat.

Ex. 2   Make dialogues on the following topics.

1. What is the relationship between humanity and nature? What is your comment on "advanced civilization"?
2. How can we improve our life while caring for our planet? Give examples.

Part Ⅳ   Watch and Debate

What Is Death?

There is one thing I can be sure of: I am going to die. But what am I to make of that fact? Are we, in some sense, immortal? Would immortality be desirable? What does it mean to say that a person has died? What kind of fact is that? And, finally, is death an evil? How should the knowledge that I am going to die affect the way I live my life? All these questions will be answered by Shelly Kagan, Professor of Philosophy at Yale.

Glossary

mortality 必死性   reappraise 重新评价
do-over 重新开始   flub 搞坏, 搞糟
sprinkle 散布, 点缀

Ex. 1   Watch the video and answer the following questions.

1. What might be the general answer to "How should we live", given that we will die?
   _____.
2. What does Kagan mean by "Mortality adds an extra risk/danger" to our life?
   _____.

Calamity Is Man's True Touch-Stone

Unit 17

3. What are two mistakes we'll make? And how can we avoid them?
   _____.
4. What are two strategies in life? How different are they?
   _____.
5. Why does Kagan prefer the third strategy?
   _____.
6. What is Kagan's conclusion of quantity and quality of life? How does he prove it?
   _____.

Ex. 2 Express your opinions on the following questions after watching the video.
1. How do you understand the nature of life and death? What is their relationship?
2. What life strategy do you prefer? Why? Give examples.
3. What kind of life do you hope for? How do you make plans and strive for your future life?

Part V Extracurricular Listening

Listen to the following 10 short dialogues and choose the best answer to each of the questions you will hear.

1. A. He has no other clothes the same color.
   B. He chose the jacket a long time ago.
   C. The jacket collar fit him very well.
   D. He didn't buy the jacket for himself.
2. A. He has made a good decision.
   B. He probably won't listen to the man's advice.
   C. He has done the right thing.
   D. He has decided not to buy that car.
3. A. She asked Prof. Adams for assistance this semester.
   B. She helps Prof. Adams with his teaching.
   C. She is doing both teaching and research this semester.
   D. She needs another assistant for her research.
4. A. She has everything done except for her last paper.
   B. She just finished writing a paper on cloud formation.
   C. She started working for a publishing firm.
   D. Her paper will be published.
5. A. He has a lot of free time.   B. He's extremely forgetful.
   C. He has been asking for his book.   D. He keeps buying books.
6. A. He wants to say good-bye at the airport.
   B. He would like her to take a day off.
   C. He likes to watch the planes take off.
   D. He thinks she should take the bus to the airport.

7. A. Convince his classmates not to argue with the professor.
   B. Talk to the class about a field trip.
   C. Get to know his classmates by talking to them.
   D. Have the professor give lectures outside the class.

8. A. She has finished only one step.
   B. She doesn't have any more time for redecorating.
   C. The redecorating is being done gradually.
   D. It's time for the work to be finished.

9. A. His teeth hurt him very much.
   B. He has no time for meals.
   C. He decided to take the course next semester instead.
   D. He finds the work harder than he expected.

10. A. Martha knows practically everybody.   B. Bob isn't hard to cheer up.
    C. Martha always knows exactly what to say. D. Bob didn't order the right thing.

Unit 18 Science and Technology Revolutionize Life

Part I Door to Wisdom

Read, think and interpret your understanding of the following proverbs and well-known sayings.

1. Our technological powers increase, but the side effects and potential hazards also escalate.

   —Alvin Toffler

2. Technology is a useful servant but a dangerous master.

   —Christian Lous Lange

3. All truths are easy to understand once they are discovered. The point is to discover them.

   —Galileo

4. An expert is a person who has made all the mistakes that can be made in a very narrow field.

   —Niels Bohr

5. Imagination is more important than knowledge. Knowledge is limited. Imagination encircles the world.

   —Albert Einstein

Part II Join in the Dialogue

During the last 100 years, humans went from walking on the Earth to walking on the Moon. They went from riding horses to flying jet airplanes. With each decade, aviation technology crossed another frontier, and, with each crossing, the world changed. During the 20th century, five companies charted the course of aerospace history in the United States. They were the Boeing Airplane Co., Douglas Aircraft Co., McDonnell Aircraft Corp., North American Aviation and Hughes Aircraft. By the dawning of the new millennium(新千年), they had joined forces to share a legacy of victory and discovery, cooperation and competition, high adventure and hard struggle. Their stories began with five men who shared the vision that gave tangible wings to the eternal dream of flight. William Edward Boeing, born in 1881 in Detroit, Michigan, began building floatplanes near Seattle, Washington. Donald Wills Douglas, born in 1892 in New York, began building bombers and passenger transports in Santa Monica, California. James Smith McDonnell, born in 1899 in Denver, Colorado, began building jet fighters in St. Louis, Missouri. James Howard "Dutch" Kindelberger, born in 1895 in Wheeling, West Virginia, began building trainers in Los Angeles, California. Howard Hughes Jr. was born in Houston, Texas, in 1905. The Hughes Space and Communications Co. built the world's first geosynchronous communications satellite in 1963. The companies began their journey across the frontiers of aerospace at different times and under different circumstances. Their paths merged and their contributions are the common heritage of the Boeing Company today.

Dialogue 1

Glossary

Smithsonian National Air and Space Museum　　史密森国家航空空间博物馆
mechanics 机械学,动力学　　　　　　　　　　　glider 滑翔机
manned-powered 人力　　　　　　　　　　　　bureaucrats 官僚,官僚主义者
rudder 舵,方向舵

Ex. 1 Listen to the following dialogue and choose the best answer to each of the questions.

1. What might be the most probable topic of their talk?
   A. The first plane toy for young boys.　　B. The first flight for earlier inventors.
   C. The first day for Sue's father at work.　D. The first day for Dick's engineering.
2. What are they probably doing?
   A. Making an investigation or survey.　　B. Watching a Television program.
   C. Discussing preparations for a flight.　　D. Analyzing government documents.
3. What was Sue's father's job?
   A. A bicycle mechanic.　　　　　　　　B. An flight engineer.
   C. A pilot in the army.　　　　　　　　　D. An office worker.
4. What helped lead to Wright brothers' early interest in flying?
   A. Influences from their father and other people's stories.
   B. Influences from their printing and traveling experiences.

C. Influences from children's crazy games and dreams.

D. Influences from government bureaucrats.

Ex. 2　Make dialogues on the following topics.

1. Invention and innovation are significant part of science and technology. Search in your memory for some inventors or innovators you know. Form groups or pairs and tell each other what you know about their life events and contribution to human history.

2. Computer science and internet provide a great many opportunities for innovation. Talk with your partner(s) about your own experiences of using them in your study or work. Focus on the obstacles you may have encountered and how you have managed to handle them.

Dialogue 2

Glossary

axis 轴　　　　dependent variable 因变量
curve 曲线　　correlation 相关性

Ex. 1　Listen to the following dialogue and choose the best answer to each of the questions you will hear.

1. What is Ann's survey mainly about?
   A. Students' sleeping habits and their study.
   B. Younger people's reading habits and study.
   C. Older people's study habits and health problems.
   D. Students' eating habits and their health condition.

2. How far has John gone about his survey?
   A. He has given up for some big problems.　　B. He has reached the middle part.
   C. He has finished all of the survey.　　　　　D. He has finished the beginning stage.

3. Which of following is NOT true about John's survey?
   A. It uses graphs and charts for measurement.
   B. It shows that young people watches TV more often.
   C. It evaluates people's TV watching and reading ability.
   D. It takes people of various ages into consideration.

4. How does John think of Ann's comment on his survey?
   A. He disagrees with Ann and thinks her a careless person.
   B. He disagrees with Ann and thinks her a forgetful person.
   C. He agrees with Ann and thinks her a fascinating person.
   D. He agrees with Ann and thinks her an intelligent person.

Ex. 2　Make dialogues on the following topics.

1. Scientific research involves data collecting and proper statistics assessment. Refer to the clues of

this dialogue and try to do a survey of your own on People's Views on Electronic Reading and Traditional Reading.
2. With the advancement of digital technology, photography has become an inexpensive daily use for people. Discuss How Digital Photography Has Changed Our Life and Work in groups or pairs. Decide on your topic and make a list of your results.

Part Ⅲ Listen and Discuss

Glossary

neutrino 微中子 gravity 地心引力
mass 质量(物理学) conceive of 构想出
bit 微粒 equation 等式
precede 领先于,早于 electron 电子

Passage 1

Ex. 1 Listen to the following passage and choose the best answer to each of the questions you will hear.

1. A. They are examples of the usual sequence of observation and explanation.
   B. They provide evidence of inaccurate scientific observation.
   C. Their discovery was similar to that of the neutrino.
   D. They were subjects of 1995 experiments at Los Alamos.
2. A. Its mass had previously been measured.
   B. Its existence had been reported by Los Alamos National Laboratory.
   C. Scientists were looking for a particle with no mass.
   D. Scientists were unable to balance equations of energy without it.
3. A. That it carries a large amount of energy.
   B. That it is a type of electron.
   C. That it is smaller in size than previously thought.
   D. That it has a tiny amount of mass.

Ex. 2 Make dialogues on the following topics.

1. The study and application of biotechnology are frequently under heated discussion. On the one hand such technology has obviously and greatly contributed to human welfare in many fields such as agriculture, medicine, public security, etc. On the other, misuse of it could supposedly lead to ethic as well as technical catastrophes as well. Find references concerned and exchange ideas with your partners on issues like **How Genetic Technology Should Be Properly Developed and Controlled.**
2. Only a few years ago, shopping on the internet was still something rarely heard of in many places. Now, offices of different express delivery companies have become a regular location on college

Science and Technology Revolutionize Life

campuses. E-commerce has become a convenient and inexpensive approach of people's personal consumption. Meanwhile security and protection have become outstanding issues. Illustrate what you believe are the necessary means to avoid any hazards or losses in E-trade.

Passage 2

Glossary

synesthesia 副感觉   pekoe 香红茶
control group 对照组   artificially 人工地,人为地

Ex. 1 Listen to the following passage and choose the best answer to each of the questions you will hear.

1. A. To explain how sense organs normally function.
   B. To point out errors in a recent study.
   C. To discuss an unusual condition of the brain.
   D. To present a creative approach to teaching language skills.
2. A. Remembering word definitions.
   B. Recognizing repeated numbers.
   C. Distinguishing between similar colors.
   D. Combining mentally tastes with sounds.
3. A. To explain the causes of synesthesia.
   B. To prove that sound and color can affect a person's mood.
   C. To determine whether or not synesthesia exists.
   D. To show how creativity can be stimulated.
4. A. Consistently associate words with certain colors.
   B. Memorize long lists of words.
   C. Use colored printing to learn pronunciation.
   D. Use words creatively in art objects.

Ex. 2 Make dialogues on the following topics.

1. With the convenience and efficiency of the internet, worldwide friend-making with a computer is no longer a myth in today's life. How do you like friend-making on the internet? Discuss in groups or pairs and list its Advantages and Disadvantages.
2. With highly developed medical science nowadays, organ transplants may be an effective means to save and prolong lives. But the implementation could be confronted with financial, ethical, legal, cultural as well as many other controversies. Discuss your view with your friends and list your reasons.

Part IV Watch and Debate

Antonio Damasio (born February 25, 1944) is David Dornsife Professor of Neuroscience at the University of Southern California. Professor Antonio Damasio is an internationally recognized leader in neuroscience. His research has helped to elucidate the neural basis for the emotions and has shown that emotions play a central role in social cognition and decision-making. His work has also had a major influence on current understanding of the neural systems, which underlie memory, language and consciousness. Damasio directs the USC Brain and Creativity Institute.

Glossary

intervene 干预,介入	convergence 集中,收敛
undue 不适当的	divergence 分歧
narrative 叙述	synapse 突触(解剖学)
superimpose 添加	fire 燃烧,激发
trump 胜过,压倒	microscopic 显微镜下可见的,精微的
unfolds 展开,进行	cellular 细胞的
ploy 策略	molecular 分子的
electrochemical 电器化学	

Ex. 1 Watch the video clip three times and fill in the missing information with either the exact words from the interview or with your own words.

In the following video clip, Professor Antonio Damasio as a celebrated behavioral neurobiologist is talking in an interview with bigthink.com. He believes that while our own personal histories happen one event at a time, our brains make sense of our lives by stringing these events together in an structured way.

Question: *How do our brains construct coherent personal narrative out of our memories of experiences?*

Antonio Damasio: You do it in very interesting ways. A first way is by taking the story as it happens. You know, our biographies happened one part at a time. There is a sequence of events in our lives and so there's a temporal aspect to our experience that brings by itself, sense into the story. In other words, you were not walking before you were born and you were not doing X and Y before you did something else first. So _____ 1 _____.

Then there's something that intervenes and is very important which has to do with value. Value in the true biological sense, which is that contrary to what many

Science and Technology Revolutionize Life

Unit 18

people seem to think, taking it at face value—sorry for the pun—_____ **2** _____. So there are things in our lives that take up an enormous importance and that become very dominant effects in our biography. And that comes out of a variety of reasons, but fundamentally comes out of _____ **3** _____. So _____ **4** _____. And so that is the next element to superimpose on the sequencing element. And in fact, that element is so powerful that very often it can trump the sequencing event, that the sequencing aspect. So something may have happened before, and yet this thing that happened just after may be so important that you don't even know about the thing that happened before and when you tell your story to yourself, or to someone else, it's going to be told _____ **5** _____.

And that value, by the way, does not need to be conscious. You know, you're not deciding, "Aha, this is very good, X-value." No, you're assigning value naturally as life unfolds and that's this very important element for the construction of one's narrative. And the other thing that is very important is that narratives are not fixed. We change our narratives for ourselves and we change them not necessarily deliberately. In other words, some people do, some people will constantly reconstruct their biography for external purposes, it's a very interesting political ploy, you know. But _____ **6** _____.

So the way we construct our narrative today is different from the way we constructed it a year ago. The difference is maybe very small or it may be huge. And they're constantly changing as a result of events that happen in your life. _____ **7** _____. Or something that happens to your health, or something that happened to somebody else's health, that is close to you, or something that happens professionally. All of those things sort of rearrange the way your story gets constructed.

Question: *Does constructing these stories change our brains?*

Antonio Damasio: Well, of course it happens, first of all, in the brain, and it's affecting the brain because it _____ **8** _____. So I know we had a chance of talking on another occasion about the architecture of convergence and divergence. All of that is constantly operating when you not only learn, but when you recall. But as you recall in a different light, _____ **9** _____. So you're constantly changing the way, for instance, synapses are going to fire very easily or not so easily. There's that effect that is very physical, very down there at the synaptic level, which really means microscopic cellular level, but also molecular level, because all of those structures are operating on an electrochemical basis and so the changes there are very important.

Ex. 2 Express your opinions on the following topics.

1. In today's high technology society, people tend to live a highly organized life with little time and space for real socializing or communication, especially when internet provides the rocketing speed for message delivery. Do you think this is partly responsible for the increasing mental and communicative problems among populations? Give your reasons.

2. Chatting online has become a regular means of communication and relaxation for many people. Yet there are a variety of choices of such instant messaging tools as MSN, QQ, Skype, Fetion, and others. Which do you prefer as your first choice for online chatting? Illustrate your reasons.

Part V Extracurricular Listening

Listen to the following 10 short dialogues and choose the best answer to each of the questions you will hear.

1. A. Move them away from the coffee cup.   B. Go over them right away.
   C. Discuss them with Professor Johnson.   D. Forget them until later.

2. A. Lock the door carefully.   B. Open the door.
   C. Fix the lock himself.   D. Call the repairman.

3. A. Buying some laces.   B. Breaking in his new shoes.
   C. Purchasing new shoes.   D. Going shopping during the break.

4. A. He considers the weekend a time to think.
   B. He knows the beach is a long way from here.
   C. He's surprised she's thinking of going away.
   D. He suggests going to the seashore.

5. A. The man should ask at the office.   B. It's too late to get tickets.
   C. There may be a package for him.   D. The office won't take his check.

6. A. It would be better to go another way.   B. They should take a different road.
   C. They won't be allowed to make that turn.   D. The other cars won't let them pass.

7. A. The machine should be cleaned.   B. He ought to have made fresh coffee.
   C. This kind of coffee isn't sold anymore.   D. The machine ought to be replaced.

8. A. The clothes don't look clean to him.
   B. He doesn't intend to get the clothes.
   C. The woman can pick out her own clothes.
   D. The woman should stop staring at his clothes.

9. A. That they watch the clock carefully.
   B. That they be careful of their handwriting.
   C. That they finish their assignment earlier.
   D. That they wait a few minutes after class.

10. A. Continue reviewing.   B. Use her notes.
    C. Time the speech.   D. Give her the correct time.

Unit 19 Best Is Cheapest

Part I Door to Wisdom

Read, think and interpret your understanding of the following proverbs and well-known sayings.

1. There is no resting place for an enterprise in a competitive economy.

   —Alfred P. Sloan

2. Success or failure in business is caused more by the mental attitude even than by mental capacities.

   —Walter Scott

3. Men are more ready to repay an injury than a benefit, because gratitude is a burden and revenge a pleasure.

   —Tacitus

4. The herd seek out the great, not for their sake but for their influence. And the great welcome them out of vanity or need.

   —Napoleon Bonaparte

5. A friendship founded on business is better than business founded on friendship.

   —John Davision Rockefeller

Part II Join in the Dialogue

The World Trade Organization (WTO) is an organization that intends to supervise and liberalize international trade. The organization officially commenced on January 1, 1995 under the Marrakech

Agreement, replacing the General Agreement on Tariffs and Trade (GATT), which commenced in 1948. The organization deals with regulation of trade between participating countries; it provides a framework for negotiating and formalizing trade agreements, and a dispute resolution process aimed at enforcing participants' adherence to WTO agreements which are signed by representatives of member governments and ratified by their parliaments. Most of the issues that the WTO focuses on derive from previous trade negotiations, especially from the Uruguay Round(1986—1994).

The organization is currently endeavoring to persist with a trade negotiation called the Doha Development Agenda (or Doha Round), which was launched in 2001 to enhance equitable participation of poorer countries which represent a majority of the world's population. However, the negotiation has been dogged by "disagreement between exporters of agricultural bulk commodities and countries with large numbers of subsistence farmers on the precise terms of a 'special safeguard measure' to protect farmers from surges in imports. At this time, the future of the Doha Round is uncertain."

The WTO has 153 members, representing more than 97% of the world's population, and 30 observers, most seeking membership. The WTO is governed by a ministerial conference, meeting every two years; a general council, which implements the conference's policy decisions and is responsible for day-to-day administration; and a director-general, who is appointed by the ministerial conference. The WTO's headquarters is at the Centre William Rappard, Geneva.

Dialogue 1

Glossary

shipment 出货   reserve 预定

Ex. 1 Listen to the following dialogue and choose the best answer to each of the questions.

1. What does the man want to do?
    A. Discuss the course with Dr. Peterson.
    B. Finish his assignment before Monday.
    C. Buy a book for his psychology class.
    D. Take the course on different days.
2. What does the woman say about Dr. Peterson?
    A. He has canceled his psychology course.
    B. He knows there aren't enough books.
    C. He has ordered a different textbook for his course.
    D. He was planning to call the students.
3. What will the man probably do next?
    A. Leave his phone number with the woman.
    B. Sign up for a different class.
    C. Talk to Dr. Peterson about the problem.
    D. Find out when the next shipment will arrive.

Ex. 2 Make dialogues on the following topics.

1. Have you ever purchased any pirated goods, such as books, software disks, film DVDs, knockoff

（仿制品，山寨货）digital products and clothes or any others? Some say that no matter how many slogans are posted or how hard companies push their claims of intellectual property, if cheaper pirated products are available, consumption still persists. In the long run, intellectual or design piracy impairs a healthy market economy. Discuss with your partner and suggest some feasible measures to completely eliminate piracy.

2. Where do you usually prefer to go shopping, in a large supermarket like the CE-Mart Mall or just at a mini-size grocery store like a Suguo or Hualian Convenience Store across the street where you live? Or both but for different reasons? Discuss with your partner and list the advantages and disadvantages about them in your view.

Dialogue 2

Glossary

charge... to 给……支付　　　credit card 信用卡
asset 资产　　　　　　　　　loan 贷款
microcredit 小额贷款　　　　rate 价格

Ex. 1   Listen to the following dialogue and choose the best answer to each of the questions you will hear.

1. A. She will be able to join the economics seminar.
   B. She has a new printer for her computer.
   C. She finished paying back her loan.
   D. She got an A on her term paper.

2. A. The importance of paying back loans promptly.
   B. A way to help people improve their economic conditions.
   C. Using computers to increase business efficiency.
   D. The expansion of international business.

3. A. It is the topic of his term paper.
   B. He would like to find a job there.
   C. His economics professor did research work there.
   D. Microcredit programs have been very successful there.

4. A. Cancel her credit card.　　　　B. Sign up for the economics seminar.
   C. Do research on banks in Asia.　D. Type the man's term paper.

Ex. 2   Make dialogues on the following topics.

1. How do you like door-to-door sales promotion? Discuss in pairs and present your views.
2. Purchasing goods on sale could be an interesting experience. What are the things to be considered to make a satisfactory purchase on this occasion? Discuss with your partner and make a list of them.

Part III Listen and Discuss

Passage 1

Glossary

laisser faire 放任,自由主义 tariff 关税
hinder 阻碍 ironically 具讽刺意味
subsidy 补贴 doctrine 学说,信条
grant 批准,提供

Ex. 1 Listen to the following passage and choose the best answer to each of the questions you will hear.

1. A. Competition in business. B. Government grants.
   C. A type of economic policy. D. International transportation practices.
2. A. American industrialists. B. French economists.
   C. International leaders. D. Civil War veterans.
3. A. The rights of private business owners should be protected.
   B. The government shouldn't interfere in private business.
   C. Politicians should support industrial growth.
   D. Competition among companies should be restricted.

Ex. 2 Make dialogues on the following topics.

1. What do you know about trade protectionism? Consult some references and share with your partner(s). Discuss with your partner(s) and list the reasons why it should be stopped. Suggest feasible measures to adopt.
2. What do you think is the Win-win Philosophy in Business Negotiation? Compare it with the win-lose philosophy in business negotiation, especially in terms of the probable cultural clashes between trading parties from different backgrounds. List the advantages and disadvantages for both and decide on the proper tactics to take in an assumed negotiating situation.

Passage 2

Glossary

grind 碾碎,毁灭 lose one's shirt 赔光老本
halt 终止 portfolio 投资组合
mortgage 抵押 blue chip stock 蓝筹股(稳而值钱的股票)
essentials 基本指标 venture capital 风险投资
current deposit 活期存款 hundredfold 百倍数
crystal ball 水晶球(西方算命器具,据传可透过预测未来)

Unit 19　Best Is Cheapest

lottery 彩票　　　　　　　　　dividend distribution 分红
dotcom bubble 互联网泡沫经济

Ex. 1 Listen to the following passage three time and fill in the missing information with either the exact words from the talk or your own words.

　　Good morning, everybody, and welcome to one of the Hong Kong Bank's lectures on money management. I'm John Rogers, and I'm the manager here.

　　Money, as they say, makes the world go round. Well, it is true that your world can come to a grinding halt if you have no money. I know you all agree, because that is why you have come here today.

　　OK, Money. What do we want to do with it? Most people want to enjoy the money they earn today, but also put some aside for a rainy day, ＿＿＿＿＿＿＿＿＿＿1＿＿＿＿＿＿＿＿＿＿. In other words, they want to invest it. So let's talk for a little while on spending money wisely today, and then I'll talk about ＿＿＿＿＿＿＿＿2＿＿＿＿＿＿＿＿.

　　The question is: How much of your income should you enjoy spending today, and how much should you save for the future? And the answer is different for different people. It depends on things like age, your health, how many children you have, et cetera. Well, my initial answer is—write out a budget for the necessities—food, rent, mortgage and loan payments, clothing, health insurance, things like that. When most people do this, they say to themselves, "My goodness! I really only need to spend 1,500 pounds a month. So how come I always spend nearly two and a half thousand?" My mother used to tell me, "Look after the pennies, and the pounds will look after themselves."

　　What to do? Discipline. I suggest ＿＿＿＿＿＿＿＿＿＿3＿＿＿＿＿＿＿＿＿＿. And you must strictly limit what you spend every month to, for example, your budget for essentials, plus an amount, say 10 percent, for a bit of entertainment if you want, and the unexpected, like house repairs, that birthday present you forgot about, things like that. If after three weeks you find that you have nearly spent your budget for the month, then stay at home for a week, no fancy restaurants or drinking with the boys. As they say, there's no free lunch.

　　OK, so what do you do with the money you don't spend? Oh, one thing I forgot to mention. It's a good idea to always have some money in a current deposit at the bank in case of big surprises, say a thousand or so. Don't be tempted to use your credit card unless you absolutely have to. And get that safety cushion back in the bank as soon as you can.

　　Right. So what should you invest in? The list is endless: real estate, stocks and shares, equity funds—did I hear someone say gambling? —well, if you have a crystal ball, maybe. The government lottery? Someone once described it as a voluntary tax on fools. But I must admit I spend a pound or two on it every week. But no more. It brings a little bit of excitement into my life, even though I know I have a better chance of being struck by lightning than winning.

　　OK, let's start off with a basic principle. In general, ＿＿＿＿＿＿＿＿4＿＿＿＿＿＿＿＿ —the one you have been told will be the next IBM in three weeks—the higher the risk. We've all heard about the dotcom bubble of several years ago. Some people ＿＿＿＿＿＿＿＿5＿＿＿＿＿＿＿＿. The majority of investors lost their shirts.

　　Another basic principle: the balanced portfolio. A balanced portfolio means you have

investments in a variety of things, from _____6_____, to the riskiest of all—venture capital-where success could increase the value of your investment a hundredfold, or failure could wipe it out.

Well, why don't we break for a coffee now, then I will talk about the most common form of share ownership. Common stock, which makes you become a part owner of the company itself, with voting rights and entitlement to dividend distribution, if there is one.

Ex. 2 Make dialogues on the following topics.

1. Have you ever made a budget plan for your present life? What do you think are the prior issues to consider while making a family budget for a Chinese family today? Discuss with your partner and decide on them. Tell reasons for your decisions.
2. The use of credit card has become pervasive in China today. However, impulsive consumption and financial frauds could emerge along with its convenience. Consult some references and try to discuss the precautions to take against the disadvantages of using credit card.

Part Ⅳ   Watch and Debate

Gary Hamel is ranked by *The Wall Street Journal* as the world's most influential business thinker, and *Fortune* magazine has called him "the world's leading expert on business strategy". For the last few years, Hamel has also topped *Executive Excellence* magazine's annual ranking of the most sought after management speakers.

Hamel's landmark books, *Leading the Revolution and Competing for the Future*, have appeared on every management bestseller list and have been translated into more than 20 languages. One of his latest books, *The Future of Management*, was published by the Harvard Business School Press in October 2007 and was selected by Amazon.com as the best business book of the year.

Glossary

take bet 下注,打赌
reverse accountability 反向负责制
（利用互联网,及时反映下级
对领导的评价,以保证
客观高效的管理策略）
iddle 虚度,荒废
margin 富余空间
pharmaceutical 药物
simulation 类似环境或事物
incremental 增加

status quo 现状
merchandising 广告推销,销售规划
variance 变异
revenue 收入
mass 群众
iteration 反复
incentive 动力,激励
ramp 迅速推展
tweak 调整

Ex. 1 Watch the video clip three times and fill in the missing information with either the exact words from the interview or your own words.

Say Goodbye to Business as Usual

I believe the companies that win over the next few years are going to be the companies that

Best Is Cheapest

_____ 1 _____. And there are a lot of reasons to believe that there are, you know, good alternatives to the status quo. One of the most successful companies over the last few years in India has been HCL Technologies, an Indian IT services company. Their entire management model is built on the principle of reverse accountability. In this company, an employee can fill out a ticket on their boss or an internal service provider, like HR, internal IT, (and) say I don't agree with this decision or I don't believe I've been treated fairly, and only the employee can close that ticket when their concerns have been addressed. Managers are measured and kind of tracked _____ 2 _____. And I could give you a half dozen other things that HCL is doing in that same spirit. Radically different management model than you find, you know, in the average company today.

So clearly, it is possible. There are alternatives to the status quo. It's hard to imagine them, because management itself has not changed much during our working lifetimes. Mostly we fiddled at the margins, but now we have to go beyond that. I think the question is though, how _____ 3 _____? And I would argue, like in any other area of human endeavor, we have to be able to experiment, right? That's the way _____ 4 _____.

If you're a drug company, you don't start out by putting a new pharmaceutical in the water supply. You start out by testing it in a simulation with rats, or whatever it may be. I think we have to think about management in the same way. Typically, when we think about changing an HR system or a budgeting system, we give that project to a big team. We _____ 5 _____. That's a very risky proposition. So risky that normally you only want to do something that's a small tweak, fairly incremental versus what you already have.

But I think _____ 6 _____, of trying things in a low cost, particular period of time, particular corner in the organization, so you don't have to take those bet the company risks. A few years back there was a vice president at Best Buy and he was looking at how the company did its forecasting. Obviously in consumer electronics retailing, forecasting is very critical, particularly around that holiday selling period. And typically those forecasts _____ 7 _____ at Best Buy.

And they got it usually about 90 percent accurate. It sounds pretty good, but when you're talking about tens of billions of dollars, companies where margins are very thin, those variances are very, very expensive either way. And so he did a little experiment. He _____ 8 _____, asked them—this was in August of 2005, asked them to _____ 9 _____. And then once they'd gotten into 2006, he went back and compared those forecasts, the wisdom of the masses versus the experts.

The experts were 93 percent right; not too bad. This much larger group had been 99.9 percent right. Now that was a little management experiment. Best Buy is now on their third or fourth iteration of this kind of prediction process and they use it in a whole variety of ways. But that management experiment started out—it _____ 10 _____.

Think about how you do something radical in two hours and for MYM100 bucks. We have to

think about _____**11**_____.
Because the companies that win are going to be the companies that _____**12**_____.
And the ones that then take the best of those experiments ramp them up into their existing management systems. You do that. You're experimenting more broadly. You're applying the lessons more quickly. You're going to have an enormous advantage in a world that is going to become increasingly hostile to management as usual.

Ex. 2   Express your opinions on the following topics.

1. You are walking on the street when someone extends you an ad. What will you do, accept it or ignore it? Why?
2. Ads descend upon us by means of TV, radio, newspapers, magazines, posters, circulars, and so on and have great effects on purchasing habit. Do these ads help you with your purchasing? Why or why not?
3. Advertising is a regular practice for marketing. But from time to time fraudulent advertising find thriving spaces in different types of media, including TV commercials boasting low quality products and deceptive websites in the disguise of a legal organization. Even some social celebrities have been found involved in such notorious manipulations. Discuss in groups or pairs the ethics in the implementation of advertising. List the necessary measures to regulate the practice of advertising. Give your reasons.

Part V   Extracurricular Listening

Listen to the following 10 short dialogues and choose the best answer to each of the questions you will hear.

1. A. Nothing was returned last night.   B. The weather wasn't bad last night.
   C. They were able to turn out the lights.   D. Last night's storm hadn't been predicted.
2. A. She wants the man to repeat his report.
   B. She wants to know the man's favorite sport.
   C. She thinks the man wants to be in the play.
   D. She wonders if the man will win his bet.
3. A. He caught Mark taking a nap.
   B. He doesn't sleep as much as Mark.
   C. Mark is trying to get as much sleep as he can.
   D. Mark won't sleep this much once he gets home from college.
4. A. She can do the job.   B. She could call a friend.
   C. She's just switched off the light.   D. She's already replaced the shelf.
5. A. The schedule should be reprinted.
   B. The train never comes when it should.
   C. The company should have a better schedule.
   D. The company has a trouble to print a schedule.

6. A. It is interesting.　　　　　　　　　B. It turned out to be easy.
   C. It's hard to judge.　　　　　　　　D. It's quite difficult.
7. A. She won't be able to come.　　　　 B. She's not going to graduate.
   C. She has a week to do the work.　　 D. She'll visit her sister in a week.
8. A. He spends too much money.　　　　　B. He bought an expensive watch.
   C. He really does like television.　　D. He should watch more television.
9. A. Mark is still studying photography.　B. Mark will have to work quickly.
   C. Mark has been hard to find lately.　 D. Mark is too busy to help them now.
10. A. Dan isn't a very good violinist.　　 B. Someone else should make the introductions.
    C. There will be other musicians to introduce. D. It's rather late to ask Dan now.

Unit 20 The Present Is Pregnant with the Future

Part I Door to Wisdom

Read, think and interpret your understanding of the following proverbs and well-known sayings.

1. Those who wish to sing always find a song.

—Swedish Proverb

2. He is the richest who is content with the least.

—Socrates

3. The future belongs to those who believe in the beauty of their dreams.

—Eleanor Roosevelt

4. You cannot step twice into the same river; for other waters are continually flowing in.

—Heraclitus

5. The greatest discovery of all time is that a person can change his future by merely changing his attitude.

—Oprah Winfrey

Unit 20 The Present Is Pregnant with the Future

Part II Join in the Dialogue

The Future of Life: An Interview with Dr. Wilson

Many species are likely to go extinct before they are even discovered and named by biologists. Of the estimated 10 to 20 million species living on Earth, only 10 percent have been described in the past 250 years. Dr. Edward O. Wilson, Professor Emeritus at the Museum of Comparative Zoology, Harvard University, proposes that the remaining 90 percent must be described in one-tenth that time to save millions of species from extinction.

Earthwatch spoke to Dr. Wilson, a world-renowned expert on biodiversity, in his Harvard office about the future of life and how people can work together to ward off imminent mass extinction.

Dialogue 1

Glossary

Hawaiian 夏威夷的	scot-free 全免的
overlapping 重叠的	interlocked 相互关联的
chaos 混乱	tropical 热带的
biodiversity 生物多样性	burgeoning 发芽的

Ex. 1 Listen to the following dialogue and choose the best answer to each of the questions you will hear.

1. A. It's easy to see that half the species of organisms are extinct forever.
   B. Only 20 percent of Pacific Island bird species has been extinguished.
   C. It's hard to figure out the situation, but it can be dangerous in the long run.
   D. We won't even know about human activities until we do studies.

2. A. Climate warming is more urgent if you're thinking for 50 years.
   B. Environmental damage is not pressing in the short term.
   C. In the long run, it can be more important since extinction is irreversible.
   D. In the short run, it can be more important in terms of our survival.

3. A. Yes, if we can give back what we possess to nature.
   B. Yes, if we can put nature upside down.
   C. Yes, if we can give a description of what we gain.
   D. Yes, if we can reverse the process of our destruction of nature.

4. A. Because we'll lose services in ecosystem if we do not invest more of our product.
   B. Because we can get services scot-free.
   C. Because we can avoid bad choices.
   D. Because we need to invest more and more domestic products.

5. A. Lack of concern about the environment   B. Failure of science education
   C. Complexity of growing biology   D. A, B, and C

6. A. Yes. If they develop their agriculture and industry accordingly.

· 135 ·

B. Yes. If they have wild environments, these countries can build them into ecotourism.

C. No. There aren't places with all sorts of attractions.

D. No. There aren't places with small animals, fish, and so on.

Ex. 2 Make dialogues on the following topics.

1. What is biodiversity? How important is it to our human beings?
2. What problems does species extinction bring to our humans?
3. What is the importance of human activities?

Dialogue 2

Glossary

shatter 粉碎,破坏   molecular 分子的
biogeographically 生物地理的   depletion 消耗,耗尽

Ex. 1 Listen to the following dialogue and fill in each blank with the word(s) you've heard.

Earthwatch: Many people view science as an "__1__," but we know that scientists are people dealing with real-world issues. How can we help shatter this __2__?

E. O. Wilson: Mapping global biodiversity is not only a major area of biology now, but this is going to be a very important part of the future of the science of biology. Its not just a way of bringing young people into biology, it's going to be a major part. The way I see it, there are three __3__ to biology. One of them is the workings of a few model species that are studied from a molecular level up to an __4__ level. We have about 20 of those species. That's just one dimension. The second dimension is the diversity of life on this __5__. Understanding it and how it all fits together, biogeographically. That's going to be a major part of the __6__ science of biology. Molecular and cell biology are looked on as directly __7__ to public health: the __8__ of people, based in their health and the quality of their lives. Therefore, we are coming out of the ivory tower. The third dimension is the Darwinian: _____ __9__ _____. Where did it come from?

Earthwatch: Are you hopeful about the future of biodiversity?

E. O. Wilson: Cautiously optimistic. After all, think of how things were 40 or 50 years ago, before you were born. So there's been a huge change in this country, and all the trends landmarked by the 1992 Earth Summit have been positive. I think we're at or close to the tipping point. That's real optimism, _____ __10__ _____. Right now I see more progress in terms of awareness and action than we've had in the last two years. Unfortunately the problems, global warming, species extinction, the coming water crisis, the depletion of fossil fuels, __11__. So I'm, in two words, cautiously optimistic.

The Present Is Pregnant with the Future

Unit 20

Ex. 2 Make dialogues on the following topics.

1. What can science and technology do to help protect our nature?
2. Are you optimistic or pessimistic about conserving biodiversity on earth? Why?

Part III Listen and Discuss

The whole idea of getting to know the space and its secrets and how it can benefit mankind is what space exploration is all about. The investment made on space exploration is sure to yield rich dividends as both human and robotic exploration of the space can benefit the earth and the people living on it.

Passage 1

Glossary

enigmatic 迷一般的,不可思议的　　opt for 选择
unpredictable 难以预料的　　　　　harness 驾驭
defy 蔑视　　　　　　　　　　　　deter 威慑,阻止

Ex. 1 Listen to the following passage and choose the best answer to each of the questions you will hear.

1. A. The more nature reveals, the less there is still to know.
   B. The more nature reveals, the more there is still to know.
   C. The more nature reveals, the more universities there appear.
   D. The more nature reveals, the more intriguing space is.
2. A. Universities offer degrees or jobs as an option of study for space technology.
   B. Universities provide fund for space exploration.
   C. Universities make satellites for space exploration.
   D. Universities provide communication for space exploration.
3. A. The government offers much fund for space exploration.
   B. The government offers facilities for space exploration.
   C. The government offers space technology for space exploration.
   D. The government offers information for space exploration.
4. A. Satellites help us cover a long distance.
   B. Satellites help us travel in a global village.
   C. Satellites help us predict and understand nature in preparing for what happens.
   D. Satellites help us connect developed and developing countries.
5. A. In the field of communication
   B. In the field of medicine
   C. In the field of climatic and ocean changes
   D. A, B, and C
6. A. It will be deterred for lack of fund.

B. It will be ended for strong criticism.

C. It will be stopped by the government for the time being.

D. It will not be deterred nor ended.

Ex. 2 Make dialogues on the following topics.

1. Why do we explore space? What are the benefits of space exploration for mankind?
2. What kind of space technology do we have in China?

Passage 2

Glossary

NASA 美国航空航天局　　　hydrogen 氢
galaxies 银河系　　　　　　remnant 残余物
evaporate 蒸发

Ex. 1 Listen to the following passage and fill in each blank with the word(s) you've heard.

Do you think mankind will ever colonise other planets?

I really hope so. I'd go to Mars for starters, and I've said this before, I'd go to Mars even if they weren't going to bring me back. The condition is that they'd have to keep me alive on the __1__, but otherwise, how cool would it be to explore a new __2__? Whether it would happen, well, it's difficult. Mars is a long way away. It takes probably, perhaps 18 months to get there. It seems a waste to spend 18 months getting there, then turn around and come back. Whether it will happen in the near future, that's a more difficult question. I hope so, but a lot will depend on what happens in the next 20 years with the __3__ of private space companies. NASA have announced they're going back to the Moon and Mars, but almost all their budget is going into manned programs. The Chinese are funding manned space programs, and how all these things interact, I'm not sure. Let's hope we're on Mars soon.

What's the future for the Sun?

Okay, well, the sun is a middle-aged star. It's been around in its current state for about four billion years, and we've got about four billion years left to go. It's fueled by hydrogen, and eventually it will run out of hydrogen at its __4__. It will then swell up to the size of the earth's __5__ and will be burning helium in the center, to produce heavier elements. And all you're left with is essentially the core of the sun cooling down. That's what we see as a white dwarf, a dense ball of material which is just emitting __6__ and gradually cooling down to the background temperature of space.

What's the future for the Universe?

Well let me tell you the bad news first, the Universe is past its __7__; there are more stars dying than are being born so the galaxies are gradually __8__. As they do, more black holes are being formed. Those that exist gradually consume more materials, and eventually, we'll end up with a universe of black holes and faint remnants of stars like the sun called "white walls," which are just cold balls of material that are gradually cooling down and that's it. That takes about a billion billion

The Present Is Pregnant with the Future

Unit 20

years and then that's it for a really really long time. Steven Hawking becomes important _____ _____**9**_____ ; and this says that black holes gradually dissolve, very very slowly. I won't go into the details but black holes gradually give out light and that uses up energy. The energy has to come from somewhere so the black hole gradually shrinks. Now all this time, the universe is expanding; _____ _____**10**_____ ; so these black holes get further and further away from each other; and while they are giving out their light, gradually you will see the universe appear to shrink, because although it's expanding, everything else disappears over our horizon, so we're left with just one little black hole that we're sitting on and then gradually the black holes evaporate, and __**11**__ .

Ex. 2   Make dialogues on the following topics.
1. Why do we explore the Moon and Mars? Do you think we can move to them one day in future?
2. What is the future life for us?

Part IV   Watch and Debate

I Have a Dream

  Martin Luther King, Jr. (January 15, 1929—April 4, 1968) was an American clergyman, activist, and prominent Afro-American leader in the African American civil rights movement. He has become an iconic figure in the history of American liberalism, best known for his dedication to civil rights. A Baptist minister, King became a civil rights activist early in his career. He led the 1955 Montgomery Bus Boycott and helped found the Southern Christian Leadership Conference in 1957, serving as its first president. King's efforts led to the 1963 March on Washington, where King delivered his "I Have a Dream" speech. There, he expanded American values to include the vision of a color blind society, and established his reputation as one of the greatest orators in American history. In 1964, King became the youngest person to receive the Nobel Peace Prize for his work to end racial segregation and racial discrimination through civil disobedience and other non-violent means. By the time of his death in 1968, he had refocused his efforts on ending poverty and stopping the Vietnam War. King was assassinated on April 4, 1968, in Memphis, Tennessee. He was posthumously awarded the Presidential Medal of Freedom in 1977 and Congressional Gold Medal in 2004; Martin Luther King, Jr. Day was established as a U.S. national holiday in 1986.

Glossary

decree 法令	beacon 灯塔
sear 使干枯,使凋谢	wither 干枯,枯萎
captivity 束缚	negro 黑鬼(对黑人的贬称)
cripple 使瘸,使残废	manacles 枷锁
segregation 隔离	languish 衰弱
promissory 约定的	promissory note 【商】本票,期票

unalienable 不可让渡的	default 不履行
hallow 使成神圣, hallowed spot 圣地	desolate 荒芜的
quicksand 流沙(区),(指不稳固的基础)	devotee 信徒
wallow 沉溺	creed 信条
swelter 使闷热,使中暑	oasis 绿洲
vicious 邪恶的	interposition 插嘴, 干预
nullification 无效	pilgrim 朝拜者
hamlet 小村庄	gentiles 非犹太教徒
protestants 新教徒	Catholics 天主教徒

Ex. 1 Watch the video and answer the following questions.

1. Why was the demonstration held in front of the Lincoln Memorial Hall?
   _____.
2. What was the condition of Negro one hundred years later?
   _____.
3. Why did Martin Luther King say "the Negro lives on a lonely island"?
   _____.
4. What are the "unalienable Rights" for the black people?
   _____.

Ex. 2 Watch the video and complete each blank with what you've heard in the video clip.

1. I am happy to _____ with you today in what will go down in history as the greatest demonstration for _____ in the history of our nation. Five _____ years ago, a great American, in whose symbolic shadow we stand today, signed the Emancipation Proclamation. This momentous decree came as a great beacon _____ of hope to millions of Negro _____ who had been seared in the flames of withering _____.

2. But we refuse to believe that the bank of _____ is bankrupt. We refuse to believe that there are insufficient funds in the great vaults of _____ of this nation. And so, we've come to _____ this check, a check that will give us upon _____ the riches of freedom and the _____ of justice. We have also come to this hallowed spot to _____ America of the fierce urgency of Now. Now is the time to make real the _____ of democracy.

3. I have a dream that one day this nation will rise up and live out the true meaning of its creed: "_____."

4. I have a dream that my four little children will one day live in a nation where _____.

Ex. 3 Express your opinions on the following questions.

1. Why did Martin Luther King address his "I Have a Dream"? Did he realize his dream? Why?
2. Try to address your dream using the title "I Have a Dream".

The Present Is Pregnant with the Future

Unit 20

Part V Extracurricular Listening

Listen to the following 10 short dialogues and choose the best answer to each of the questions you will hear.

1. A. At a boat dock.
   B. At a weather station.
   C. At an airport.
   D. At a sports arena.

2. A. The woman would like to join the man the next time.
   B. Neither of them has had a chance to see the play.
   C. The man regarded himself as a good traveler.
   D. The man brought his pet along on the trip.

3. A. He's afraid to work at night.
   B. He's afraid the work will be really hard.
   C. He doesn't want to work tomorrow night.
   D. He can't find the way out of the student center.

4. A. Brenda has borrowed her car.
   B. She came with Brenda today.
   C. She parked her car in a safe place.
   D. Her car ran out of gas.

5. A. How to turn on a furnace.
   B. Repairing a switch.
   C. How to play a trick.
   D. Exchanging furnaces.

6. A. Andy will help if he's there this summer.
   B. West Virginia has many unexplored areas.
   C. Andy would probably be a good person to ask.
   D. The campers should try to get a lot of information.

7. A. Someone fixed it.
   B. Louise repaired it.
   C. It's been thrown out.
   D. Louise sold it.

8. A. He'll make up his mind tomorrow.
   B. Shirley's leaving tomorrow.
   C. Shirley will find a way to go.
   D. He's been unable to ask Shirley.

9. A. She didn't remember to take her checkbook.
   B. She couldn't get a locker.
   C. She has a temporary locker.
   D. She will check out the locker next to Jim's.

10. A. She's been extremely successful.
    B. Her success is hard to understand.
    C. She owes some of her success to her personality.
    D. She's less successful now than she was last year.

Scripts and Keys

Unit 1   Communication Is the Key to Success

Part II   Join in the Dialogue

Dialogue 1

A: Have you met Jonathan?

B: No, I haven't. Please introduce me.

A: Jonathan, this is Maggie. She works in the Research Department.

C: Nice to meet you, Maggie. How long have you been here?

B: With the company? Oh... too long... nearly fifteen years. What about you?

C: I don't work here. I'm just on a visit for a couple of days.

B: Oh? Where are you staying?

C: Greg is putting me up.

B: And have you seen much of the city?

C: Well, not as much as I'd like to...

Questions:

1. What kind of occasion do you think the conversation is about?

2. How many speakers are there in the conversation?

3. How will you describe the conversation?

4. What is the most probable relationship between Maggie and Jonathan?

5. Where does Maggie work?

6. How long may Jonathan have been here, according to the conversation?

Keys:

Ex. 1   1. A   2. B   3. C   4. D   5. A   6. D

Ex. 2   Open

Dialogue 2

W: Hey, Joe, that was really a great presentation you just gave.

M: You think so? I was really worried about it. My hands were shaking in everything.

W: To me, you sounded really natural and well prepared.

M: Oh, I'm relieved to hear you say that. It took me over a month to put that presentation together.

W: It sounds like it. Hey, before you forget, are you free tonight?

M: Yeah, I guess so. Why?

W: My mother and my little brother are in town and my mom bought these theater tickets months ago and...

M: What show?

W: It's called... A *Metamorphosis* by Ovid. It's a play written back in ancient Rome. It is supposed to be really great.

M: Don't say another word, I'd love to go.

W: Oh, Er, I don't know how to tell you this but I'm actually going with my mother. And I was wondering if you could babysit my little brother while my mom and I go to the play.

M: Ah. How embarrassing. Ah, sure, no problem. What time should I show up?
W: At seven o'clock in my place. He won't be any trouble. You can just watch a video with him or something.
M: Yeah, that sounds OK. I'll see you tonight then.
W: Ah, Joe, I'm really sorry about the misunderstanding. I know you thought I was waiting for you and... well I apologize if I misled you.
M: Actually I think it's kind of funny. Don't worry. We'll laugh about it later.
W: Oh, thanks a million. See you at seven.

Questions:
1. What does the woman want the man to do?
2. What does the woman say about the man's presentation?
3. What does the man say about misunderstanding?
4. What are the woman's plan for the evening?

Keys:
Ex. 1 1. B 2. C 3. A 4. C
Ex. 2 Open

Part III Listen and Discuss

Passage 1

Listen to part of a lecture in a physical geography class:

We only have a few minutes left so I'd like to go over a couple of points before we move on. Remember that although there are both horizontal and vertical movements of air. The term wind is applied only to horizontal movements and that more air is involved in those horizontal movements than in vertical movements. And what causes these horizontal movements? Ultimately, it's solar radiation, because the unequal heating of the earth than the atmosphere produces horizontal differences in air pressure. These differences set winds in motion. Essentially, winds are a nature's way of balancing out the uneven distribution of air pressure over the earth. Secondly, let me repeat my answer to the question we had before about wind direction. Many people get confused by what they hear in weather forecasts. We talk about wind direction in terms of where the wind's coming from, not where it's blowing to. There is a good reason for this. To weather forecasters, the origin of the wind is more important than its destination. The wind's origin helps them predict the weather. Logically, in the northern hemisphere, a north wind tends to bring colder weather, and a south wind warmer weather. I haven't forgotten vertical movements of air, but we don't have time today to talk about them in depth. In our next class then, I'll begin by discussing updraft(上升气流) and downdraft and how they affect the weather. I suspect most of you can guess which of the two brings warm weather, and which brings cold.

Questions:
1. According to the speaker, how is wind defined?
2. Why does the speaker mention solar radiation?
3. According to the speaker, which weather forecast information can be confusing?
4. What will the speaker probably discuss in the next class?

Keys:
Ex. 1 1. C 2. A 3. D 4. D
Ex. 2 Open

Passage 2

A deep national crisis faced the United States in the year eighteen-fifty. It threatened to split the nation in two. It arose over the issue of slavery in the new territories of California and New Mexico. The president of the United States,

General Zachary Taylor, had no clear policy on the issue. Taylor tried to be neutral, hoping that the problem would solve itself. But it did not solve itself. The split between the north and south got wider. There was a real danger that the south would try to leave the Union. Then, Senator Henry Clay of Kentucky stepped forward to save the Union.

Clay was a firm believer in the idea of compromise. He once said: "I go for honorable compromise whenever it can be made. Life itself is but a compromise between death and life. The struggle continues through our whole existence until the great destroyer finally wins. All legislation, all government, all society is formed upon the principle of mutual concession, politeness, and courtesy. Upon these, everything is based."

Clay was sure that a compromise between north and south was possible. Near the end of January, Clay completed work on his plan. Most parts of it already had been proposed as separate bills. Clay put them together in a way that both sides could accept.

Senator Jefferson Davis of Mississippi declared that Clay's compromises did not offer anything of value to the south. He said the south would accept nothing less than extending the Missouri compromise line west to the Pacific Ocean. This meant that land south of the line would be open to slavery.

Clay answered that no power on earth could force him to vote to establish slavery where it did not exist. He said Americans had blamed Britain for forcing African slavery on the colonies. He said he would not have the future citizens of California and New Mexico blaming Henry Clay for slavery there.

Clay began his speech by talking of the serious crisis that faced the nation. He said that never before had he spoken to a group as troubled and worried as the one he spoke to now. Clay listed his eight resolutions. Then he said: "No man on earth is more ready than I am to surrender anything which I have proposed and to accept in its place anything that is better. But I ask the honorable senators whether their duty will be done by simply limiting themselves to opposing any one or all of the resolutions I have offered."

"If my plan of peace and unity is not right, give us your plan. Let us see how all the questions that have arisen out of this unhappy subject of slavery can be better settled more fairly and justly than the plan I have offered. Present me with such a plan, and I will praise it with pleasure and accept it without the slightest feeling of regret."

Clay said there was equal justice in his resolutions (1) <u>ending the slave trade in the District of Columbia and strengthening laws on the return of runaway slaves.</u> He said the south, perhaps, would be helped more than the north by his proposals. But the north, he said, was richer and had more money and power.

To the north, slavery was a matter of feeling. But to the south, Clay said, it was a hard social and economic fact. He said the north could look on in safety while (2) <u>the actions of some of its people were producing flames of bitterness throughout the southern states.</u>

Then Clay attacked the south's claim that it had the right to leave the Union. He said the Union of states was (3) <u>permanent, that the men who built the Union did not do so only for themselves, but for all future Americans.</u>

Questions:
1. What did President Zachary Taylor do in response to the splitting crisis in the United States in 1850?
2. What were the three key words in Senator Henry Clay's principle of compromise?
3. What was Senator Clay's attitude toward slavery?
4. According to Senator Clay, what would cause him to give up his resolutions?

Keys:
Ex.1   1. D   2. C   3. A   4. B
Ex.2   Refer to the script
Ex.3   Open

Scripts and Keys Unit 1

Part IV Watch and Debate

Keys:

Ex. 1 Refer to the script

1. decoding noises that you hear, converting them into a system that matches your own representations
2. we don't have many... I don't have problem decoding you and you don't have problem decoding me
3. be in England last week and I can find myself in places in England where I don't understand what they're saying
4. teenage cultures
5. wear different clothes
6. Our societies are very, very busy, technological societies
7. you're finding basically stone-age tribes, there's a lot of innovation in language
8. has to do with playing games with languages and constructing a lot of kinship systems, things with probably no or little function or utility

Ex. 2 Open

Part V Extracurricular Listening

1. M: Operator, I'd like to place a call to Athens, Greece. How much will it cost?
   W: $9 for the first three minutes, and $3 for each additional minute.
   Q: How much would a ten-minute call cost? (D)

2. W: How did Bill finally get to New York? First he was going to fly, then to take the bus, but the last minute I talked to him, he hasn't really decided.
   M: He ended up driving his own car. The plane was too expensive and the bus was too slow.
   Q: How many times did Bill go to New York? (A)

3. M: Susan told me you were on a diet. How much weight have you lost?
   W: Well, to start with, I weighed 160 pounds. The first month I took off fifteen pounds, but then I gained back three pounds over the holidays.
   Q: How much does the woman weigh now? (B)

4. W: I bought this $200 washer at a 30% discount.
   M: It's a very good washer. I think that's a real bargain.
   Q: How much did the woman pay for the washer? (C)

5. M: I'm afraid I wasn't paying attention to what you were saying.
   W: I said that we must hurry because we're already late for the show. It starts at 8:30, it takes us 45 minutes to get there and it is five minutes to eight right now.
   Q: If they leave now, how late will they be for the show? (C)

6. W: My baby is having his first birthday party this month. He is one year junior to Jamie and Jamie is two years junior to the twins.
   M: That means that your children are all still young.
   Q: How old are the twins? (A)

7. M: Could you tell me how many of your employees are women?
   W: Yes, certainly. We have a very high percentage of female staff. We employ about 160 women, which is eighty percent of all our staff.
   Q: How many of the employees in this organization are men? (C)

8. W: How many people showed up for the meeting yesterday? Twenty-five?

M: Fifty were expected to come, but the number was double that.

Q: Actually how many people attended the meeting? (C)

9. M: Here is the money.

W: That's four thirty-nine for the shirt, and here is your change: four forty, four fifty, five and five make ten.

Q: How much is the change? (B)

10. W: My family and I are visiting Washington for a few days. We'd like two rooms with a bath between, and a large room with a double bed.

M: Very good, mamma. The two rooms are 18 dollars a day, and the large room is 15 dollars a day.

Q: How much would the woman pay for the rooms if she and her family stay there for three days? (B)

Unit 2   Emotions Have Taught Mankind to Reason

Part II   Join in the Dialogue

Dialogue 1

W: Cheer up, Mike, you look really down in the dumps. What's the matter?

M: I've seen the Dean and the Professor this morning. They've advised me to resign as Chairman of the Students' Union.

W: Resign! But you've done it so well.

M: Yes, I know. But it takes too much of my time. I can't get through my studies and I am in my final year. I intended to work really hard last vacation, but you know what happened.

W: I suppose it is best to resign, Mike. Jim can take over.

M: That's not all. There's a bigger blow.

W: Money, I suppose.

M: Well, I owe Peter $100.

W: What for? The car, was it? You are a fool, Mike. I can't see how an economist can be so silly about money.

M: I'll just have to sell the car!

W: Well, cheer up! You can always use my bike.

Questions:

1. What is Mike's main problem?
2. What year is Mike in?
3. Why should Mike resign?
4. What do you suppose Mike is majoring in?

Keys:

Ex.1   1. A 2. B 3. D 4. D

Ex.2   Open

Dialogue 2

W: May I help you, sir?

M: You certainly can. I don't know why you put things on that recording that aren't true.

W: What do you mean, sir?

M: I called your tourist information recording and it said that *Fiddler on the Roof* was playing last night.

W: Yes, that's true, and tonight is the last performance.

M: Well, I went to the theater and they said they didn't have any tickets left for last night.

· 146 ·

Scripts and Keys — Unit 2

W: Oh, that's too bad. I'm sorry you didn't call the theater before you went. It would have saved you the trip.

M: Never mind that. Why do you tell people about a play when they can't buy tickets to see it?

W: I'm sorry you couldn't see the play, but that tape was made a week ago and there were plenty of tickets available then. It's impossible to know beforehand which nights will be sold out, but—would you like to see *Fiddler on the Roof*?

M: Well, that's what I tried to do.

W: Let me call the theater and see if there are any ticket for tonight's performance. If there are, would you like to go tonight?

M: I guess so, but there won't be any tickets anyway.

W: Well, let me try. (Sounds of dialing) How many do you want?

M: Just one.

W: Hi, Maryann. This is Janet at the Visitor Information Center. How are you? (Pause.) Fine. Do you by any chance have a single for tonight? (Pause.)... I see. OK, just a minute... She has one ticket that somebody just turned in. It's in the first row of the balcony, in the center section. Would you like it?

M: Yes.

W: OK, Maryann. Would you put it aside for him or do you want him to come and get it now? (Pause.) Just a minute... Sir, she'd like you to pick up the ticket now. Is that OK?

M: Yes. I'll go right over.

W: OK, he'll be right over. And thanks a lot, Maryann. Bye... (Sound of phone being put back in the cradle.) OK, sir, she'll hold that ticket for an hour. Just tell her we sent you. And I hope you enjoy the play!

M: Well, thank you—listen, I guess I owe you an apology. It's just that I don't get to Phoenix very often and I really wanted to see that play.

W: That's all right, sir.

M: Well, I'm sorry. And I really do appreciate your taking the time and trouble to help me. You don't usually find that in the city.

W: Oh, I don't know. The people here aren't so bad.

M: Well, I guess I'd better go pick up that ticket. Thanks again. And I am really sorry.

W: That's quite all right.

Keys:

Ex. 1   1. T   2. F   3. T   4. T   5. T   6. F   7. F   8. T   9. F   10. T

Ex. 2

1. At a tourist information center.
2. From the tourist information recording.
3. The woman works at the center; the man is a tourist.
4. He has been angry at and rude toward the woman and accused the visitor center, and now he feels he was not fair.
5. The man is not polite at first; the woman is polite throughout.

Ex. 3   Open

Part III   Listen and Discuss

Passage 1

American men don't cry because it is considered not characteristic of men to do so. Only women cry. Cry is a "weakness" characteristic of the female, and no American male wants to be identified with anything in the least weak or feminine. Crying, in our culture, is identified with childishness, with weakness and dependence. No one likes a crybaby, and we disapprove of crying even in children, discouraging it in them as early as possible. In a land so devoted to the pursuit of happiness as ours, crying really is rather un-American. Adults must learn not to cry in situations in which it is permissible for child to cry. Women being the "weaker" and "dependent" sex, it is only natural that they should cry in certain emotional situations. In women, crying is excusable. But in men, crying is a mark of weakness. So goes the American belief with regard to crying.

"A little man," we impress on our male children, "never cries. Only girls and crybabies do." And so we condition males in America not to cry whenever they feel like doing so. It is not that American males are unable to cry because of some biological time clock within them which causes them to run down in that capacity as they grow older, but that they are trained not to cry. And so the "little man" controls his desire to cry and goes on doing so until he is unable to cry even when he wants to. Thus do we produce a trained incapacity in the American male to cry. And this is bad. Why is it bad? Because crying is a natural function of the human organism which is designed to restore the emotionally disequilibrated person to a state of equilibrium. The return of the disequilibrated organ systems of the body to steady states or dynamic stability is known as homeostasis. Crying serves a homeostatic function for the organism as a whole. Any interference with homeostasis is likely to be damaging to the organism. And there is good reason to believe that the American male's trained incapacity to cry is seriously damaging to him.

It is unnecessary to cry whenever one wants to cry, but one should be able to cry when one ought to cry—when one needs to cry. For to cry under certain emotionally disequilibrating conditions is necessary for the maintenance of health.

To be human is to weep. The human species is the only one in the whole of animated nature that sheds tears. The trained inability of any human being to weep is lessening of his capacity to be human—a defect which usually goes deeper than the mere inability to cry. And this, among other things, is what American parents—with the best intentions in the world—have achieved for the American male. It is very sad. If we feel like it, let us all have a good cry—and clear our minds of those cobwebs of confusion which have for so long prevented us from understanding the natural necessity of crying.

Keys:
Ex. 1   1. B   2. A   3. C   4. A
Ex. 2   Open

Passage 2
Keys:
Ex. 1   1. emotional health   2. gathered   3. stroke   4. physical distance   5. lasted   6. contagious   7. happier
8. married   9. spread   10. your emotions can be affected by someone you do not directly know   11. the effects of social networks on obesity and efforts to stop smoking   12. happiness spreads through social networks like an emotional virus
Ex. 2   Open

Part IV   Watch and Debate

What self-esteem is? There is a research suggesting that it is connected with our well-being, to our success, that is inversely related to crime, substance abuse, unhappiness, anxiety, depression. So self-esteem is important, we know that. However, not all was well in self-esteem land, as we discussed last time. Part of the problem is there is contradictory evidence. On the one hand, self-esteem is associated with benevolence, generosity, and empathy. On the other hand, high self-esteem has been shown to be associated with hostility, lack of cooperation, defensiveness. There's also misunderstanding about or how self-esteem affects performance, how it affects happiness, and where that comes from.

The paradox of self-esteem. Sometimes, we feel like we are doing so well, we are getting so many accolades, our self-esteem increases. Only to go back to go its base level. Only worse, because now we have to do more to come back

Scripts and Keys

to our base level of self-esteem. Have to get more accolades, more achievements. Nothing is enough anymore. So there are these contradictory evidences. Where self-esteem comes from and its consequences, and one of the ways to explain it is by drawing on the work of people like Maslov, people like Nathanial Brandon, people like Carl Rogers, Rollo May, Lovinger, to see how we can perhaps break down self-esteem to its components. That's what my dissertation did. This is what I presented to you in the previous classes. Basically, take the ideas of these selected field researchers who have been thinking about people like Robert Kegan across the road from the Ed school, thinking about self-esteem more developmentally and presented the epigenetic model. Epigenetic once again, meaning one level has to be fulfilled or at least partly fulfilled before we can go to the next level.

The three levels are dependence self-esteem, independence self-esteem and unconditional self-esteem. Dependence self-esteem, the two components are first of all persons with high dependence, needs the accolades of others' constantly chooses whether it is a career path or what to do in the afternoon, based on how much approval that will gain him or her. Person with dependence self-esteem, when it comes to competence, always compares him or herself to others. Am I better or am I worse? Superior or inferior? independence self-esteem is self-esteem that is contingent on the self. In terms of how I evaluate myself, it is my internal voice that's speaking. In terms of how my levels of competence are determined, it depends on how much I have improved, how much better I have got, how much I feel I have fulfilled my potential. That's independence self-esteem, not contingent on what other people say or think. Unconditional self-esteem is the highest level, the level that Maslov would talk about self-actualization, what David Schnarch talks about as "differentiated" or at the level of being known rather than desiring to be validated. Unconditional self-esteem is when our self-esteem is high enough. We feel good enough about ourselves, not to be concerned with evaluations with others or even with self-evaluations. In terms of comparison, we don't compare; we are interdependent connected to others. So the example I gave last time is of a book.

Let's say I published a book, and I have high dependent self-esteem, first of all, I write it, I publish it so that I can get accolades. My primary motivation is external approval. My primary motivation is to publish a book that is better than the other books out there so relative competence as well as externally other-determined. If I bring in a book or write a book, and I have high independence self-esteem, I write it and I evaluate it myself, "this is good work" or "this is not so good, we need improvement." It terms of comparison, I compare to myself. "I've improved a lot since I started writing. This book is actually better than my previous book. My work is becoming more authentic, more real" that's independent self-esteem evaluation. Unconditional self-esteem, the highest level that we know of, "I write a book, I am not concerned with evaluation, whether it is good or bad, of course I want to be better and better, but that doesn't affect how I feel about myself. I simply exist. I write the book, I am in a state of flow, experiencing the experience." In terms of whether it is better than others, or better than I've written, it doesn't matter. What I am happy about is bringing a good book into existence and I would be as happy if someone else wrote the book. I would be happy or happier if someone else wrote a better book that can help others more. Important thing to understand about his model, the three levels, is that we all have the three basically from a very young age. It is not that the Dali Lama or mother Teresa or Nelson Mandela or Magaret Mead, the people we know have been self-actualized. It is not that they don't care about what other people say. However, they are mostly, most of their lives, most of the time, self-determined: do what they believe in, feel a sense of connection toward others, want to make the world a better place. But it is not that they don't care, not that they don't evaluate themselves relative to themselves, or relative to others. That's part of human nature.

Keys:

Ex. 1

1. On the one hand, self-esteem is related to positive things, on the other hand, it is also related to unhappiness and hostility.
2. By reading people's researches.

3. Dependence self-esteem, independence self-esteem, and unconditional self-esteem.
4. His self-evaluation of the book is more important to him than others' evaluation. He is not contentious of what other people say. He focuses more on how much he has improved.
5. Unconditional self-esteem is the highest level.

Ex. 2   Open

Part V   Extracurricular Listening

1. M: Mrs. Johnson, you must take these capsules every four hours without fail.
   W: It's noon now and I just took my first one. I'll follow your instruction carefully so that I can get well soon.
   Q: When should the woman take her next pill? (A)

2. M: You've been here for five years. Have you had much of a chance to travel?
   W: Not much. In November last year I planned to go Yellow Stone Park at Christmas, but when that day came, I had to postpone the trip. Then one and a half months later, I finally made it there.
   Q: When did the woman go to Yellow Stone Park? (C)

3. M: Hello. Miss, I'm William Smith. Please tell me the time difference between America and China. I'm in America. I'll call my Chinese friend at Beijing time 7:00 p.m.
   W: China is 5 hours later, sir.
   Q: When should the man place his call to China? (A)

4. W: Excuse me, when is the next train from Washington due to arrive?
   M: It's scheduled to arrive in 5 minutes, but there will be a delay of 15 minutes because of some repair work along the line. We feel sorry for any inconvenience this might have caused the passengers.
   Q: When is the next train from Washington to arrive? (C)

5. M: Is dinner ready? Grandfather always starts eating at seven on the dot.
   W: I just have to add the vegetables and cook everything for five minutes. Afterwards, we'll have ten more minutes to serve everything.
   Q: What time is it? (A)

6. M: Hurry up. It's already 8:30 and the Smiths will be arriving any second now.
   W: Oh, I forgot to tell you. Mr. Smith called at 7:15 to say they'd be half an hour late. He didn't get off work until 6:30.
   Q: When will the Smiths arrive? (D)

7. M: How long can I keep this book?
   W: Today is Tuesday. You'll have to return the book the day after tomorrow.
   Q: When should the man return the book? (B)

8. W: Could you tell me the starting time for both concerts?
   M: The first begins at a quarter after seven and lasts two hours and fifteen minutes. The second follows after a five-minute intermission.
   Q: At what time does the second concert start? (B)

9. W: It's surprising that John finished first in the 1500-meter run.
   M: Well. That's just what I expected. He had practised so hard.
   Q: When does this conversation most probably take place? (D)

10. W: Oh, no. It's five o'clock already, and I haven't finished typing these letters.
    M: Don't worry, that clock is half an hour fast, you still have time to do them.
    Q: When does this conversation take place? (A)

· 150 ·

Unit 3　Education Is the Transmission of Civilization

Part Ⅱ　Join in the Dialogue

Dialogue 1

A: Interviewer;
B: Dr. Wu;
C: Mr. Carl

A: Well, the students are taking exams and the society is paying huge attention to them. Now in China, cars are banned from blowing their horns and construction sites stop their construction because they are not allowed to disturb the students when they are taking exams. Is it too much care or just right?

B: I think in China this national entrance exam is like a big "party" for the next generation of grown-ups. The whole society is mobilized to move away to create an involvement for them to take the exam. And it's actually not just an exam but also imposes an extra pressure on them.

A: Exactly right. So, you think it's the right proportion, or a little bit too much, or not enough?

B: A little bit too much right now, especially when you consider 30 years ago when China just began this national entrance exam. During that age, only 5 % of exam takers could actually pass this admission test, but right now over 80% can get this entrance. So, I don't think it's justifiable right now to have this kind of overstretch.

A: 80%! So what is the legitimacy of this test. I mean 80% of students, after taking their exams, can go in. What is the point now?

C: Well, after all, the goal is try to have people go to college, not try to discourage them from going. I think, when we see all these preparations going in society, as Dr. Wu said, this creates in some way perhaps an artificial sense of pressure on the students because they feel it's not just their own future and their families' hope, but in fact, all of society has sort of put some measure of fate in their abilities.

A: You've made me think of an interesting neighborhood near Confucius Temple here in Beijing. I heard some interesting stories over there. Are there many parents and their children going there and praying for their exams?

C: Absolutely! In the last days we've seen traffic in the neighborhood climb because lots of people go to Confucius temples or whatever worship authorities they can.

A: Sure. A mother of someone who is taking the college exam this year is telling me she is going everywhere, you know, going to churches, temples, whichever place to pray. But the thing is, is this really the way for us to push forward the best education for our kids, or rather only protecting the original educational system which many think needs to be reformed?

B: I think right now the whole educational system is exam-oriented or exam-driven, and especially they have only this one opportunity to make it or maybe just break it. So, this do-or-die type position not only gives them a lot of pressure. That is quite different from, for example, the case in the United States. You can take SAT for a couple of times and also admission criteria are not only based on one exam but also based on a wide range of other activities, even including those extra-curricular activities.

A: Mr. Carl, before you went to college, you didn't go to church to pray for the best school. Isn't it?

C: No. Most preparations I did was to sharpen my pencil and got prepared for going. But the truth is, you know, there is a value in making a decision as to who should go to the best schools. After all, it's not just about the test we concentrate on. We want our students well-rounded and socially well-adjusted after their 12 years of study and preparing wisely for their exam.

Keys：

Ex. 1　1. A　2. C　3. B　4. D　5. C　6. D

Ex. 2　Open

Dialogue 2

Keys：

Ex. 1

1. related to　2. 220,000　3. exact number　4. engaged　5. in terms of　6. self-relied　7. impressive　8. flexible　9. maintain the capability to recruit the best talents　10. those students bringing back the elements of the West will broadly encourage universities here to take a move　11. foreign students are trying to come here to study Chinese language and Chinese culture

Ex. 2　Open

Part Ⅲ　Listen and Discuss

Passage 1

　　The first thing Chua wants you to know is that she is not a monster. "Everything I do as a mother builds on a foundation of love and compassion," she says. Love and compassion, plus punishingly high expectations: this is how Chua herself was raised. Though her parents are Chinese, they lived for many years in the Philippines and immigrated to America two years before Chua was born. Chua and her three younger sisters were required to speak Chinese at home; for each word of English they uttered, they received a whack with a pair of chopsticks. On the girls' report cards, only A's were acceptable. When Chua took her father to an awards assembly at which she received second prize, he was furious. "Never, ever disgrace me like that again," he told her.

　　One more way in which the tiger mother's approach differs from that of her Western counterparts: her willingness to drill. When Sophia came in second on a speed test at school, Chua made her do 20 practice tests every night for a week, clocking her with a stopwatch. "Practice, practice, practice is crucial for excellence; repetition is underrated in America," she writes. In this, Chua is right, says Daniel Willingham, a professor of psychology at the University of Virginia. "It's impossible to become proficient at a mental task without extensive practice," he notes.

　　More than anything, it's Chua's maternal confidence that has inspired many who have read her words. Since her book's publication, she says, e-mail messages have poured in from around the globe, some of them angry and even threatening but many of them grateful. "A lot of people have written to say that they wished their parents had pushed them when they were younger, that they think they could have done more with their lives," Chua recounts. "Other people have said that after reading my book they finally understand their parents and why they did what they did. One man wrote that he sent his mother flowers and a note of thanks, and she called him up, weeping."

　　Among those who are decidedly not following Chua's lead are many parents and educators in China. For educated urban Chinese parents, the trend is away from the strict traditional model and toward a more relaxed American style. Chinese authorities, meanwhile, are increasingly dissatisfied with the country's education system, which has long been based on memorization. They are looking to the West for inspiration—because they know they must produce more creative and innovative graduates to power the high-end economy they want to develop.

Keys：

Ex. 1　1. D　2. B　3. A　4. C　5. D　6. D

Ex. 2　Open

Passage 2

Keys：

Ex. 1

1. shocking　2. best-seller　3. describes　4. survive　5. insisting　6. defensive　7. ill equipped　8. marketplace

· 152 ·

9. in a nation where such dreams are still possible   10. Knowing the sacrifices he and my mother made for us made me want to uphold the family name, to make my parents proud   11. that sounds like a prescription for success with which it's very difficult to argue

Ex. 2   Open

Part IV   Watch and Debate

1.   One thing that the piano and violin have in common—with each other but also with many sports—is that you can't play extraordinarily well unless you're relaxed. Just as you can't have a killer tennis serve or throw a baseball really far unless you keep your arm loose, you can't produce a mellifluous tone on the violin if you squeeze the bow too tightly or mash down on the strings—mashing is what makes the horrible scratchy sound. "Imagine that you're a rag doll," Mr. Shugart would tell Lulu. "Floppy and relaxed, and not a care in the world. You're so relaxed your arm feels heavy from its own weight…. Let gravity do all the work…. Good, Lulu, good."

  "RELAX!" I screamed at home. "Mr. Shugart said RAG DOLL!" I always tried my best to reinforce Mr. Shugart's points, but things were tough with Lulu, because my very presence made her edgy and irritable.

  Once, in the middle of a practice session she burst out, "Stop it, Mommy. Just stop it."

  "Lulu, I didn't say anything," I replied. "I didn't say one word."

  "Your brain is annoying me," Lulu said. "I know what you're thinking."

  "I'm not thinking anything," I said indignantly. Actually, I'd been thinking that Lulu's right elbow was too high, that her dynamics were all wrong, and that she needed to shape her phrases better.

  "Just turn off your brain!" Lulu ordered. "I'm not going to play anymore unless you turn off your brain."

  Lulu was always trying to provoke me. Getting into an argument was a way of not practicing. That time I didn't bite. "Okay," I said calmly. "How do you want me to do that?" Giving Lulu control over the situation sometimes defused her temper.

  Lulu thought about it. "Hold your nose for five seconds."

  A lucky break. I complied, and the practicing resumed. That was one of our good days.

2.   Here's a question I often get: "But Amy, let me ask you this. Who are you doing all this pushing for—your daughters"—and here always the cocked head, the knowing tone—"or yourself?" I find this a very Western question to ask (because in Chinese thinking, the child is the extension of the self). But that doesn't mean it's not an important one.

  My answer, I'm pretty sure, is that everything I do is unequivocally 100% for my daughters. My main evidence is that so much of what I do with Sophia and Lulu is miserable, exhausting, and not remotely fun for me. It's not easy to make your kids work when they don't want to, to put in grueling hours when your own youth is slipping away, to convince your kids they can do something when they (and maybe even you) are fearful that they can't. "Do you know how many years you've taken off my life?" I'm constantly asking my girls. "You're both lucky that I have enormous longevity as indicated by my thick good-luck earlobes."

  To be honest, I sometimes wonder if the question "Who are you really doing this for?" should be asked of Western parents too. Sometimes I wake up in the morning dreading what I have to do and thinking how easy it would be to say, "Sure Lulu, we can skip a day of violin practice." Unlike my Western friends, I can never say, "As much as it kills me, I just have to let my kids make their choices and follow their hearts. It's the hardest thing in the world, but I'm doing my best to hold back." Then they get to have a glass of wine and go to a yoga class, whereas I have to stay home and scream and have my kids hate me.

3. Red Square

  Two days after Lulu's Bat Mitzvah, we left for Russia. It was a vacation I'd dreamed of for a long time. My parents had raved about St. Petersburg when I was a girl, and Jed and I wanted to take the girls somewhere we'd never visited ourselves.

We needed a vacation. Katrin, my sister, had just passed through the worst danger zone of acute graft-versus-host disease. We'd basically gone ten months without a day's break. Our first stop was Moscow. Jed had found us a convenient hotel right in the center of the city. After a short rest, we headed out for our first taste of Russia.

I tried to be goofy and easygoing, the mood my girls most like me in, refraining as best I could from making my usual critical remarks about what they were wearing or how many times they said "like". But there was something ill-fated about that day. It took us more than an hour standing in two different lines to change money at a place that called itself a bank, and after that the museum we wanted to visit was closed.

We decided to go to Red Square. Lulu and Sophia kept sniping at each other, which irritated me. Actually, what really irritated me was that they were all grown up—teenagers my size (in Sophia's case, three inches taller), instead of cute little girls. "It goes so fast," older friends had always said wistfully. "Before you know it, your children will be grown and gone, and you'll be old even though you feel just like the same person you were when you were young." I never believed my friends when they said that, because it seemed to me they were old. By squeezing out so much from every moment of every day, perhaps I imagined that I was buying myself more time. As a purely mathematical fact, people who sleep less live more.

"That's Lenin's Tomb behind the long white wall," Jed told the girls, pointing. "His body is embalmed and on display. We can go see it tomorrow." Jed then gave the girls a short tutorial on Russian history and cold war politics.

After roaming around for a bit, we sat down at an outdoor café. It was attached to the famous GUM shopping mall, which is housed in a palatial, arcade-lined nineteenth-century building that takes up almost the entire east side of Red Square, directly across from the fortresslike Kremlin.

We decided to get blinis and caviar, a fun way to start off our first evening in Moscow, Jed and I thought. But when the caviar arrived—thirty U.S. dollars for a tiny receptacle—Lulu said, "Eww, gross," and wouldn't try it. "Sophia," I snapped my oldest daughter, "Don't take so much; leave some for the rest of us." I then turned to my other daughter, "Lulu, you sound like an uncultured savage. Try the caviar. You can put a lot of sour cream on it."

"That's even worse," Lulu said, and she made a shuddering gesture. "And don't call me a savage."

"Don't wreck the vacation for everyone, Lulu."

"You're the one wrecking it."

I pushed the caviar toward Lulu. I ordered her to try one egg—one single egg.

"Why? Lulu asked defiantly. "Why do you care so much? You can't force me to eat something."

I felt my temper rising. Could I not get Lulu to do even one tiny thing? "You're behaving like a juvenile delinquent. Try one egg now."

"I don't want to," said Lulu.

"Do it now, Lulu."

"No."

"Amy," Jed began diplomatically, "Everyone's tired. Why don't we just—"

I broke in, "Do you know how sad and ashamed my parents would be if they saw this, Lulu—you publicly disobeying me? With that look on your face? You're only hurting yourself. We're in Russia, and you refuse to try caviar! You're like a barbarian. And in case you think you're a big rebel, you are completely ordinary. There is nothing more typical, more predictable, more common and low, than an American teenager who won't try things. You're boring, Lulu—boring."

"Shut up," said Lulu angrily.

"Don't you dare say shut up to me. I'm your mother." I hissed this, but still a few guests glanced around. Then I said, knowing Lulu well, "Stop trying to act tough to impress Sophia."

Scripts and Keys Unit 3

"I hate you! I HATE YOU." This, from Lulu, was not in a hiss. It was an all-out shout at the top of her lungs. Now the entire café was staring at us.

"You don't love me," Lulu spat out. "You think you do, but you don't. You just make me feel bad about myself every second. You've wrecked my life. I can't stand to be around you. Is that what you want?"

A lump rose in my throat. Lulu saw it, but she went on. "You're a terrible mother. You're selfish. You don't care about anyone but yourself. What—you can't believe how ungrateful I am? After all you've done for me? Everything you say you do for me is actually for yourself."

She's just like me, I thought, compulsively cruel. "You are a terrible daughter," I said aloud.

"I know—I'm not what you want—I'm not Chinese! I don't want to be Chinese. Why can't you get that through your head? I hate the violin. I HATE my life. I HATE you, and I HATE this family! I'm going to take this glass and smash it!"

"Do it," I dared.

Lulu grabbed a glass from the table and threw it on the ground. Water and shards went flying, and some guests gasped. I felt all eyes upon us, a grotesque spectacle.

I'd made a career out of spurning the kind of Western parents who can't control their kids. Now I had the most disrespectful, rude, violent, out-of-control kid of all.

Lulu was trembling with rage, and there were tears in her eyes. "I'll smash more if you don't leave me alone," she cried.

I got up and ran. I ran as fast as I could, not knowing where I was going, a crazy forty-six-year-old woman sprinting in sandals and crying. I ran past Lenin's mausoleum and past some guards with guns who I thought might shoot me.

Then I stopped. I had come to the end of Red Square. There was nowhere to go.

Keys:

Ex. 1　1. B　2. D　3. B　4. A　5. A　6. C

Ex. 2

1. refraining as best I could from making my usual critical remarks
2. what really irritated me was that they were all grown up
3. that takes up almost the entire east side of
4. I felt my temper rising
5. how sad and ashamed my parents would be
6. You don't care about anyone but yourself
7. the most disrespectful, rude, violent, out-of-control kid

Ex. 3　Open

Part V Extracurricular Listening

1. M: I want to see about getting a private room as soon as possible. Also, please put a "No Visitors" sign on my door when you leave.
   W: I'll take care of both things, but first I have to give you an examination so that I can fill out your chart.
   Q: Where is the man in the dialogue? (C)

2. W: Look at those colorful birds over there. I think you can teach them to talk.
   M: Yes, but look at the price tag on them. Frankly, I'd rather have a hamster for two-fifty.
   Q: Where did this conversation take place? (D)

3. M: How do Jane and Bill like their new home?
   W: It's really comfortable, but they're tired of having to hear the jets go over their house at all hours.

Q: Where is Jane and Bill's new home located? (B)

4. W: Good morning. Do you have anything to declare?

   M: Only these two cartons of cigarettes, a bottle of brandy and some silver jewelry. That's all.

   Q: Where is this conversation most probably taking place? (D)

5. M: I understand that the art and music section was assigned to Sue, and the sports page to Charles. What's your responsibility?

   W: I have the editorial to write, as well as several book reviews.

   Q: Where do the speakers work? (C)

6. W: Stop for a minute, I want to look at this display in the window.

   M: I see some books are on sale. Let's go inside and see if we can find something on art.

   Q: Where are the two people standing? (D)

7. W: This doesn't look at all familiar. We must be lost. We'd better get some directions.

   M: Let's pull in here, while I'm filling the tank, you ask about the directions and get me a soft drink.

   Q: Where will the man and woman go for assistance? (A)

8. M: Your Honour, I would like to bring to the jury's attention some points that I feel are relevant to the case at this time.

   W: Counsellor, you may address the jury this afternoon. The court will now recess for one hour for lunch.

   Q: Where is this conversation taking place? (C)

9. M: Good morning. I'm looking for wire and nails to hang a picture.

   W: They're in the second aisle over there. We also have a good selection of hammers and other tools.

   Q: Where does this conversation probably take place? (C)

10. W: I'm here to pick up Taffy. Is she all right?

    M: I think she ought to stay here for at least another twenty-four hours. She still has an infection in her hind leg that should be watched carefully. Why don't you telephone tomorrow morning?

    Q: Where does this conversation most likely take place? (C)

Unit 4 Work to Become, Not to Acquire

Part II Join in the Dialogue

Dialogue 1 Babysitter

(Kelly, who wants to find a job as a babysitter, is interviewed by Mr. Adams.)

Kelly: Hi, Mr. Adams?

Adams: Ah, Yes. You must be Kelly. Thanks for coming.

Kelly: Here's my card.

Adams: Oh, the entrepreneurial spirit. It's hard to find a good babysitter on a Friday night.

Kelly: Well, I like watching kids, and I need the extra money.

Adams: Well, I heard you were one of the best and most affordable babysitters in the area, and…

Kelly: Uh, well, I'd like to talk to you about my new rate increases.

Adams: Rate increases?

Kelly: You see, Mr. Adams. I've consulted with my financial advisor, my mother, and she says I should charge more per child since I do cook and clean your house while you're away.

Adams: Oh, I see. So, what do you have in mind?

Kelly: Well, as I see it, I'd like to ask a dollar more per child per hour, and overtime after midnight. Based on my calculations, that's only 10.23% above the going market, and I'm now a certified babysitter with training in

Scripts and Keys

CPR.

Adams: Oh, I never knew there were courses and certifications in babysitting.

Kelly: Times are changing, Mr. Adams. I have to figure in expenses for a benefits package to cover college tuition, retirement, and my stock portfolio. Well, I tell my dad what to do.

Adams: Ah now, you're pulling my leg. I mean, how old are you anyway?

Kelly: Old enough to be a tough negotiator.

Keys:

Ex. 1 1. B 2. A 3. A 4. C 5. A

Ex. 2 Open

Dialogue 2 Job hunting

(Kelly and Josh are good friends. They are chatting in a bar about Josh's new job.)

Kelly: So, have you found a job yet?

Josh: No, but, I have a few leads, so things are looking up.

Kelly: But isn't that what you always say?

Josh: Well... uh... this time is different.

Kelly: What are you looking for this time, then?

Josh: Actually, I want to work for a Web hosting company.

Kelly: What would you do there?

Josh: Well, in a nut shell, Web hosting companies provide space for people to store and run their Websites. Does it sound like I know what I'm talking about?

Kelly: Oh, yeah, sort of.

Josh: Well, And then, sort of? Well, they allow people to run their Websites without having to buy and maintain their own servers, and I'd like to work in technical support, you know, helping customers resolve computer-related problems with their sites. And you know I'm a good communicator.

Kelly: So, how's the pay for that kind of job?

Josh: Well, most people start out with a very reasonable salary; you can earn pay increases depending on your performance.

Kelly: So, what about benefits?

Josh: Oh, the benefits are pretty good. They provide health insurance, two weeks (of) paid vacation a year, and opportunities for advancement. And in the end, I'd like to work in a management position.

Kelly: Well, is there any long-term job security in a job like that?

Josh: Uhh. That's hard to tell. I mean, the Internet is booming, and these kinds of companies are sprouting up everywhere, which is a good thing, but just like the dot-com era, you never know how long things will last.

Kelly: Well, have you ever thought about going back to school to improve your job skills?

Josh: Wait, wait. What are you suggesting?

Kelly: Well, you know, more training might help you land a better job.

Josh: Wh... wh... Are you trying to say something about my current job? I mean, is there something going on here? I mean, what are you saying?

Kelly: You know, you did drop out of college.

Keys:

Ex. 1 1. C 2. A 3. B 4. A 5. D

Ex. 2 Open

Part III Listen and Discuss

Passage 1

Today I'm going to talk to you about my internship with the advertising company "Flash". The handout you have includes *erm* some vocabulary related to international sales. If you have any questions about advertising or sales you can ask them at the end. In my presentation I'll explain what work I did and what I learnt from my internship.

First of all, I'd like to introduce the company. It was founded in 1985 by two brothers in Paris and they now have four offices worldwide. They have a turnover of 800,000,000 euros per year and employ over 200 people in France, London, and Chicago. These two slides show you some examples of the adverts they have designed for their clients.

So, to explain what work I was doing. I helped out in the international sales department in Paris. I had to contact potential clients by phone and e-mail and *erm* present our company to them to find out if they might be interested in our services. Then a more experienced member of the sales team followed up the initial contact I had made *erm* to *erm* try and eventually secure an advertising deal.

There were some positive and negative sides to my internship but on the whole I really enjoyed my work. I used my English every day as many of the phone calls I made were in English and *erm* I also had to send and receive e-mails in English. I sometimes observed the design team as they brainstormed ideas for advertising a new product but as this isn't my main area of interest I mostly stayed with the sales team. However, as I was the intern I also had some tasks to do that no one else wanted like sorting out a cabinet of old files and *erm* checking up-to-date e-mail addresses and websites for companies we had worked for in the past.

The working conditions were very good and I was in an open-plan office with seven other people from sales who were all very friendly and welcoming. We had an hour and a half break for lunch and most people ate at the restaurant next door to the head office. It was a great opportunity to meet with other people from different departments and to find out how the company worked.

So to conclude my presentation, I'd say the main disadvantage of my internship was that I didn't get to follow up any of the sales. *Hmm*, some of my colleagues let me sit in with them on meetings with some already established clients, and although I did go to some presentations given by my boss to potential clients, I wanted to be more involved. I still have a lot to learn and I intend to work at the same company next summer to gain even more experience. I hope that next time the job I do will quickly progress into something a little more challenging.

Keys:

Ex. 1

1. The company was founded in 1985.
2. They have a turnover of 800,000,000 euros a year.
3. Malcolm helped in the international sales department in Paris.
4. A more experienced member of the sales team had to secure the advertising deals.
5. He spoke English on the phone every day.
6. He observed the design team brainstorm ideas for advertising new products.
7. He ate lunch in the restaurant next door.
8. The main disadvantage was that he didn't get to follow up any of the sales.

Ex. 2 Open

Passage 2

In our job, we may encounter some angry customers who are hard to deal with. The first thing to remember about angry customers is that while their behavior is directed at you, the real source of the anger is elsewhere. The angry person is not usually angry at you as a person. He or she is usually angry at you as an employee of an organization that is perceived as cold, unfeeling, and unhelpful. Since it is difficult to yell or abuse an entire organization, the angry customer will direct anger towards you.

One of the half-truths about hostile customers is that they want their problem solved. This isn't the whole story. When a person is initially denied something from an organization, they get to a point where the problem becomes secondary. Yes, they want the problem solved, but after a point, they get so angry that they are unwilling to work positively to get what they started out wanting. It is important to realize that very angry people want an opportunity to vent their anger, and they want to be heard and acknowledged. If you don't acknowledge their anger, and move too quickly to try to solve the problem, you will likely make them angrier and more abusive.

There are specific things you can do to take control of potential hostile situations so that they don't escalate into major time-consuming conflicts.

First, you need to observe customers as they approach, and prepare yourself for the possibility that they may show hostile behaviors.

People who are irritated or upset will show signs even before they open their mouths. You need to look for these signs so that any outbursts do not surprise you. Many hostile situations get out of hand because the employee reacts too quickly to hostile behavior, because he or she did not expect it.

Second, when you are in contact with a hostile customer, you must strive to present yourself in as un-bureaucratic a way as possible. If the customer perceives you as an object, a piece of the bureaucracy, they will be more likely to be more abusive. However, if the customer sees you as a human being who doing the best you can, it is more likely that he or she will show less aggressive behavior.

Keys:
Ex.1 1. B 2. C 3. A 4. A 5. B
Ex.2 Open

Part IV Watch and Debate

Hi, welcome to Video Jug. I am Rikki Hansen from career Concierge and I am going to show you how to ace a job interview.

Step 1: Put the job interview into perspective. Try to think this as an exchange between two people, rather than a one way interrogation. You know, they have an interest in you, and you have an interest in them. It should be a two way thing. It is very helpful to actually think it is like a first date. You know you want to make sure you show something of your best side, but you also want to make sure they are surviving for both of you.

Step 2: Be clear. Be absolutely clear about Why should they hire you? What are your unique selling points? And how you can match that to what they are looking for. Think about that upfront and really give examples throughout the interview to just how good you are and how relevant your experience is. It is up to you to show them you are the right candidate for the following reasons. So take every opportunity to get your selling points across.

Step 3: Give examples. Examples, examples. , examples. An example is proof, the proof that you have already done what the interviewer is asking for and you can do it for them again. so really, throughout the interview, give as many examples as you can and think about them in the following way. Each example should illustrate: what's the problem? what you did and what was the result? The great thing about using examples is it helps you avoid cliché, or answering the questions like everybody else would. Your experience and example is unique. By giving them examples, you are really saying that you are a unique candidate.

Step 4: Never assume. Never assume the interviewers have read your CV. So feel free to talk about things in the CV. Elaborate on them, expand them, use some examples there. On the other hand, make sure you know your CVs well. There is nothing worse than, oh, did I really put that in my CV?

Step 5: Never slag off. Don't ever slag off any former employees, products, colleagues or experiences. Be very positive about your experiences, so far.

Step 6: Prepare at least three questions. Prepare at least three potent questions that they may ask you. Think about what you really want to know. Do you want to know the management style, the culture of the company, what is important for you to know, and may it prepared and know exact what you are going to ask.

Step 7: Listen. Listen and read between the lines as to what they are really asking. If you have any doubts, then ask them to clarify. But listen and answer the questions asked.

Step 8: Don't talk too much. Don't talk too much or go to excessive details. You know, keep it brief, keep it thin. If they want more detail, they will ask you. On the other hand, don't sit there like a lemon and give them very short answers. So do engaged in the conversation.

Step 9: Do you research. Know the company, research research research. Make sure you've done your research before the interview. So you know all the things that are relevant about the company. And make sure that throughout the interview, you bring about little slippys about their products, their competitors to show them you know what they are about.

Keys:

Ex. 1

1. elaborate   expand
2. potent   management style   prepared
3. relevant   products   competitors

Ex. 2 Open

Part V Extracurricular Listening

1. W: This is Mrs. Jones. My heater isn't getting any power and the temperature is going to get down below freezing. Could you come over and fix it?
   M: This is our busiest time of the year, but I'll speak to one of our men about getting over there some time today.
   Q: Who has Mrs. Jones called to come over? (B)

2. W: Your room is mess! Your clothes are all over the floor and your bed is unmade. And when was the last time you picked up your toys?
   M: You ought to try to be neater. Clean it up now, and when you're finished, we'll all go on a picnic.
   Q: Who might these two speakers be? (A)

3. W: This is the third time you've been late this week, Robert. You'll have to do better than that, or I might find it necessary to let you go.
   M: It won't happen again. I assure you.
   Q: Who spoke to Robert? (D)

4. M: If you can make your mind up about the color, I can start on the outside of your house by early next week.
   W: Well, right now, I think I want white for the window frames and yellow for the sliding, but I'll let you know tomorrow for sure.
   Q: Who is the woman talking to? (C)

5. M: Your hair looks very lovely. Did you style it yourself?
   W: I wish I had, but I can't do it this way. My neighbor gave me the name of a new beauty salon.
   Q: Who fixed the woman's hair? (C)

6. W: It's always been hard to get this car into first gear, and now the clutch seems to be slipping.
   M: If you'll leave the car with me, I'll have it fixed for you this afternoon.
   Q: To whom is the woman speaking (B)

7. W: Pardon me, Mr. Brown, where are these vitamins located?

M: You need a prescription for those. If you have one, I can fill it for you right away.

Q: Who is Mr. Brown? (A)

8. M: Hello, will you please send me someone to my room? The hot water is running and I can't turn it off.

    W: There's no one in the office now. I'll send someone as soon as possible.

    Q: Who will be sent to the man's room? (C)

9. M: I think I have exactly the house you're looking for, Mrs. James. It's in a very good neighborhood.

    W: Fine. Is it near a shopping center?

    Q: Whom is Mrs. James talking to? (D)

10. M: I was hoping that we could see George here today.

    W: He was planning to come, but then his wife's father fell down and they had to take him to a doctor.

    Q: Who was injured? (C)

Unit 5   While There's Life, There's Hope

Part II   Join in the Dialogue

Dialogue 1

Anchor: Lots of Americans, you know, you are one of them, dream about owning a shiny new car. But before you spend your hard-earned cash on some hot wheels, you definitely want to hear what personal finance guru Dave Ramsey has to say. As you know, he is a syndicated radio talk show host and the author of the best selling book *The Total Money Makeover*. Hey, there, good to see you, Dave.

Dave Ramsey: Good to see you.

Anchor: So, we never ever buy a new car?

Dave Ramsey: Well, I am like everybody else, I am a boy, I like new cars, but they go down in value like a rock. I mean, Kiplinger's *Personal Finance Magazine* says you lose 60% of the value in the first 4 years, the worst car accidents happen on the show room floor.

Anchor: Oh, and the minute you drive it off the show room floor, of course the value plummets right away, right?

Dave Ramsey: All right. Sure it's the wheels break the curb, you know, you really have to change, you know.

Anchor: Oh my god, so maybe not a wise use of your money. What about employee discount for the cars?

Dave Ramsey: Well, certainly it's pulled people back into that and 0% interest before that, but even then, you got to consider by the time you get it home, you've still lost money. So, a wise use of your dollars, unless you've got just piles of cash, is to really pay cash for a high-quality 1 or 2 or 3 year-old used car, let someone else take the butt-kicking on depreciation.

Anchor: Oh, you have done it then break it down with a lease payment, it sounds reasonable, what about leasing a car? Come on!

Dave Ramsey: We call it a fleecing. You know, Consumer Reports says it is the most expensive way to operate a vehicle, (OK.) because in fleecing, what you've done is to quit asking "how much", (OK), now, you just asking "how much down, how much a month" (mm, right) and when you start asking that, you are gonna live in endless payments the rest of your life, and again, like I always say, you tie up your most, your most powerful wealth building to, which is your income, with no car payments, you can have some money.

Anchor: Alright, now, tell us about how to buy a used car then, you say that's a way we go, right? how, how used is used?

Dave Ramsey: Well, it depends on how much money you have. (OK). And, you should pay cash. Again, grandmother's rule: If you can pay cash. I can't believe this guy's said I pay cash for a car. Look, just for a short period of time, drive like no one else, so later you can drive like no one else. The average Car Payment in America is 378 dollars over 84 months right now. (Wow.) If you took that and invest it from age 25 to age 65 in a mutual fund, you'll have 4.4 million dollars. (Holy pal! All right.) Hope you like the car. (All right.) So, let's take that money, set them in a cookie jar, pay cash for a little used car, and then move up, and then do it again, and then move up and work your way out.

Anchor: OK, And how do we, how do we move up? So we are saving money, ok so we are buying our nice resolvable car right, for cash, then we are putting away money each month for a nicer car? (Pay yourself a car payment.)

Dave Ramsey: Pay yourself a car payment, (all right) and then you've got 4,000 dollars every 11 months or so.

Anchor: How do we know how much we can afford?

Dave Ramsey: You should never have vehicles, cars, boats, trucks, sedan and their sisters that add up to more than half your annual income. Cause then you got too much tied up and things are going down in value. It's the most expensive thing we buy, but it's all about prestige. I mean, we spent a minimum amount of money to impress somebody at the stoplight we'll never meet.

Anchor: I know, it is a big ego buy, isn't it? It really is. (It really is.) All right, what about people who are afraid of getting stuck with problems if you buy a used car, you know, it is a lemon.

Dave Ramsey: Well, that's an old car dealer's myth. I mean, really, if you buy a car from 50s to 60s, that might be true, but the cars that we build today, are fabulous cars. And they've got a lot of life in them, used to if you had one at 60,000 miles, it is about to fall apart. Now it's got 260 thousand miles if it is about to fall apart, they got a lot life in them. And you can get services like car factory, you can check the history of the car, make sure you're getting a good car, have your mechanic check it, there are good cars out there.

Anchor: All right, let's take a look at your tips here, just by way of your views, so, you said, don't buy a new car, unless you are rich. What, what's rich?

Dave Ramsey: Well, usually you need at least a million bucks, (OK) I mean the bottom line is can you lose 20,000 dollars and not miss it?

Anchor: Wow, I don't think anybody can say that. All right, you say, don't lease a car ever ever ever? (Never.) Nerver? (It's never a good deal.) OK, buy a car that is 2 years old or more. Why is it 2 years?

Dave Ramsey: Again, because that is where the most of that appreciation, most of that value lost in the first two years.

Anchor: OK, pay cash.

Dave Ramsey: Absolutely, always. Because, then you have that control of your earned money. We get in the thing of all the money goes out and all the money comes in, all the money goes out, only the names that changed your protecting in this otherwise.

Anchor: Save up for that better car, all right, great advice as always, thanks a lot.

Dave Ramsey: Thanks. Don't forget we are gonna be on 60 *Minutes* Sunday night.

Anchor: I hey, man. I was just getting ready to say that. Oh, dear, I am sorry, (you're always doing my job). I am sorry, Don't forget you can see more of Dave Ramsey on 60 *Minutes* this weekend, good to see you.

Dave Ramsey: Thank you.

Keys:

Ex. 1 1. B 2. B 3. D 4. C 5. B 6. B

Ex. 2 Open

Dialogue 2

Anchor: Technology is impacting how we live in a more positive way with the growth of networked homes. South Korea is leading the way as it becomes one of the most wired countries in the world. Sohn Jie-Ae takes a look at a super-connected apartment.

Reporter: This may seem like an every-day domestic scene, but look closely. As she cooks dinner, Chung Sung-young is reading the recipe from a community chat room off her web pad, a portable Internet appliance. The web pad offers much more. Chung shows us how she uses the Internet device earlier in the day to order groceries from South Korea's largest super-market chain. Several tabs on the panel display allow her to compare prices and pay using her credit card.

Chung Sung-young: It's just like going to the store in the chair. I hardly ever go to the food market any more. It's very convenient.

Reporter: Chung says her husband takes the web pad into the bathroom in the morning, to read the newspaper and check the stock market. Her daughter can play games and exchange email with the neighbors. All 800 households in this apartment complex are networked. The home of the future has indeed become a reality in South Korea.

Refrigerators that order food as it runs out, and TV sets that show you who's at the door, seem to be no sci-fi dream for about 10,000 homes in the country, that offers some sort of connected environment.

Industry officials credit the advances to the unique Korean conditions.

Korea's population density is very high, and already half the people live in apartment buildings that look like match boxes. This used to be a handicap, but not now. This allows us to provide the infrastructure like cyber-optics at low cost.

Reporter: The Korean government has already issued regulations that require all the apartments to be equipped with speedy Internet access. And South Korean construction firms are looking at spreading their know-how to other Asian countries that share similar characteristics. It's the same of systems, not just products. And that promises to be a big market, which means more people like Chung, across Asia, could be able to turn their high-tech fantasies into reality.

Keys:
Ex.1   1. B   2. C   3. D   4. A   5. B   6. C
Ex.2   Open

Part III   Listen and Discuss

Passage 1

If you plan to remain in the United States for any length of time, you will soon find it too expensive to stay in a hotel and will want to find another place to live in. As is true in cities everywhere in the world, the farther you live outside the city, generally the lower the rents will be. However, travelling to and from the city by bus, car, or train may make it as expensive as living in the city.

Naturally, it is easier to join in the life of a city if one is close to the centre. For this reason, you may prefer to live as close to centre of the city as possible. Or, you may prefer to rent a place for only a month or two until you become more familiar with the area.

Your best source of information about either houses or apartments is likely to be the local newspaper. Usually, the week's most complete listing of houses or apartments to rent appears in the Sunday newspaper, which in many cities, can be obtained late Saturday night. Many people looking for houses or apartments believe that they have a better chance of finding a place to live in if they have all the information as soon as possible. On Sunday morning, they are ready to call or visit.

Questions:

1. If you would like to pay lower rents, where should you live?
2. What's the benefit of living close to the city center?
3. What is the best source of information about houses?
4. When do most people go visiting houses or apartments?

Keys:

Ex. 1 1. A 2. C 3. A 4. B

Ex. 2 Open

Passage 2

Keys:

Ex. 1

1. suburb 2. raise 3. retirement 4. vacation 5. positive 6. appreciation 7. constitutes 8. casual
9. For a Frenchman, a German or an Englishman friendship is usually more specific and carries a heavier burden of commitment
10. to someone known for a few weeks in a new place, to a close business associate, to a childhood playmate
11. But to a European, who sees only our surface behavior, the differences are not clear

Ex. 2 Open

Part Ⅳ Watch and Debate

New York and Its Skyscrapers

New York, more than any other city, is defined by skyscrapers. They are not towers standing alone in open space. They are big buildings that come together to fill streets, to make streets, to make a whole urban environment of total skyscraperdom, of a sort that you see in Manhattan but almost no where else in America. The buildings are built right out to the street. They kind of jostle each other for position, and together form a whole complete streetscape of towers. In these New York towers, of course, the view from a lot of windows, is only of somebody else's windows.

Getting those windows up in the sky fast enough was one of the problems for the revolutionary Empire State Building.

The Empire State Building is more than 70 years old. It's still the most famous skyscraper in the world. It's a long time since it's been the tallest building in the world. But it's still the archetypal skyscraper, the building that symbolizes the New York skyline, and symbolizes the very idea of skyscrapers all over the world.

The 1920s were boom years. Pressure for office space on the crowded island of Manhattan was leading to taller and taller buildings. Building the biggest brought the prestige and also profits.

For a time, it seemed that the prize would go to the car-marker Walter Chrysler, with his magnificent Lexington Avenue office block, at a 1048 feet the tallest building in the world, and still one of the most beautiful. But even as the Chrysler building opened its doors in 1929, architects would work on an even taller skyscraper. Legend has it that William Lamb held up a humble pencil, and decided that was how his new building should look.

When Lamb got this assignment to design the Empire State Building, New York was already full of skyscrapers. How to make another one that would not only be bigger and taller than all the others but would be memorable. What Lamb came up with was a solution that was elegant, simple and subtle, and turned out to be incredibly powerful. Lamb decided that only the bottom five floors would cover the whole sight. The main part of the building would be a tower set back 60 feet from the street. A smart move! From the sixth floor the tower soared up 700 feet in an unbroken rise to the 80th floor. Light streamed in from all sides. No office desk was farther than 28 feet away from a big window. It guaranteed a premium rental for office space all the way up the building.

It's one thing to come up with the design for the world's tallest building, and it's quite another to get it built, especially when you considered that the financier behind the Empire State Building told Lamb that they wanted it built in 18 months to be ready for tenants to start paying rent by May of 1931. But the challenge for the architect was to build the world's tallest building in record time.

It was due to open on May 1st, but the building was in fact complete on April 16th. To this day no skyscraper had ever been built so fast. Despite all the publicity, it was hard for the owners to fill the building. They ordered lights to be left on at night to suggest the skyscraper was fully rented when it was actually only 40% occupied. The Empire State Building didn't show a profit until well after the Second World War. Today the Empire State Building stands majestically above the mid-town skyline. Only once did New York build anything taller—the twin towers of the World Trade Center. Due to their destruction, the Empire State Building once again reigns as the tallest building in New York.

Keys:

Ex. 1   1. D   2. A   3. C   4. B   5. B   6. A

Ex. 2

1. is defined by   2. in open space   3. no where else   4. in the sky   5. tallest   6. all over the world   7. leading to   8. 1048   9. the most beautiful   10. held up

Ex. 3   Open

Part V   Extracurricular Listening

1. M: My family and I will be leaving on January 5. Is there anything we need to do to the apartment before we leave?
   W: If you want your fifty-dollar deposit back, you'll have to clean the stove and the refrigerator. Also, we ask that you vacuum carefully before leaving.
   Q: What does the woman in the dialogue do for a living? (A)

2. W: Paul is so busy lately, I never have a chance to talk to him any more. How's he doing?
   M: He had a collection of verse published last year, and now he's trying to get a novel about the automobile industry accepted.
   Q: What does Paul do? (B)

3. M: Anne, my morning meeting may last longer than planned, would you call my wife and tell her I won't have lunch at home?
   W: Yes, sir. If anyone calls while you're out, I'll take the message.
   Q: What do you think is the woman's profession? (C)

4. W: Hold it right there. Put your hands against wall.
   M: But I was just checking to be sure the door was locked.
   Q: What does the man do? (A)

5. W: My, you must get nervous hanging up in the air outside the window like that. Are you sure you're all right?
   M: Yes. I'm just doing my job. It's okay.
   Q: What is the man's occupation? (B)

6. M: You know, I've tried to even up the legs of my typewriter table, but I just don't seem to be able to get them right.
   W: If I were you, I'd get Mr. Roberts to come and do them.
   Q: What does Mr. Roberts do? (C)

7. W: Hello, this is Betty Howard. May I speak with my son please?
   M: Sorry, he's still out on his route delivering letters. Shall I have him call you?

Q: What does the woman's son do? (A)

8. M: Do you make connections with the Maple Avenue line?
   W: Yes, sir. Pay your fare and I'll give you a free transfer and call you before we get to Maple Avenue.
   Q: What's the woman's occupation? (C)

9. W: How do you like you new job, Jim?
   M: Fine. This week I have been reading financial reports and studying the books. Next week I'll probably start to handle some of the accounts.
   Q: What does the man do for a living? (D)

10. W: Can you come to my birthday party tomorrow afternoon, Uncle Smith?
    M: I'd like to, Mary, but I can't. I'll be in surgery at 3 o'clock, I'll be operating on a patient then.
    Q: What's the profession of the man? (D)

Unit 6   Life Well Spent Is Long

Part II   Join in the Dialogue

Dialogue 1

White: And you have a first class honors degree in Public Health Management from Keele University.
Jones: Yes.
White: What made you choose this major, Ms. Jones?
Jones: Well, both my parents are doctors, and I got my interest in health and things from them. But I wasn't sure that I wanted to be a doctor myself. At the same time I wanted to be involved in the health field. And I thought public health management would be ideal. Also, I've always been interested in politics and the environment, so I figure this would allow me to satisfy various interests.
White: I can't disagree. As workers in the country public health department are often faced with a health threat from pollution or unsafe working conditions, we try to do something about it, and most companies or government departments are very cooperative, but it's not unusual to find a company that isn't. They start threatening things like loss of jobs. And of course, that's always a political hot potato, especially with unemployment running around 11 percent in the country. So what do you think about such things, Miss Jones?
Jones: Well, I think the first thing is that some companies think meeting environmental standards is expensive. But so many companies find that they can reduce costs by adopting cleaner technologies, seeing wastes as resources, that sort of thing. And as for dangerous or unhealthy working conditions, if they don't get fined, then sooner or later there will be a big lawsuit, which is always expensive, even if they win.
White: Good. I agree. Oh, how rude of me. Would you like a cup of tea, coffee, or something?
Jones: Coffee would be lovely.

Questions:
1. Why did Miss Jones choose the public health management as her major?
2. According to Mr. White, for the public health department what is a big threat to health?
3. Why do some companies mention the unemployment issue as a threat?
4. What does Miss Jones say about cleaner technologies?
5. According Miss Jones what could be the final result of keeping dangerous or unhealthy working conditions?

Keys:
Ex.1   1. A   2. C   3. D   4. B   5. D
Ex.2   Open

· 166 ·

Scripts and Keys

Dialogue 2

A: Hey, Janet, you are so lucky to be done with all of your final exams and term papers. I still have two more finals to take?

B: Really?

A: Yeah. So what are you doing this summer, anything special?

B: Well, actually yeah. See, my parents have always liked taking my sister and me to different places in the United States. You know, places with historical significance. I guess they wanted to reinforce the stuff we learned in school about history. And so even though we are older now, they still do once in a while. Oh, so where are you going this summer?

A: Well, this summer it's finally going to be Gettysburg.

B: Finally? They... you haven't been there yet? I mean Gettysburg. It's probably the most famous civil war site in the country. It's only a couple of hours away. You think that would be one of the first places that they'd have taken you. I have been there a couple of times.

A: Well, We were going to go about ten... well, no, it was exactly ten years ago, but I don't know. Something happened. I cannot remember what.

B: Something changed your plans?

A: Yeah. Don't ask me what it was, but we ended up not going anywhere that year. I hope that doesn't happen again this year. I eh... wrote a paper about Gettysburg last semester for a history class I was taking, well, about the political situation in the United States right after the battle at Gettysburg, So I'm eager to see the place.

Questions:

1. What are the students mainly discussing?
2. What does the man find surprising about the woman?
3. What is the woman unable to remember?
4. What does the woman imply about Gettysburg?

Keys:

Ex. 1 **1.** D **2.** A **3.** B **4.** D

Ex. 2 Open

Part III   Listen and Discuss

Passage 1

Some of the most practical lessons coming out of research in psychology are the area of memory. People ask, why can't I remember that term from the physics chapter or the date my library book is due? Well for a lot of people, memory may be weak, because they don't use it enough. It's like a muscle, if you don't exercise it, it won't stay strong. That's why it's important to keep our minds active, to keep on learning throughout our lives. We can do this by reading, playing memory games and seeking out new experiences. It's my guess though that the lack of mental stimulation isn't a problem for students like you. More likely, the lives you all live are so busy and stimulating that this in itself may sometime interfere with learning. Later on we will be discussing how information is recalled from memory. But, first, the information needs to be recorded, in other words, learned. And for busy people like you and me, that's where the real problem often lies. If we are distracted, or we are trying to think what we are going to do next, the incoming message just might not be getting recorded effectively. And that leads to the first tip for students who want to improve their memories. Give your full attention to the information you hope to retain. Research clearly shows the advantages of this, and also of active learning, of consciously trying to visualize a new fact, perhaps to make a mental picture, even a wildly ridiculous one, so the new fact will stick in memory. Let me illustrate that for you here a little more concretely.

Questions:

1. What's the talk mainly about?
2. What does the speaker illustrate with the example of a muscle?
3. What does the speaker suggest students do to learn new information more effectively?
4. What will the speaker probably do next?

Keys:

Ex. 1　1. A　2. A　3. C　4. B

Ex. 2　Open

Passage 2

Keys:

Ex. 1

1. getting your bronze on at the tanning salon may be addictive
2. commonly used to assess patients for alcohol abuse and substance-related disorders
3. focus on indoor tanning habits
4. greater symptoms of anxiety, and were more likely to use drugs and alcohol
5. drugs and tanning lamps might hook you through similar means, including peer pressure

Ex. 2　Open

Part Ⅳ　Watch and Debate

Keys:

Ex. 1

1. we're going to see ice sheets begin to disintegrate
2. increases the temperature gradient between low latitudes and middle and high latitudes
3. there's no practical way to escape from this planet
4. we could transplant life from our planet to another planet
5. once the planet gets warmer and warmer, then the oceans begin to evaporate
6. the oceans will begin to boil, and the planet becomes so hot that the ocean ends up in the atmosphere
7. go unstable either toward a cold climate or toward a hot climate
8. volcanoes put carbon dioxide into the atmosphere, and it builds up more and more until there's enough to melt the ice
9. with continued rapid increase in greenhouse gases, that—you could melt the ice sheets in less than a century
10. the methane hydrates on the continental shelves melted and went into the atmosphere and caused global warming

Ex. 2　Open

Part Ⅴ　Extracurricular Listening

1. M: The telephone company says that they can send a man between one and three tomorrow afternoon. But someone has to be at home to let him in.

   W: Well, I guess I'll have to take off from work at noon. We can't go any longer without a telephone.

   Q: What's the probable relationship between the two speakers? (A)

2. W: These trousers turned out to be too small for my son, so I have brought them back for larger ones.

   M: Certainly, Madam. We can take them back if you have your receipt with you.

   Q: What's the probable relationship between the two speakers? (C)

3. W: I'd appreciate your professional opinion. Do you think that I should sue the company?
   M: Not really. I think that we can settle this out of court.
   Q: What is the probable relationship between the man and woman? (D)
4. M: Well, we need some temporary labour in our packing department, just for a short time, but the job will be rather monotonous.
   W: I only want something for two or three weeks anyway. I don't mind monotony.
   Q: What's the probable relationship between the two speakers? (A)
5. W: I got such a bad start in the last race, it was hard to catch up. I tired myself out trying too hard. All I could see was the backs of the others' heads.
   M: We'll work on your start. The most important thing is concentration.
   Q: What is the probable relationship between these two speakers? (C)
6. W: I don't know how you can eat so much yet stay so slim, son. I can't take a bite without mentally calculating how many calories I'm eating.
   M: Don't forget Aunt Louise. She ate like an elephant and never gained a pound.
   Q: What's their relationship? (B)
7. M: Dad is angry because we're on the phone too much.
   W: Why don't we chip in and get our own private line?
   Q: What's the probable relationship between these two people? (A)
8. M: Will this keep me from playing basketball for very long?
   W: Not too long. I thought you might have broken your ankle, but the X-ray shows that it's just a bruise.
   Q: What is the probable relationship between the two speakers? (B)
9. W: Is Aunt Margaret in? I've got something important to tell her.
   M: Sorry. Mom has gone shopping. She won't be back until noon.
   Q: What do you think is the relationship between the two speakers? (A)
10. M: Good afternoon, Madam. Would you like to sit here? I'm afraid there are no other seats free at the moment.
    W: I'd prefer to sit alone, but I suppose this will do. Have you a menu, please?
    Q: What are the man and woman? (B)

Unit 7 All Holidays Can Be Good Times

Part II Join in the Dialogue

Dialogue 1

Reporter: Now on Culture Shock coming to you from the BBC World Service. It's time for our trends track down in which we pursue the latest happenings in some of the world's most hip cities. Christina Cordero joins me on the line from New York. Christina, I understand that you're about to get some help in reconfirming your flight out of New York to Chile but from an unconventional source.

Christina Cordero: That's right yeah, well I need to reconfirm my flight and make a special request.

Reporter: And so how are you planning to this? Because usually when you call an airline it's fight your way through the voice mail tree and then hold for twenty minutes.

Christina Cordero: Yeah, I don't really want to bother with that so I'm going to call an online personal assistant that I've signed up with and see if they can handle the job so that I can do some other things like talk on the radio with you guys.

Alex: Thank you for calling Cernet, this is Alex, how may I help you?

Christina Cordero: Hi. This is Christina Cordero. I need to make a request.

Alex: OK, one moment please. What's your request today?

Christina Cordero: I need you to call the airline Land Chile and I need you to reconfirm a flight that I have going out on Saturday. But I also need to make a little request which is I want to know if you could ask them to order a bassinette for my baby.

Alex: OK.

Christina Cordero: What they do is they give you the front row seat and they stick this bassinette on the wall in front of you.

Alex: OK, I'll do that.

Christina Cordero: Alright, how soon do you think they'll be able to do it?

Alex: Pardon me.

Christina Cordero: How soon do you think they'll be able to find out?

Alex: OK, we'll do our best. OK is there anything else I can now do?

Christina Cordero: Nope, that's all.

Alex: OK, thanks. Bon Sunday. Have a nice day.

Christina Cordero: Call me back as soon as you can.

Alex: Yeah, sure.

Christina Cordero: OK, bye.

Reporter: Christina that didn't sound like an American you were talking to.

Christina Corpero: No it definitely was not an American.

Reporter: Yet you dialed a New York number.

Christina Cordero: Yes, you dial numbers from cities all over the United States. You can just dial a local number, you connect with an operator who is out in another country, I believe they're usually in India and occasionally in the Philippines. And they take care of your request from there and then they get back to you either by email or by telephone.

Keys:

Ex. 1   1. C   2. A   3. C   4. B   5. D   6. C

Ex. 2   Open

Dialogue 2

Azuz: Americans may be changing their donating habits, too. We've probably heard of Toys for Tots. There might be a donation bin at your school. This group has been collecting and handing out Christmas gifts for decades. But as Barbara Starr explains, this year, the program designed to help those in need is in need of some help, itself.

Ebony: Thank you. Merry Christmas to y'all, too.

Barbara Starr: Ebony desperately needs Christmas toys for her children. She has come to the Marine Corps Toys for Tots center to get them.

Ebony: There is no money. I wrote my letter early, in October, and I was able to come to pick up my toys today.

Starr: The toy program began 61 years ago. This year, with the economy in shambles, the Marines are anxious; there are not enough toys. Here in the nation's capital, these were the only toys the Marines collected the night before we arrived.

Starr: How far behind are you from where you want to be?

Master Sergeant Timothy Butler, U. S. Marine Corps: We are tens of thousands of toys behind. Tens of thousands.

Starr: Master Sergeant Timothy Butler says unless something changes and soon, all the toys in these crates, donated over the summer by companies, will be gone in five days. Butler has to find enough toys for 82,000 children in the Washington, D. C. area. These bare containers, which should be full, are not.

Butler: Here we are in the nation's most powerful city, and we have those kinds of needs. We have folks that last year lived in a nice home, this year are homeless.

Starr: And over at Union Train Station, people getting off the trains are giving what money they can. But it's not enough.

Staff Sergeant Johnny Noble, U. S. Marine Corps: Last year here, from just the morning time frame, we collected just over $13,000. This year, right now, we're lucky to get about half that.

Starr: Even as toys are packed up and shipped out every day, the worries grow.

Starr: What's it gonna mean to the U. S. Marine Corps if they can't give every child who needs a toy a toy?

Butler: Well, to be honest, it's gonna break my heart.

Starr: Marines are used to responding to crises all over the world. But what the Marines didn't expect was that their latest crisis might be making sure every needy child has a toy this Christmas. Barbara Starr, CNN, Washington.

Keys:
Ex. 1 1. B 2. D 3. A 4. C 5. B 6. C
Ex. 2 Open

Part III Listen and Discuss

Passage 1

A lot of people travel to foreign countries in the summer time and it's really a good experience. I've done a lot of that myself and I've seen a lot of interesting things when I've traveled.

One time I was sitting in a restaurant watching the people come in and out, just drinking some coffee, and kind of enjoying the experience of being in another place. I watched at one point two people come in and sit down at a table. They didn't quite know what to order and they didn't speak the language at all, but there were pictures in the menu and they thought, well, they could probably get by just pointing at things so they pointed at something and the waiter seemed to think that was reasonable because he didn't ask any questions. So he brought the sauce for the meat that they were going to eat first and put it on the table. The two people who were eating didn't understand what they'd ordered so they didn't know what he'd brought. They looked at it and since it was in a small bowl, they thought, "Well, this must be the soup." And they drank it. You can imagine their surprise to find out that it was almost a hundred percent chilly sauce!

Questions:
1. What was the speaker doing in the restaurant when this incident took place?
2. How did the two people who came into the restaurant order their food?
3. Why did the two people drink the sauce?

Keys:
Ex. 1 1. D 2. C 3. B
Ex. 2 Open

Passage 2
Keys:
Ex. 1
1. procedure 2. ensure 3. purchased 4. counter 5. security 6. prohibited 7. everyone's 8. manually

9. you will go to the designated boarding area and gate to wait for your plane

10. the plane is equipped with emergency exits in case you have to leave the plane

11. Be sure to read the safety instruction card located in the pocket of the seat in front of you

Ex. 2　Open

Part Ⅳ　Watch and Debate

Tahiti Island

On the fable island of Tahiti', it is not the land which is endangered of disappearing but the culture. The outside world has refused to leave this place alone. Since 1842, Tahiti and its neighboring islands have been the colony of France. Wherever you look at the capital Papeete, the French language. French culture and French merchandise give it the atmosphere and the appearance of a provincial town somewhere in France itself.

It was a very different scene which greeted the old European mariners when they first dropped anchor in Matavai Bay. Here is the way of life completely at odds with their own. It is the description the glorious brought back to Europe that inspired the artists and writers with the philosophical ideal of the "noble savage" which still maintain its appeal in our modern over-regulated world. They painted the pictures of feasting and dancing, and above all, the beauty of the women, so free with their favors. These young Tahitians of today have just one purpose to preserve the rich variety of their own unique culture, so mighty with their expressing dance before it is too late. Each one of these carefully rehearsed movements reflects the traditional pattern of Polynesian life and all has its root in the ancient legend. Dance is the very language of the soul, passed from one generation to the next.

"At least in the last years, people like me, the youngsters, are searching for their own identity. Because we have a mix of French identity and Tahiti identity, so we search for our ancestor roots."

Today these students on the threshold of adulthood have to attend classes to learn their own language. For years the policy of the French government towards the islands was one of the assimilation. It was deemed a privilege bestowed on the Polynesian people that they were allowed to regard themselves the citizens of France. The Tahitian mother tongue was never used in classroom and the children knew more about French history than they knew of their own.

"More and more young people have not the opportunity to really speak Tahitian in their own family, and we know that. And that's why it's very important for efficient teachers to know how to give them the chance, the chance to learn how to speak the language, and also to give them their own, uh, somewhat culture. So we are not only teaching them the language, we are also giving them the love for the language."

Ex. 1　1. C　2. A　3. D　4. A　5. B　6. C

Ex. 2

1. endangered of　2. culture　3. 1842　4. Wherever　5. somewhere　6. different scene　7. the way of
8. free with　9. variety of　10. to the next

Ex. 3　Open

Part Ⅴ　Extracurricular Listening

1. W: The guests are leaving for New York today at ten. We need someone to get them to the airport on time.

   M: Ordinarily, I'd be happy to, but my car is in the garage.

   Q: How are the guests going to New York? (B)

2. W: I've got to go to Boston this afternoon, but I'm too tired to drive and the bus is so uncomfortable.

   M: No problem. I'll save you the cost of a taxi by dropping you off at the train station on my way to work.

   Q: How will the woman get to Boston? (B)

3. W: I hardly ever go shopping by car now. The shopping center is within walking distance.

   M: Well, you are lucky. The nearest store I can go to is about 3 miles away.

· 172 ·

Q: How does the woman go shopping? (C)
4. M: When I go on a diet, I eat only grapefruit and that takes off weight quickly.
   W: I prefer to eat whatever I want and then run to lose weight.
   Q: How does the woman lose weight? (D)
5. M: I hope you can understand my reasons for deciding to leave, Mrs. Harrison.
   W: Do I have to remind you that we have invested a lot of time and money in your career here?
   Q: How did Mrs. Harrison respond? (C)
6. W: Have Todd and Lisa Taylor started a family yet? They've been married for two years now.
   M: Todd indicated to me that they'd postpone having children until he gets his law degree.
   Q: How do the Taylors feel about children? (D)
7. W: Professor Horton, have you heard the morning news report? Lindsay resigned his post as defense secretary.
   M: I didn't turn on the radio this morning, but I did see the headlines. If you remember, he threatened to leave office at the last cabinet meeting.
   Q: How did the professor learn that the defense secretary had resigned? (A)
8. W: Vincent decided to speak to his boss's mother about his problem at work rather than to go directly to his boss.
   M: That was certainly an unusual way of handling the situation, but it did bring good results.
   Q: How did Vincent solve his problem? (D)
9. W: Do you like your new room?
   M: It's nice to have enough space for all of my books, so I'm glad I moved. But I miss my friendly neighbors and the beautiful surroundings. I especially miss living so close to the campus.
   Q: How is the man's new room, compared with his old one? (A)
10. M: This is ridiculous. I've been waiting for my meal for more than half an hour.
    W: I know, but you see the restaurant is full and we're shorthanded today.
    Q: How does the man feel? (B)

Unit 8 Travel Is More Than the Seeing of Sights

Part II Join in the Dialogue

Dialogue 1 Check-in

(Robert is travelling to London on business. He and the ticket agent have several things to discuss before he goes through the security and get on the airplane.)

Agent: Hello, can I help you? What's your destination today?
Robert: Hi, I am headed to London, but I have connecting flight in Chicago.
Agent: OK, could I have your flight reservation and passport please?
Robert: Certainly, here you are. I've just got one bag to check and I wasn't sure about the baggage allowance on international flight. I might be over the limit.
Agent: The allowance is 20 kilograms. If you could just place your suitcase up here on the scale, you could find out. And now, did you pack your own bags today? And has it been your possession all the time?
Robert: Oh, yes, I packed it myself, and yes, and I had it with me all the time.
Agent: OK, 19.2 kilos. There was no problem. Let me tag that. And do you have a seating preference? Window or isle?
Robert: Isle. I prefer an isle seat. Near the front of the plane if possible. So I can get off fairly quickly. And there was something behind the bellgate with extra leg room. That would be great.

Agent: Let's see what I can do. It can put you in 11C. That's an isle seat in an emergency exit room, so you have a bit more leg room.

Robert: Great.

Agent: And I suggest you have a carrier over there. Please make sure you don't have those prohibited items on this list. OK, you should be departing at 10:30 at gate B4. And you should be at the gate at least half an hour before the departure. Here is your boarding pass.

Robert: A. Sounds great. That's Gate B4, half an hour before departure. So should I go through security now or do I have time to do a bit looking around?

Agent: There is a lot to see at the departure areas. I suggest making your way through security now. It is backed up with increased alert level and new body scan systems. Just up there to your left.

Robert: Oh, sounds like fun. Thanks a lot.

Keys:

Ex. 1 1. B 2. A 3. D 4. B 5. C

Ex. 2 Open

Dialogue 2 Take a Taxi

Passenger: Hey Taxi! Ah great. Thanks for pulling over.

Driver: Where to?

Passenger: Well, I'm going to the National Museum of Art, and…

Driver: Sure. Hop in. No problem. Hang on!

Passenger: Uh. Excuse me. How long does it take to get there?

Driver: Well, that all depends on the traffic, but it shouldn't take more than twenty minutes for the average driver. And I'm not average. I have driving down to an art, so we should be able to cruise through traffic and get there in less than twelve minutes.

Passenger: Okay. Uh, sorry for asking, but do you have any idea how much the fare will be?

Driver: Oh, it shouldn't be more than 18 dollars… not including a… uh-hum… a tip of course.

Passenger: Oh, and by the way, do you know what time the museum closes?

Driver: Well, I would guess around 6:00 O'clock.

Passenger: Uh, do you have the time?

Driver: Yeah. It's half past four. Uh, this is your first time to the city, right?

Passenger: Yeah. How did you know?

Driver: Well, you can tell tourists from a mile away in this city because they walk down the street looking straight up at the skyscrapers.

Passenger: Was it that obvious?

Driver: Well…

Passenger: Oh, before I forget, can you recommend any good restaurants downtown that offer meals at a reasonable price?

Driver: Umm… Well, the Mexican restaurant, La Fajita, is fantastic. It's not as inexpensive as other places I know, but the decor is very authentic, and the portions are larger than most places I've been to.

Passenger: Sounds great! How do I get there from the museum?

Driver: Well, you can catch the subway right outside the museum. There are buses that run that way, but you would have to transfer a couple of times. And there are taxis too, but they don't run by the museum that often.

Passenger: Okay. Thanks.

Keys:

Ex. 1 1. C 2. D 3. A 4. A 5. C

Ex. 2 Open

Part III Listen and Discuss

Passage 1 Travel Agent

Good afternoon. My name's Carl, I'm a travel agent. And I have been working as a travel agent for about ten years.

People often ask me why I decided to be a travel agent. When I came back to the UK ten years ago, I decided to stay within the travel industry because I love travelling. and my experience of working in resort abroad helped me get a job as a travel agent. I have to admit that one of the major reasons to be a travel agent was that we can get cheap flight and holidays.

Basically I'm a sales person. I advise people on the holiday options available to them, you know, different destinations, types of holiday, ways to get there, and so on. When a customer has decided what they want, I book it for them and make any other arrangements they might need, such as car hire or tours. My responsibility doesn't end there, though. I have to make sure that clients know if any visas are necessary, or if they will need vaccinations, and how to get them. If they are flying, I need to tell them what time they have to check in, and make sure they know what time they will be arriving. I also give information on likely weather conditions and anything else I think will be useful for them. I'm finding that more and more customers want a tailor-made holiday, not just a package from a brochure. It's a lot more interesting for me if I can organise the whole thing—make out an itinerary, book flights, accommodation and everything. I love providing a personalised service, especially if it's to places that I know. I can really help customers get a great holiday that will be ideal for them.

Sometimes I get difficult customers. One man came in wanting a flight to Venice the next day. I checked out times and fares on the computer, and found a very reasonable flight at a suitable time, so we booked it there and then. A week later he came in and he was absolutely furious. He wanted to know why I had flown him to Venice, in Italy, when he had had an important meeting in Vienna, which is in Austria. I didn't know what to say, but since then I've always been careful to check that people really know where they want to go.

Keys:

Ex. 1

1. travel agent   2. cheap flights   3. available   4. destinations   5. books   6. arrangements   7. make sure
8. visas   9. vaccinations   10. check in   11. weather   12. make out   13. accommodation   14. personalized service
15. difficult   16. times and fares   17. reasonable   18. suitable   19. furious   20. flown

Ex. 2 Open

Passage 2

Mark Twain, who wrote the story we're going to read, traveled quite a lot often because circumstances, usually financial circumstances, forced him to. He was born in Florida, Missouri in 1835 and then moved to Hannibal, Missouri with his family when he was about 4 years old. Most people think he was born in Hannibal but that isn't true. After his father died when he was about 12, Twain worked in Hannibal for a while and then left so that he could earn more money. He worked for a while as a typesetter on various newspapers and then got a job as a river pilot on the Mississippi. Twain loved this job and many of his books show it. The river job didn't last, however, because of the outbreak of the Civil War. Twain was in the Confederate Army for just 2 weeks and then he and the whole company went west to get away from the war and the army. In Nevada and California Twain prospected for silver and gold without much luck, but did succeed as a writer. Once that happened, Twain traveled around the country giving lectures and earning enough money to go to Europe. Twain didn't travel much the last 10 years of his life and he didn't publish much either. Somehow his travels even when forced inspired his writings. Like many other popular writers, Twain derived much of the materials for his writing from the wealth and diversity of his own personal experiences.

Questions:

1. The speaker focuses on which aspect of Mark Twain's life?
2. Where do most people think Twain was born?
3. What job did Twain especially love?
4. Why did Twain go West?
5. What connection does the lecturer suggest between Twain's travels and his writings?

Keys:

Ex. 1   1. A   2. D   3. B   4. C   5. A

Ex. 2   Open

Part Ⅳ   Watch and Debate

A new home exchange member, Pieere Jean, lives near Touloust in the south of France, Lori, an experienced member from—in southern California, got in touch with him. 'We put in our listings that we wanted to go to California or Florida and received many enquiries including one from Lorri. We looked into the photo in the website, and it looked like a lovely home." Their own home, gave Pieere Jean, his wife, and two daughters the opportunity to live as Californians for one month. They kept souvenirs, this photo album. "We actually arrived at their home, we thought unbelievable". "It looked exactly like on a site, and it was real." The magic of home exchange is that you are immersed in the culture, and you live as the people would in the country. So there was no way to experience the country in the same way by going to a five-star hotel."

The president of home exchange, ED Kushins, from California, pioneered home exchange on the web in 1996. "My main objective was to share the opportunity to do home exchange and have the same benefit and experience that I have. First year home exchange, we had about 100 members. It was really a hobby and I had a day job. It was really an adventurous room of open-minded travelers." Open-minded, that certainly describes Redondo Beach, of home California. Home exchange changed the way of vacationing. "For me, it is with home exchanging, you looked at travel differently." "Before, we went some places, usually, frequently, cramped up in a hotel. With three kids, the five of us need privacy whatsoever. So it was just really tight. When you have a home exchange, now we are living in a home environment." Three kids, and a dog, even pets love home exchange. "It is great for pet owners because basically, we never have to leave our dog in a canal at all. We either take our dog with us, or we left him in the house with the family who stayed here to take care of him."

Before they tried, almost everyone has the same concern: the fear of having a stranger in their own house. "It is natural for people who haven't done home exchange to think that they are going to do home exchange with a stranger and that stranger may steal something or do damage to their home. But the reality is no one ever does a home exchange with a stranger. The whole process serves to make sure that it doesn't happen. The first family, and it was also their first time, so we were both equally anxious about that, about the risks involved. And we talked a lot about that. After some phone calls, you started to feel a connection with the family." "That was the first in Canada, it was one of the best vacations we had. I mean, the Canadians are fantastic. And Van Couver was an amazingly beautiful city."

Pierre Jean remembers how difficult it was to convince his wife. "Leave my home to strangers, that was very hard for me to imagine. And in the end, I say, ok. Forget my fear. Let's do it. And it was better than we ever imagined. It was a dream, a dream to be repeated each year. On July 4th, that was so impressive. We felt involved. Ever being standing up when US lines were passing." We felt like demifact.

Our exchangers did a very good job lining out the maps of the area, how to get down to Toulous, how to get to the market, to go out. To look out the wineries, all the points of interest in the towns, what is a lot to learn about is the history, the history goes back millennium while our history goes back to three or four hundred years. So every town has some history. It is fascinating to discover the history in each town.

Scripts and Keys Unit 8

"Every Thursday, there is a local outdoor market, and we are so enchanted with the market and all the fresh fishes, and all the meats and fresh vegetables, and all the things favoring out. We are actually arranging our other activities around this day."

The president of home exchange gets testimonials like this almost each day from members wanting to share their stories. "I love talking to our members. They have such great stories about some 20, 30, 40 home exchangers. Some had met lost relatives; some had made great friends with their home exchange partners. Every single home exchanger had a great story to tell."

The Holiday movie director got ideas for her scripts when surfing homeexchange.com and the reality copied fiction. "We had seen the movie, the holiday, and when we arrived in California, it was exactly the same type of house. We had the same experience in the movie. It was unbelievable."

"Our home has never been the reason for the exchange. The home size we selected has never been an issue for us. We were really looking for a certain area of the world that we wanted to learn about. It was more about the culture than it was about the house."

Besides saving money, home exchange offers the benefits that make the mainstream holiday alternative. "Home exchange has followed the trend of internet dating, which 5 years ago, was probably a little scaring. Wait and meet the people, and the people were not sure this is a good idea. But now internet dating is like the good place to meet someone. Home exchange five years ago was a fear of stranger coming to the house, but now home exchange is becoming the mainstream way to travel. Almost everybody knows someone who has done home exchange and people feel very comfortable using the internet as the way to do home exchange which is just like internet dating for your house. And even with its hundreds of members joining every week from all around the world, home exchange is still a very personal experience.

Whether we have 200 member or 200,000 members, each home exchange is still between two members", Members who feel at home any place in the world.

"We have done five home exchanges."

"We had roughly about eight exchanges now in about 2.5 years."

Keys:

Ex. 1   Free, with reference to the script

Ex. 2   Open

Part V   Extracurricular Listening

1. W: Where did you and Sue go on your vacation?
   M: We planned to spend our holidays in Switzerland, but finally we spent three days in Denmark, one week in Spain and five days in Scotland.
   Q: Which of the following countries didn't the man and woman visit? (B)
2. M: Washington is the most important city in the United States, isn't it?
   W: Yes, it is, in the political sense, although it can not compete with cities like New York, Chicago, Philadelphia or Los Angeles in size and population.
   Q: Which city are they talking about? (D)
3. W: Are you going to watch the movie on TV tonight?
   M: No, I think I'll watch the soccer game and then the documentary on volcanoes.
   Q: Which is the first program the man is planning to watch? (B)
4. M: Did you know that the hot dog did not originate in the United States but in Germany?
   W: Yes, and there is even something similar to it in Finland. It's made out of reindeer meat.
   Q: Which of the following is not true about the hot dog? (B)

5. W: Have you been to the new supermarket that just opened?

   M: Yes. The prices are quite rational. They have a great variety even in meats and vegetables, but you have to bag your own groceries.

   Q: Which of the following is the drawback of the new supermarket according to the man? (A)

6. W: Why do we always have to argue about money? I would rather go out and spend it all so that we wouldn't have to argue about it.

   M: Of course, you'd like to go spend all the money, you don't spend five days a week in a factory. Besides, if it wasn't money, you'd argue about something else. I think you enjoy arguments.

   Q: According to the man, which statement best describes the woman? (D)

7. W: Excuse me, sir, where is Dr. Brown's office?

   M: The Doctor's office is on the sixth floor, but the elevator only goes to the fifth. So you have to use the stairs to reach there. It's the ninth room on the right.

   Q: On which floor is the doctor's office? (B)

8. M: Hello, Jane, I hear that you've got a new job as a typist at the university.

   W: Yes, I work at the office. I also do filing and sometimes write letters.

   Q: Which of the following does the woman not do? (C)

9. M: You still have a social science requirement to fulfill. Jean. You can take history, psychology, anthropology or sociology. Which do you think you'd like?

   W: Well, I've always been fascinated by the conscious and unconscious reasons people have for acting as they do, and I'd like to learn more about how memory works.

   Q: Which course will the woman probably enroll in? (B)

10. W: Let me get you some coffee or tea, or would you rather have something cold like Coca-Cola?

    M: Well, there's nothing like water when the weather's hot.

    Q: Which drink does the man prefer? (C)

Unit 9   Sports Are a Microcosm of Society

Part II   Join in the Dialogue

Dialogue 1

Jim Stevenson: The theme of the Beijing Olympics was 'One World, One Dream.' And the world did come together in competition, and for the closing ceremonies Sunday, filled with performers, music and fireworks. International Olympic Committee chief Jacques Rogge says victories were measured by wins, and simply by showing up.

Jacques Rogge: The Games is not only about winning, not only about being triumphant and winning gold. It is about the struggle of every athlete every day to achieve his or her own limits. And having this resilience in saying, 'I will not give up. And I will come back.'

Jim Stevenson: Countries like Bahrain, Togo, Sudan, Mauritius and Afghanistan won their first-ever Olympic medals. And the Beijing Olympics had no shortage of star performances by teams and individuals. Usain Bolt of Jamaica displayed unparalleled speed on the track on the way to winning three gold medals.

Usain Bolt: I just blew my mind and blew the world's mind.

Jim Stevenson: American swimmer Michael Phelps made a strong case for claiming the title of greatest Olympian of all time. He is the first athlete to win eight gold medals at a single Olympics.

Scripts and Keys Unit 9

Michael Phelps: To have ups, to have downs, to go through everything and be able to accomplish everything you have ever really dreamed of. It is fun.

Jim Stevenson: On August 8 inside the iconic Birds Nest stadium, the opening ceremonies featured an elaborate depiction of 5,000 years of Chinese history. The closing ceremonies Sunday were a simple reflection of the Olympic spirit and the joy of competition. U.S. silver medal fencer Erin Smart reflected the sentiment heard from many of the athletes who competed in China.

Erin Smart: It is really not a political event. It is about being an athlete, and bringing the most you can to the table. Whether you are the strongest or fastest, that is what we believe going into it.

Jim Stevenson: And for some of the more seasoned Olympians, like American 25-year-old and 100-meter backstroke bronze medalist Margaret Hoelzer, the games have redefined their outlook on sports.

Margaret Hoelzer: I feel like I have gone full circle. You go from having a love of the sport, to competing and feeling pressure. And, getting older, I feel like I have almost gone back around the other half of it in getting back to that primal joy.

Jim Stevenson: The Olympic flag was lowered, and handed from the mayor of Beijing to Boris Johnson, the mayor of London, which will host the 2012 Summer Games. The Olympic flame, which has burned continuously over the Bird's Nest for the past 16 days, was slowly extinguished, and fireworks lit the night sky, as the Beijing Olympics officially closed.

Keys:
Ex. 1 1. B   2. C   3. D   4. A   5. D   6. A
Ex. 2 Open

Dialogue 2

Azuz: Jessica Cox says a lot of people have doubted her because of a congenital disease, but she hasn't let that hold her back. And now, the 25-year-old is a certified pilot. But what's really impressive is how she handles the plane. Lorraine Rivera of affiliate KVOA in Arizona launches into the details of this exceptional feat.

Lorraine Rivera, KVOA Reporter: From the runway to the sky, this flight is like most others. Flying the pattern is a breeze; the landing, smooth. The only thing that's different: The pilot in command of this Air Coupe is a 25-year-old woman without arms.

Jessica Cox: A lot of people have maybe doubted me or don't believe that a girl without arms, or a woman without arms, can do much.

Rivera: But she can. Jessica Cox, a certified pilot, does it all and alone, even her pre-flight inspection.

Cox: It's full.

Rivera: She checks the oil with a screwdriver, her foot and head; fills out her own log book.

Cox: OK, today is the second.

Rivear: Really, the only tricky part...

Cox: This was my first challenge in flight training, was how to buckle the seat belt. So, I figured out, well, you don't always have to buckle the seat belt until after you sit down.

Rivear: Born with a congenital birth defect, she's accepted who she is. For eleven years, she used prosthetic arms, then decided she didn't need them. Then three years ago, a pilot with Wright Flight, an aviation company, offered her the chance to fly.

Parrish Traweek, Flight Instructor: Well, when she came in here, we knew she'd be able to do it, just because of the drive she has. Absolutely.

Cox: Yeah, Parrish, he has this undying faith in me.

Rivera: She's already logged close to 100 hours in the sky.

Cox: When you're behind the yoke and you're soloing the airplane for the first time, and you look over and don't see your instructor there, you're forced to accept that you're flying the airplane. You realize at that moment that you literally have your life in your own hands, or in my case, my own feet.

Keys:
Ex. 1　1. D　2. B　3. A　4. B　5. A　6. D
Ex. 2　Open

Part Ⅲ　Listen and Discuss

Passage 1

When John Weston awoke that morning, he remembered that his mother was going into hospital. He hadn't worked out quite what was wrong with her. He knew, though, that she hadn't been well for some time now. Their own doctor, who she had finally gone to for advice, had sent her to a specialist who knew all about these things, and had told her that just as soon as there is a bed for her, she would have to come into his hospital where he could look after her himself.

During the weeks since then the pains had come even more frequently. And his mother began losing her temper over little things, thus John's father kept his thoughts to himself more and more. John, always considerate, tried to think what it would be like to have toothache all the time and how bad-tempered that would make you.

So his mother would go into hospital for a few days. John was going to stay with his Aunt Daisy till his mother came back, and his father would stay on at home by himself. That was the arrangement, and John didn't care much for it. Apart from missing his mother, he wasn't very fond of his Aunt Daisy because she was even more bad-tempered than his mother.

Questions:
1. When did John's mother go to see her doctor?
2. What did their own doctor decide to do?
3. How did John's father react to his mother's frequent bad temper?
4. What was the arrangement during John's mother's stay in hospital?

Keys:
Ex. 1　1. C　2. A　3. D　4. C
Ex. 2　Open

Passage 2

Keys:
Ex. 1
1. determination　2. leak　3. suspected　4. decide　5. investigate　6. excuses　7. pressure　8. intense
9. The logic is not reliable, just because someone is available to be bribed doesn't mean you should bribe them
10. five to eight of his colleagues had asked for bribes from potential host cities
11. Whether or not more offences are uncovered, the Games will go on—and they will certainly be held in America

Ex. 2　Open

Part Ⅳ　Watch and Debate

Jeffrey Brown: In Vancouver today, mourners gathered at a memorial service for the Georgian luger Nodar Kumaritashvili, who was killed in a crash during a training run on Friday.

　　The incident brought into focus the dangers of some Olympic competitions. In newer sports and older ones, in their pursuit of the Olympic motto, "faster, higher, stronger", athletes in these Winter Games continue to push the limits of human performance and, in some cases, raise new questions about safety.

David Wallechinsky has chronicled the evolution of the Olympics in several books, including "The Complete Book of the Winter Olympics." He joins us now from Vancouver.

Well, let's start with Friday's accident and its aftermath. You have been talking to people there. Where do things stand now?

David Wallechinsky: Well, right now, what concerns me is that the International Luge Federation seems to be trying to cover up the causes of this accident.

They quickly put the blame on the athlete himself, which was rather shocking. First of all, it was insensitive. But, also, they tried to say that it was because he—he wasn't an accomplished athlete, when, in reality, the best lugers have been crashing also.

Armin Zoeggeler, who is the defending Olympic champion, won a medal here in Vancouver. He had crashed. So, when you start getting the athletes themselves questioning a course, that is when you—you should step in and do something.

Jeffrey Brown: Now, you have followed the Olympics for a long time, as I said.

Do you see them, especially the Winter Olympics, more thrills, more spills? I mean, is it getting more dangerous?

David Wallechinsky: It is almost as if they have added a fourth category to faster, higher, stronger, which is most—more dangerous. And it is true.

And part of this goes back to about 20 years ago, when the International Olympic Committee, the IOC, discovered that they were losing the youth audience for the Winter Olympics. The Summer Olympics wasn't a problem.

And, so, they sought out snowboarding, a youth sport, and then the short-track speedskating, aerials, moguls, these different more X Game—like sports that appeal to younger people. But what they also have done is, they brought in more of a danger element, and they have also added that danger element to even alpine skiing.

So, yes, I think it is a disturbing trend, actually.

Jeffery Brown: A disturbing trend, but did it work? I mean, is this what they think people wanted?

David Wallechinsky: Yes, it definitely worked. The ratings have been up. So, in that sense, I guess they got what they wanted.

But, sometimes, you get a little something that you didn't ask for. And, in this case, it was a really tragic something they didn't ask for.

Jeffrey Brown: Presumably, though, the technology changes as well, the—the ability to control some of these sports, the equipment, all of that advances at the same time.

David Wallechinsky: Well, it's true.

But, if you take the luge, sticking to the luge, yes, the technology advances all the time. But it—it advances in a way that, not only makes them go faster, but also gives them more control. And, so, what you had with this problem—the problem we had here in Vancouver was the course itself.

It was a new course. And it was designed by somebody who had designed the last three Olympic courses, who is very knowledgeable. In his early interviews after the tragedy, he said that he had designed the course to go a certain speed, and, in reality, it was going 20 miles an hour faster.

So, the question that, if you are going to have a real investigation, not like the whitewash that we saw the Luge Federation do, you have to ask yourself, is this designer of the course, is what he said the truth? Did something happen between his design and the construction? What is the story here?

When you have even the major athletes worrying about the course, you really should—that should have been a red flag that they had to deal with it before the Olympics.

Jeffrey Brown: Well, to the degree that there is this line between the thrill and—and real danger, who is supposed to—how is it supposed to be governed? Who is supposed to be finding that line?

David Wallechinsky: The International Olympic Committee is the umbrella organization that runs the Olympics. But, in reality, the competition themselves are run by the international sports federation in charge of each sport.

So, the Ski Federation is in charge of everything about skiing, the Skating Federation skating, and, in this case, the Winter Olympics and Risk was supposed to make sure that the course was safe and that everything was going well.

Of course, the International Olympic Committee can criticize the sports federations, but, in the end, it is the sports federation that takes responsibility.

Jeffrey Brown: And, when you look at what's to come here in terms of audiences, in terms of governing bodies, do you expect any change, or does it all fade away over time?

David Wallechinsky: I'm a little concerned about what is going to happen in the luge situation, primarily because of the initial way that the Luge Federation dealt with it.

I can see delaying a full investigation until after the Games are over. But when they just quickly came out and said, "OK, we have done an investigation, there is nothing wrong with the course, it was all the athlete's fault, but, by the way, since you mentioned it, we're going to change the course," I think there is something wrong here.

And, at this point, I'm not confident that the International Luge Federation realizes that they have to make some changes, or at least they have to regulate themselves.

Jeffrey Brown: And is there any way of bringing those concerns to the federation?

David Wallechinsky: I would say that, other than public protest and the media calling attention to them, it is the International Olympic Committee who is going to talk to them, I'm sure, in private after the Games are over and go, this was outrageous. You got us into trouble. You need to—we're going to have to put you under stricter controls if you want to keep your sport in the Olympics.

Keep in mind that luge was added to the Olympics in 1964, and, two weeks before the opening of those Games, a luge athlete was killed on the Olympics course. Now, it was two weeks before the Games. We didn't have so much television, so it wasn't a big story.

But, here, you would have thought that they would have learned after 26 years. And here we had it on the opening day.

Jeffrey Brown: All right, David Wallechinsky in Vancouver, thank you very much.

David Wallechinsky: Thank you.

Keys:

Ex. 1   1. A   2. D   3. B   4. A   5. D   6. C

Ex. 2

1. be governed   2. in reality   3. in charge of   4. responsibility   5. in terms of   6. concerned about   7. because of
8. delaying   9. nothing wrong   10. not confident   11. regulate   12. public protest   13. in private

14. into trouble   15. big story

Ex. 3　Open

Part V　Extracurricular Listening

1. M: Everyone hide in the next room and when John comes in, jump out.
   W: Perhaps we should turn on a few lights so he won't be too suspicious.
   Q: What are the people in the conversation most probably planning? (A)

2. W: I was terribly embarrassed when some members of the audience got up and left in the middle of the performance.
   M: Well, some people just can't seem to appreciate live drama.
   Q: What did the people in the conversation attend? (C)

3. W: The X-20 model is an excellent buy. The price includes the tripod.
   M: The lens seems to be excellent and the tripod is not bad. However, the price on this model seems a little steep. Does it include the flash attachment?
   Q: What is the man probably going to buy? (C)

4. M: They may be proud of their new facility, but frankly I'm disappointed. The nurses are friendly, but everything seems to be running behind schedule.
   W: Not to mention the fact that it's noisy because no one observes visiting hours.
   Q: What are the people in the dialogue discussing? (C)

5. W: Does everything look right to you? I want it to be perfect.
   M: I think you've made a mistake. Don't the napkins go on the left and the silverware on the right?
   Q: What are the two people discussing? (A)

6. M: If you had signalled your intention to turn a little sooner, this wouldn't have happened.
   W: But I signalled in time! Just look at the mess you've made of my car! You were driving carelessly and your speed was above the limit!
   Q: What are they talking about? (B)

7. M: When did you first discover the window broker' and your belongings missing?
   W: Right after getting up, around 6:30. That's when I reported the break-in and called the police station.
   Q: What is the topic of this conversation? (D)

8. W: My shoes are too new, I even wore thick socks and I got blisters.
   M: Perhaps you walked too far. You should wear new shoes only an hour a day.
   Q: What caused the blisters? (C)

9. M: I hope to get a job during summer vacation and earn some money. How about you?
   W: I'm going to take a correspondence course so I can graduate sooner.
   Q: What are the man and woman discussing? (B)

10. W: I'm furious with Tommy! He kicked this football through the bedroom window. There was broken glass everywhere.
    M: I hope no one was hurt.
    Q: What is the man concerned about? (C)

Unit 10 Character Is Long-Standing Habit.

Part II Join in the Dialogue

Dialogue 1 Motivation

Professor Bevan is interviewed on a radio by interviewer Tony White on the importance of motivation for managers.

Tony: Professor Bevan, how important is motivation for a manager?

Prof. Bevan: Oh motivation is extremely important. I'd say it's the most important aspect of a manager's job. A manager's job is to get the job done. So a manager has to motivate the workers as a team and also on an individual basis. Without motivation the job just won't get done.

Tony: So how do managers go about doing this? It doesn't sound very easy.

Prof. Bevan: No, it is a complicated issue. But managers have special tools. They are trained to boost motivation and increase production to a maximum.

Tony: Tools?

Prof. Bevan: Yes, tools like praise approval and recognition. And then there is trust and expectation. They are all important for workers.

Tony: And money? What about money?

Prof. Bevan: Yes, money is a factor but you might be surprised to learn that it comes out last on list of these tools that we are talking about.

Tony: So, what comes before money? What sort of things are more important for workers?

Prof. Bevan: Well… all of the things that I have already mentioned, and then job enrichment and good communication between the workers and the bosses.

Tony: And have you got any examples of real life situations to back up your claims?

Prof. Bevan: One good example is the firm Western Electric. When managers started taking an interest in their workers there was a huge increase in production. They started to talk to the workers and encouraged them to get involved in decision making. Workers began to feel that their contributions were important. And it paid off.

Tony: Productivity increased?

Prof. Bevan: Yes, hugely. The Swedish company Kochums is another example. The company was on the verge of collapse when managers decided to try a change in motivation practice.

Tony: What did they do?

Prof. Bevan: Well, basically it was a change in attitude towards their workers. Managers decided to stop giving orders and to try persuading them instead.

Tony: And it worked?

Prof. Bevan: Absolutely. In just ten years they managed to turn a 15 million dollar loss into a 100 million dollar profit.

Tony: So, let's get this straight… are you saying that workers are not interested in earning more money?

Prof. Bevan: I'm saying they're not just interested in money. It is important of course.

Keys:

Ex.1 1. C 2. D 3. A 4. A 5. C

Ex.2 Open

Dialogue 2 Ideal Women

(Jack and Rocky are in a party.)

Jack: Hey Rocky! You've been sitting around all night. Get out and dance with someone like that woman over there.

Rocky: No way! She looks like the intellectual type.

Jack: Oh come on man! What kind of woman do you like?

Rocky: I want a woman who's affectionate and fulfills my every need, and that woman over there is just not the right type.

Jack: Hey. Where have you been? Times are changing, and you're never going to find a woman who will shine your shoes and pick up after you all the time. Wake up.

Rocky: Oh really? I meet a lot of women like that, but not at this party. I also prefer a woman who'll stay home, cook, clean, and watch the kids.

Jack: Okay, but what are your household responsibilities once you get home from work?

Rocky: Hmm. Eat, watch TV, and throw out the garbage.

Jack: Wait, wait, wait. I can't believe I'm hearing this. In fact, you're never going to get married. I recently read a news report that said 40 percent of women don't think their husbands do their share around the house, and you seem to be that type.

Rocky: Well, that's the way I am, but what's your idea of the perfect woman?

Jack: Well, I like a woman who's outgoing, caring, and non-judgmental about people's differences, and it bothers me when people think they are the center of the universe... like someone I know.

Rocky: Well, that's nice for you, but that doesn't change my point of view. I guess I'll have to go home to a TV dinner and my dog, Rusty.

Keys:

Ex. 1   1. C   2. A   3. C   4. C   5. A

Ex. 2   Open

Part III   Listen and Discuss

Passage 1 Good Study Habit

The first and most important, study habit is recognizing that you are responsible for your successes and also your failures. Taking on this responsibility entails the understanding that your priorities, decisions, habits, and resources all determine the success you have, or do not have, with studying. Having a clear sense of who you are, including your beliefs and values, instead of letting others dictate what you say, do, and believe, will also help you to be more successful on the path you choose.

Next, you need to establish your goal. What is it that you are trying to accomplish through studying? What is motivating you? After these questions are answered, you can better arrange your priorities in order to be successful at reaching your goal. Remember, your goal and priorities should be dictated by you, not by the people who surround you.

Finding the times and places when and where you do the best work is essential to being successful and reaching your goals. Are you more alert in the morning or the early evening? This will help you decide when you should schedule study time. Also, make sure you have a room or quiet place that is set up for studying. It should be free from distractions, climate-controlled, and hold everything you need to have an effective study session.

If you are studying for a class, then chances are you will have interactions with a teacher or professor. Learning to communicate with the instructor can be a key to your success. Before you approach an instructor, put yourself in the teacher's position and ask yourself how you would like to be approached if you were the teacher. This will help you choose the manner, tone, and words to use when speaking with him or her.

Finally, follow the old adage—if at first you don't succeed, try, try again. For example, if you are working on a math problem that you cannot figure out, staring at the page probably will not help. Can you draw it out conceptually? Can you discuss the problem with another student or the teacher? The point is that to succeed, you need to exhaust all possibilities and paths to success until you reach your goal.

Keys:
Ex. 1 1. A 2. B 3. D 4. A 5. C
Ex. 2 Open

Passage 2 Success Personality

Is there a 'success personality'—some winning combination of qualities that leads almost inevitably to achievement? If so, exactly what is that secret success formula, and can anyone develop it?

At the Gallop Organization we recently focused in depth on success, probing the attitudes of 1,500 prominent people selected at random from who's who in America. Our research finds out a number of qualities that occur regularly among top achievers. Here is one of the most important, that is common sense.

Common sense is the most prevailing quality possessed by our respondents. Seventy-nine percent award themselves a top score in this quality. And 61 percent say that common sense was very important in contributing to their success.

To most, common sense means the ability to present sound, practical judgments on everyday affairs. To do this, one has to sweep aside extra ideas and get right to the core of what matters. A Texas oil and gas businessman puts it this way: "The key ability for success is simplifying. In conduction of meeting and dealing with industry, reducing a complex problem to the simplest term is highly important."

Is common sense a quality a person is born with, or can you do something to increase it? The oil man's answer is that common sense can definitely be developed. He attributes his to learning how to debate in school. Another way to increase your store of common sense is to observe it in others, learning from their—and your own—mistakes.

Besides common sense, there are many other factors that influence success: knowing your field, self-reliance, intelligence, the ability to get things done, leadership, creativity, relationships with others, and of course, luck. But common sense stands out. If you develop these qualities, you'll succeed. And you might even find yourself listed in who's who someday

Keys:
Ex. 1 1. C 2. C 3. B 4. C 5. B
Ex. 2 Open

Part Ⅳ Watch and Debate

Ran Hanson, a psychologist at New York University, wanted to find out more about how our perception of people is altered by what we know about them. "It is not the case that we read treats on faces, we also read treats into faces. So for example, you fall in love with someone, and you think that his face or her face, is really beautiful or amazing and they convey happiness or all the things you like in men or in women. And then, suddenly, as it happens from time to time, you fall out of love, suddenly the face looks really different. It is not the faces anymore. Now it is of course sure thing that nothing about the face that has changes. It is something about the information that you had about the person." Hanson and his colleagues conducted an experiment with his colleagues where they attached different character descriptions to the same face. "For one group, they give the description, let's say, of a very mean-heated person, for another group, about the exact picture, but with descriptions of a kind-hearted person. The information to be had about the personality of the person changed his attractiveness. So although the faces were the same, the mean hearted person was perceived as less attractive than the kind-hearted person. So, the perception of faces really changes as the result of the information that we had about the personality of the person." We may be buyers towards beauty, but we are not always deceived by looks. A pretty package can go a long way in life, yet true beauty will always lie beyond.

Keys:

Ex. 1 1. perception 2. altered 3. psychologist 4. attached 5. character 6. kind-hearted 7. attractiveness 8. perceived 9. buyers 10. deceived

Ex. 2 Open

Part V Extracurricular Listening

1. M: Have you decided where you are going to live when you get married?
   W: I'd like to live in the city near my work, but my fiancé wants a house in the suburbs to save on expenses.
   Q: Why does the woman want to live in the city? (C)

2. W: Why do you always put on slippers when you go into your apartment?
   M: It saves wear and tear on the carpet.
   Q: Why does the man wear slippers? (B)

3. W: I don't understand how you got a ticket. I always thought you were a careful driver.
   M: I usually am, but I thought I could get through the intersection before the light turned.
   Q: Why did the man get a ticket? (B)

4. M: I was sorry to hear about Bill's being fired. I know he was sick a lot and that he usually got to work late.
   W: Oh, it wasn't that. Bill made a big error in last month's accounting. Even though it wasn't really his fault, his boss was very angry.
   Q: Why did Bill lose his job? (D)

5. W: Are you going to the post office for stamps or pick up a package?
   M: Neither. I left a letter for the postman to take yesterday, but he left it clipped to the mailbox. And this check has got to be in the mail today. I'd better hurry.
   Q: Why is the man going to the post office? (A)

6. M: I have to take a beginning Spanish course next term. Do you know any of the professors in that department?
   W: Oh sure. Do you want someone who will make you work hard?
   Q: Why is the man asking for advice? (D)

7. W: I haven't seen Calvin lately.
   M: I wish I could say the same. He frequently drops by just at supper time. I wouldn't be so angry if called to warn us, but always claims that he forgot our number.
   Q: Why is the man angry at Calvin? (D)

8. M: Did the boss say anything about my not being here at eight?
   W: He said that if he were you, he'd make a habit of being on time.
   Q: Why did the man ask if his boss said anything about him? (A)

9. W: I think this history course is interesting, but it's very difficult. I'll never get through the reading list.
   M: Don't worry. You'll find the time somehow.
   Q: Why is the woman worried? (A)

10. M: I'm a little tired, so I think I'll go to the student lounge and listen to some music. Care to join me?
    W: I'd love to, but I have to go to the library to look at a book on reserve.
    Q: Why can't the woman go with the man? (B)

Unit 11 Love Is the Fruit of Marriage

Part II Join in the Dialogue

Dialogue 1

Interviewer: How long have you been a marriage guidance counselor, Mr. Thurber?

Mr. Thurber: Over thirty years.

I: You must have gained a deep insight into the problems of married couples.

T: I think I have, yes.

I: What do you consider to be the most common problem?

T: Well, many people become disillusioned with their partners, their roles, or with marriage itself, especially in the early stages.

I: What exactly do you mean by "disillusioned"?

T: They start off with idealistic images of their partners and of married life. Gradually these romantic fantasies give way to cold reality as they find out their partner's weak points and start to compare their own dull lives with those of their unmarried friends. They become less willing to make concessions.

I: Concessions?

T: Yes. Marriage involves a great deal of give and take. For the husband, this may mean sacrificing an important promotion in order to spend more time with his family; for the wife, it may take the form of accepting the tedious, soul-destroying life of a housewife. In many marriages, one or both partners find themselves unable to make these concessions and begin to blame each other.

I: Is it possible to save a marriage when it has reached that stage?

T: Through counseling, yes.

I: One more question, Mr. Thurber. Are you married?

T: No, not at present. My fifth wife divorced me last month.

Ex. 1 Refer to the script

Ex. 2 Open

Dialogue 2 Condolence

Heather: Hi, Tim. I'm really sorry to hear about your dad. My sincerest condolences go out to you and your family. He was such a great man.

Tim: Thanks. As you know, he had been sick for some time before he passed away, so we were somewhat prepared.

Heather: So, how's your mom taking it?

Tim: Oh, it's been really hard on her. I don't think you get over something like that.

Heather: Yeah, I'm sure. My heart really goes out to her. Uh, so how's your mom going to be able to manage things alone?

Tim: Well, financially, mom will be able to live a secure life from now on. I mean, Dad had life insurance and substantial investments in property and stocks, so returns on those should take care of her. But our main concern at this moment is her emotional state. She's really down, so a call now and again should brighten her day.

Heather: So, what are the funeral arrangements? The obituary in the paper didn't mention much about the funeral.

Tim: Well, some of the family members will get together on Tuesday morning for a private memorial service, but there will be a viewing in the afternoon from 2:00 to 3:00, followed by the funeral service. One of my uncles will be giving the eulogy.

Heather: I wish there was something I could do for you.

Tim: Well, actually, there is. You know, Dad really admired you a lot, and before he died, he asked if you'd sing a musical number at the funeral.

Heather: Really? I'd be honored.

Tim: It would really mean a lot to the family.

Heather: Sure. Then, see you on Tuesday.

Tim: Okay, see you then.

Keys:

Ex.1 1. C 2. A 3. C 4. B 5. B

Ex.2 Open

Part III Listen and Discuss

Passage 1

Loving a child is a circular business. The more you give, the more you get, the more you want to give, Penelope Leach once said. What she said proves to be true of my blended family. I was born in 1931. As the youngest of 6 children, I learn to share my parents' love. Raising 6 children during the difficult times of the Great Depression took its toll on my parents' relationship and resulted in their divorce when I was 18 years old. Daddy never had very close relationships with his children and drifted even farther away from us after the divorce. Several years later, a wonderful woman came into his life, and they were married. She had 2 sons. One of them is still at home. Under her influence we became a blended family and a good relationship developed between the 2 families. She always treated us as if we were her own children. It was because of our other mother, Daddy's second wife, that he became closer to his own children. They shared over 25 years together before our father passed away. At the time of his death, the question came up of my mother, Daddy's first wife, attending his funeral. I will never forget the unconditional love shown by my stepmother, when I asked her if she would object to mother attending Daddy's funeral. Without giving it a second thought, she immediately replied, "Of course not, honey, she is the mother of my children."

Questions:

1. According to the speaker, what contributed to her parents' divorce?
2. What brought his father closer to his children?
3. What message does the speaker want to convey in this talk?

Keys:

Ex.1 1. B 2. D 3. B

Ex.2 Open

Passage 2 Same-Sex Marriage

Keys:

Ex.1 1. approved 2. limiting 3. violated 4. lesbians 5. announcement 6. cheers 7. opponents 8. signatures 9. overturn 10. interracial 11. ended 12. recognize 13. century 14. amendment 15. destroy

Ex.2 Open

Part IV Watch and Debate

Hostess: Lately, we see the grocery stores are all pink and red. Yes, Valentine's Day is just a few weeks away and we want to help you get ready, so where should we just start? The bedroom, of course. Our new fengshui consultant, Kent Lawher is here with us: Fengshui are lovelight. So Kent, thanks very much for coming in.

Kent: Well, thanks for having me.

Hostess: We have three weeks to get ready.

Kent: Yes. Well, some people practice it all their life.

Hostess: That's good. Well, at the age of 7, you remember moving furniture around your bedroom and this really made a difference. At one point, you were done Wall Street, and then you really get trained to be a Fengshui…. Would you call yourself a master?

Kent: I don't think I am old enough to be called a master, Fengshui expert and consultant.

Hostess: OK, very good. You helped people from actors and actresses, performers, CEOs of big business, and now you are here to help us. You say there are areas at home that should really focus on, the entrance, the kitchen and the bedroom.

Kent: Right, so the three most important areas for a home or apartment are the entrance, which is how the opportunity comes to you in life, the kitchen, which represents how you are seen in the world, also it has to do with your career, how you make money, and then the bedroom, which we are going to focus on on this close to you, a personal energy.

Hostess: Yes, zero in on the bedroom. So the first thing is "be aware of the relationship corner in your bedroom." What's that?

Kent: So what we want to focus on is how the energy comes in to a space. So when you are standing in the doorway of your bedroom looking in, the back right corner is refer to the relationship corner. So what you want to look at is really what you've located in the relationship corner. A lot of the time, people have exercise equipment, and that can really mean their relationship is a workout.

Hostess: So what should you put in that corner?

Kent: You can have different variety of things. Obviously, pictures of you and your significant other having happy time.

Hostess: OK. I am taking bridal pic in the right back corner. What are the other kind of the things? Happy pictures, maybe a light? I don't know.

Kent: Lights, plants, things like that, that would actually activate the energy. Also, make sure you just don't have a lot of things just cluttered in that area in the space of the corner.

Hostess: OK, you also said a smaller bed is actually better than a, sometimes, a big bedroom.

Kent: Yes. The bigger is not always the better. So, for example, the ideal bedroom size for a couple is a queen size bed. A king size bed has too many box frames, which split the energy and can be said that it is only a matter of time before you sleep alone if you had a king size bed.

Hostess: Interesting. Oh, also make sure you had a head board.

Kent: Yes, a headboard firmly attached to the bed is about not only the potential relationship, but also about the stability in the relationship and it has also to do with the protection. So a firm solid headboard can be wood, can be fabric, is OK, but should be solid and attached to the bed.

Hostess: OK, there are something about the symmetry, having match night stand is good.

Kent: That's right. Ideally, what you want to have is two matching night stands, with matching table lamps on them beside the bed. Also what you want to do is make sure the bed is not against the wall. So ok, if the headboard is against the wall, but you want to be on the walk around both sides of the bed.

Hostess: What's the meaning of the matching bed lamp?

Kent: Well, it is about the other person in the relationship, so not one side actually has the control, or the romance or the incentive. Both are really equal.

Scripts and Keys

Hostess: Oh, I got the feeling why the lamp is on my side. I got the control. OK, I am just kidding. OK, there is something called a command position. What's that? That's important too.

Kent: OK. There are roughly three positions for a bed in a room. So, ideally, you want to have a view of the door, but not in the direct line with the door. If you are in the direct line with the door, that can cause potential foot problems, that can cause lack of sleep and other things. So, when you look at the bed, you want a position so that it is up to a side, so it can be a bar wall, it can be a side wall, but ideally, you don't want to be in a direct line with the wall or have the bed on the same side as the door.

Hostess: We are running out of time. We did want to talk about colors. Pink is good, if you look for love. You said, peach is good for a guy with money. You want a guy with money, use each. Thank you so much…you have a lot of information, and there is a lot of information on your website, so people want to find out more, they can go to Kentlawher. com. Thanks for coming in.

Keys:

Ex. 1   1. B   2. B   3. C   4. C   5. A

Ex. 2   Open

Part V Extracurricular Listening

1. W: The lights are blinking, but I'd like to buy a program before the play starts.
   M: Shall we take our seats now? We can always get one later.
   Q: What does the man want to do? (C)

2. W: Here's this week's schedule. On Monday, there's the board meeting. Your speech at the Lion's Club is on Tuesday. Then on Wednesday, you're supposed to see the dentist.
   M: I'm glad I don't have to travel to the business conference until next week.
   Q: What will the man do on Tuesday? (B)

3. M: Your yard is always so beautiful, Cathy. You must have a gardener.
   W: Oh no. It would cost at least $50 a month to hire someone to do the work, so I do most of it myself. The flowers I enjoy taking care of, but I have to force myself to do the weeding and cut the grass.
   Q: What does Cathy like to do? (C)

4. M: If you hadn't mentioned their dinner party, I would have gone home.
   W: That would have been the third time you've disappointed them this month.
   Q: What's the man going to do? (A)

5. W: Here's an ad for an apartment with two rooms. It's near the campus and not too high.
   M: What's the number? I'll find out if it's available for immediate occupancy.
   Q: What are the man and the woman doing? (D)

6. W: Did you turn off the lights and checked the locks on all the doors and windows?
   M: Yes, and I told the neighbors we'd be gone for two weeks. They'll keep an eye on the house for us.
   Q: What are the man and the woman going to do? (B)

7. W: Have you had a chance to talk to your landlord yet?
   M: No, I don't know what I'm going to say. Do you think he'll try to evict me?
   Q: What is the man afraid he'll have to do? (D)

8. M: There must be an electrical storm some place, because the picture isn't very sharp, and the sound isn't very clear.
   W: I think you're right. They said on the radio last night that a storm was coming in from the mountains and the morning paper forecast heavy rain.
   Q: What are the man and the woman doing? (B)

9. M: When I was in college, I used to know the names of all the football players, the dates of all the games, and which teams were winning, but now I don't keep up with football, baseball, or any of the sports.

   W: Now, you're busy with your own golf games, aren't you?

   Q: What did the man do when he was in college? (C)

10. M: I can't seem to tune into the station I want. Funny, I found it last night.

    W: Maybe you should put the antennae up. I hope you find it soon, the program is about to begin.

    Q: What are the man and the woman doing? (D)

Unit 12　Money Isn't Everything

Part Ⅱ　Join in the Dialogue

Dialogue 1

Anchor: We're all paying more for groceries than ever before except for one family. They had nearly cut their grocery bill in half while everyone else's just keeps going up. So, how do they do it? How could you do it too? Our Mike Von Fremd reveals the answer in our latest Recession Rescue.

Mike Von Fremd: To the aptly named Economides family, shopping is a game. The thrill of victory is to find the cheapest food.

Mr. Economides: Entertainment for you, it seems like. I know, you like the deal. It's a fun you get the deal.

Mrs. Economides: Well, it is. I mean, If your job is to stretch your dollars and you can do it and have success at it, and wouldn't you?

Mike Von Fremd: Steve and Annette Economides feed their family of six for just $350 a month--something you have to see to believe. At the first store, they used coupons for almost every item, buying more than $140 worth of food for just $53. (Thank you all.) The typical American family buys only a few bags of groceries for $100. So at our next stop, I challenged the Economides to see how much they could buy with $100. And the race was on.

Mr. Economides: Wait, wait, we'd better check and make sure you didn't short us. Trust but verify. It's all there.

Mrs. Economides: OK, good, we are ready.

Mike Von Fremd: And they did not disappoint, buying 13 bags of groceries, everything from Global Mart, yogurt to fruits and vegetables for only $101.77.

Mr. Economides: An average person would have spent 200, 250, what do you think.

Mrs. Economides: At least 200, I'm thinking. Coz of all the price match. Think about the price match.

Mr. Economides: You're convincing you got about at least 50 percent off? (Yah.) Proud of yourself? (Yeah.)

Mike Von Fremd: She did good. Price match means the store will match the lowest price from any competitor. It's a good way to stretch your dollars. And the Economides have some other tips. No. 1, don't go to the grocery store often.

Mr. Economides: A lot of families are going three, four, five times a week. We're gonna take a challenge, let's say, I'm gonna plan the menu, I'm gonna plan five dinners. And I am gonna go shopping once this week, and buy the stuff I need, use what's in my pantry, whatever, and not go back to the store, no matter what.

Mike Von Fremd: The Economides planned for each grocery trip. They bring coupons which save them $87.57 on this trip. And they write down price match items, saving $42.18. No. 2, leave the kids at home.

Mrs. Economides: You'll save three times the price of the baby-sitter if you have time to really think and walk through

	the store and get and pick up the things you need.
Mike Von Fremd:	No. 3, have the deli slice your lunch meat.
Mr. Economides:	I need you to slice this up for me, real thin, can you do that? Yes.
Mike Von Fremd:	By buying a chop of meat and asking the deli to slice it for you, you can save $1 to $5 a pound. And finally, the Economides recommend: You grind your own meat.
Mrs. Economides:	You can buy the cheapest cuts of like, chuck roast or chuck steak at $1.50 pound, and leave most of the fat on there, put it through the grinder and the stuff will come out looking like and cooking up as if you have bought the $5 a pound lean ground beef.
Mike Von Fremd:	Total savings? $3.50 a pound. This family wins the gold medal when it comes to saving money.
Mr. Economides:	I mean, this is like your moment of glory, when you look and see that you tripled your money, isn't it.... (Yes.)
Mike Von Fremd:	And they'd like to teach you how to do the same. For Good Morning America, Mike Von Fremd, ABC news, Phoenix.

Keys:
Ex. 1   1. C   2. D   3. D   4. C   5. A   6. C
Ex. 2   Open

Dialogue 2

Anchor:	And this morning, on today's Money marriage and your finances, you've spent your life building your nest egg, and protecting your assets and then it happens. You fall in love. But is marriage a good financial move for you? Here with some advice is Money in Today's Financial editor Jean Chatzky. Jean, hey!
Jean Chatzky:	Hey!
Anchor:	So marriage is a beautiful thing. [It can be.] But look at it from sort of like a cold hard financial perspective, is it a smart thing just kind of a broad question to get married?
Jean Chatzky:	It rolls a lot of people's assets into a risky position. Because think about it this way, we are getting married later, which means we are coming at marriage by the time that we have houses, we have, think, retirement accounts, we may have kids from a previous marriage, we wanna take care of all of those things, and just tying the knot can actually put those assets in a precarious position.
Anchor:	And having that money talk when you are in love is so hard, isn't it?
Jean Chatzky:	It's hard when you are not in love. I mean, I only say I do what I do for a very specific reason, talking about money used to and still does at some point make me completely nuts and if you don't have these conversations, then you are going to really do yourself serious financial damage.
Anchor:	So painful it is, you gotta have the talk.
Jean Chatzky:	You gotta get to the line and have a talk?
Anchor:	Okay! First, let's talk about income. Now here is a question for you. Can getting married lower your income?
Jean Chatzky:	It absolutely can. Because if let's say you are toward retirement age, and you are earning money in retirement, your social security benefits will get taxed you can earn up to 25,000 dollars a year as a single person, but you get married you can only earn up to 32,000 before you get taxed. And it can actually lower the amount of money that you have to draw on from alimony. (Oh, yes) and, you know, if you get alimony, if you are getting social security benefits, or pension benefits from a previous spouse. Those could completely go away. You have to sort of compare what you could be eligible from, from your new spouse.

Anchor: Now, I always thought according to taxes, like everyone say, oh getting married is so good for your taxes, you always end up saving money on taxes, is it true or not true?

Jean Chatzky: Not necessarily. If you file jointly, that's probably the best way to go, but there is the thing called marriage penalty and it doesn't go away when you get older. You can actually lose money to taxes. If you get married and again you have to look at your individual situation. If you get married, your spouse is going to inherit all of your assets without paying any taxes on them once you get married. But that may mean that your kids do not.

Anchor: That's scream's prenup right, I mean, you should just get a prenup.

Jean Chatzky: Well, a lot of people really do need to look at the prenup question. The older you are, the more you come to the party with, particularly if you come to the party with either kids from a previous marriage or a business, you gotta protect that, and that means getting a lawyer in your court and a lawyer in his and sitting down at the table.

Anchor: Well, Let's talk about kids. How, let's say you have kids in college, pretend, or you have a grown kid, how does getting married later in life affect them?

Jean Chatzky: If you have kids who are about to go to the college, your new spouse's income can be taken into consideration to form those financial aid formulae. So you might marry somebody who's earning a boatload of money, all of a sudden this child who you thought would be eligible for financial aid may not be. And that may make it difficult to, you know, pay for school, depending on how you've set up the finances. You also have to look at the question of inheritances. If your new spouse is ganna all of a sudden inherit everything that you have, your kids are all of a sudden not going to unless you take care of that in your wills and with the prenup.

Keys:
Ex.1   1. B   2. C   3. A   4. C   5. D   6. D
Ex.2   Open

Part Ⅲ   Listen and Discuss

Passage 1

Michael Dell, the 39-year-old chairman and founder of Dell Computer, was at the top of the annual list of the "40 Riches Americans under the Age 40". His first business idea was to take apart an Apple computer in the bedroom of his parents' Houston, Texas home. From there, he went on selling computers out of his dorm room. He had developed a brand new approach to do business: sell computers directly to the consumers without going through retailers. And, in the process, he decided to design and deliver a computer based upon the customers' special needs. Prior to this there was absolutely no idea about make the PC special for each customer. In 1984, he founded the Dell Computer corporation with US $1,000.

Dell gave a short version of his success secrets at a conference in Texas. He said: "First of all, don't start a business just because everybody else is doing it or it looks like it's a way to make a lot of money. Start a business because you found something you really love doing and have a passion for. Start a business because you found something unique that you can do better than anyone else. And start a business because you really want to make a big contribution to society over a long period of time."

Questions:
1. Which age group does Michael Dell belong to?
2. What is unique about Dell's doing business?
3. What advice does Dell give to those who want to start a business of their own?
4. What is the main idea of this passage?

Scripts and Keys

Keys:
Ex. 1 1. B 2. A 3. C 4. D
Ex. 2 Open

Passage 2
Keys:
Ex. 1
1. issued 2. current 3. payments 4. welcome 5. charged 6. victim 7. opened 8. credit
9. that company developed a way to represent credit risk with a number based on information gathered by credit reporting agencies
10. However, according to a largest survey, lenders are not the only ones interested in these numbers
11. People with high scores can expect lower interest rates for loans because the higher the score, the lower the risk
Ex. 2 Open

Part IV Watch and Debate

Jim Lehere: There were new signs today that the great recession may be over. The most encouraging was about retail sales for February. Economists had been expecting a dip, but sales actually were up three-tenths-of-a-percent overall, despite the major snowstorms. But other data showed the effects of the financial crisis linger on.

Judy Woodruff: In fact, a monthly survey showed consumer confidence slipped. And while a private report this week found new home foreclosures are slowing, more than 300,000 households were put on notice last month, and three million homes are expected to face foreclosure this year.

Meanwhile, the Federal Reserve reported that total U. S. household debt fell last year for the first time since 1945. Much of that was due to a wave of defaults, people walking away from their obligations.

Well, to help us unravel these varied economic signals, we turn to Diane Swonk, chief economist and senior managing director at Mesirow Financial, a diversified financial services firm based in Chicago.

Diane Swonk, good to see you again.

We seem to have arrows pointing in a lot of different directions. Let's start with these retail sales number—number—up better than people expected, but—so, is this something—does this say the economy is stronger than we thought?

Dianf Swonk: Well, it's nothing to pop champagne corks over. That's for sure. I think we are still cracking beers, at best, out there.

What we seeing is the level of consumer spending fell to such a low level, there is almost nowhere to go but up. We are seeing a lot of pent-up demand. And, in fact, a lot of the spending we're seeing is coming from transferred income, which is everything from Social Security to unemployment insurance being continued, a lot of spending on—not the spending on discretionary, but on necessities out there.

And we are seeing repair and replacement of things that we have just postponed for so long. There is just nothing else we can do. So, the level of spending is still extremely low, but the momentum in the right direction.

That said, the data for January will revise down. And so, even though we are moving up, it is sort of two steps forward, one step back. And we could still see this data get revised down as well.

So, it really is that level vs. momentum. It kind of feels like we're moving forward in a traffic jam.

Judy Wppdruff: How do you square those retail sales numbers, though, with consumer confidence being down?

Diane Swonk: Well, that's exactly it. We're not getting enough growth to feel good about it. We are still at a very low level of economic activity. We are talking about recession lows.

On the consumer confidence data, we are not at the lowest levels of the height of the crisis during the fall of 2008, but we are back at levels consistent with the 1980s recessions, which was very, very bad economy. People still feel terrible about an economy with 10 percent or more real unemployment in the economy.

And it's a very frustrating economy, because we're not moving anywhere rapidly. And it's hard to see a lot of light on the horizon. So, this is an economy that is still a lot of troubles in it, a lot of potholes along the road. We are on a very rocky road to recovery. But it's not a very easy road. And it's going to remain that way for some time to come.

Judy Woodruff: And then you also have the report that consumers are shedding debt, the fastest rate since the Depression, but mainly due to defaults. They are just walking away from the bills that they owe. So, is this a good sign or a bad sign?

Diane Swonk: Well, deleveraging is part of the process of going into too much debt, but it is a bad thing when you have to walk away from it.

In fact, I think, moving forward, what we going to have to see is, we now see a lot of households that put 20 percent down. They are underwater on their mortgage and they lost their job. The only way they can stay in the house is not just to renegotiate the terms of the loan. They are going to need some principal forgiven. And that is a very controversial issue, but it is our only way to really deleverage and move forward.

And, frankly, I think everybody knows now it's better to keep their neighbors in their home, even if it means forgiving some of that debt, than letting that home go vacant, and be vandalized over the next year, and destroy the value of your home.

Judy Woodruff: Well, what about the foreclosure numbers? It did slow a bit, as we said, but, overall, we are told millions more this year. So, how do you factor that in?

Diane Swonk: Yes, again, less bad is good news.

The rate of deterioration in the foreclosures is slowing. But they're still up, and they are still going to a record high. In fact, I think we will see another record high. In addition to those three million expected, we have 4.6 million homes 90 days or more delinquent. The only good news out there is that the shorter-term delinquencies, 30-day delinquencies, have slowed down quite dramatically.

That could be good news for 2011. But I think we are still going to see a peak in 2010 of foreclosures, or at least of these loans needing—need some help in restructuring. That said, it's also one of the reasons why you are seeing so many banks, over 400 banks on the troubled bank list right now by the FDIC.

And you are going to see a lot more bank failures this year as well.

Judy Woodruff: So, foreclosures continuing to hold back a more robust recovery?

Diane Swonk: You know, and this is what we always see, is, we tend to see the legacy. We saw the first part of the crisis was the subprime crisis, which was something structural that happened. It shook us all up.

The result of that was a recession. And now we are having the residual effects on defaults and foreclosures of the recession, of—people actually lost a lot of jobs, and they simply are in a worse economic situation. That forces this credit card they took on, they are now just defaulting on it, because they can't keep up the payments on the other three or four that they are keeping up the payments on.

Judy Wppdriff: So, finally, is the story this sort of the same mixed economy story we have been telling for the last few months, or is there something positive we can hang on to underneath all these statistics?

Diane Swonk: The one thing that I think is positive out there is, we are seeing a new technology investment boom. And it's not just in the investment sector by businesses. Consumers are also turning to technology as well.

I think we are on the precipice of another technological revolution that really is finally the fruition of the Internet boom or the dot-com boom that was sort of the false start to it in the 1990s. That is the one piece of good news out there.

Consumer electronic sales are up, very robust. In fact, people are renewing their technology. They skipped Vista. They moved into 2007. They are buying laptops. They're buying flat-screen TVs. So, hopefully, they are watching you in high definition right now.

Judy Woodruff: Well, we will take every little bit of good news where we can find it. Diane Swonk, thanks very much.

Diane Swonk: Thanks, Judy.

Keys:
Ex.1 1. B 2. B 3. A 4. D 5. C 6. D
Ex.2
1. confidence 2. 300,000 3. 1945 4. away from 5. turn to 6. based in 7. stronger than 8. at best 9. up 10. being continued 11. replacement 12. so long 13. right direction 14. one step back 15. forward in
Ex.3 Open

Part V Extracurricular Listening

1. W: Can you accompany me on the piano while I sing?
   M: I don't play very well, but I'll give it a try.
   Q: What does the woman want the man to do? (A)

2. W: Sometimes I think you have no heart.
   M: Just because I laughed at your breadmaking efforts? If it's too hard, you can purchase it.
   Q: What does the man recommend the woman do? (B)

3. M: I need some new clothes. None of my blue jeans fit, and I can't even button my suit jacket.
   W: Maybe you should first start counting your calories and then worry about your wardrobe.
   Q: What did the woman suggest the man do? (B)

4. M: I'd like to take a trip to Florida for my spring vacation. Can you give me any ideas on where to go?
   W: I could tell you about the places I've visited, but I think you'd better get a professional to make your arrangements.
   Q: What did the woman advise the man to do? (D)

5. W: I would really like to know why Donna is always so hostile toward me.
   M: Did you ever think of just coming right out and asking her?
   Q: What does the man suggest the woman do? (B)

6. M: I think I'll break down and get myself some new towels.
   W: I'd hold off, if I were you. There are some good sales next month.
   Q: What does the woman suggest the man do? (B)

7. M: Carla, I can't take this job any longer.
   W: If you need the money, you'll just have to grin and bear it.

Q: What does Carla suggest the man do? (D)

8. M: I can't find a kind of jogging shoes I want anywhere in town.

   W: Why not order them from the catalog? It's easier than running around town looking for them.

   Q: What does the woman suggest the man do? (C)

9. M: I can't seem to reach the tea at the back of the cupboard.

   W: You might strain your shoulder. Why don't you use the step stool?

   Q: What does the woman suggest the man do? (B)

10. M: I have trouble concentrating when my roommate plays loud music.

    W: Why don't you just ask him to turn down the music, Harry?

    Q: What does the woman suggest Harry do? (B)

Unit 13 Success Is Sweet

Part II Join in the Dialogue

Dialogue 1

Glob glob glob, around the Watercooler this morning, the question is simple, but the answer may be complex. What do you think is the happiest country on the planet? Ladies, some guesses?

Somewhere in the South Pacific, perhaps. Fiji was a guess over here (one of our...), any place with steel drums. Yes, over there.

So we're going with a happy cultural environment?

It would have to be an island, I would think, Yes, (yeah) I would think, if not the South Pacific, maybe the Caribbean? I don't know.

And you?

I know the answer, go.

Oh, I would, I would still say America. I'm an Ameri-can, (Oh, you are...) not an Ameri-can't. But let's take a look. David M with the researchers who came up with the answer. Let's see what it is.

Yes.

The happiest country on earth? Denmark. Researchers at the University of Leicester in England looked at 178 countries. What mattered most? Health, wealth, and education. "Precisely", says the Danish Embassy.

We are happy because we have a balance between our work and our private life.

How many weeks of vacation?

Do you really wanna know?

Let me know.

5 to 6 weeks.

But vacation, she says, is only part of it, there're shorter work weeks, 37 hours on average and higher education and health care for all and when it comes to the people, well, they say they are humble.

You say they don't like to brag—, (no) and yet, you'll be happy to tell us that you're happy.

We'll be happy to tell we're happy, but then nothing more and we'll do it together.

But no bragging?

No bragging.

But they have reason to and who's behind them? Switzerland, Austria, Iceland and the Bahamas. Where's the US? 23rd, not so bad out of 178.

But Denmark is not as big as the United States, by any means.

Scripts and Keys — Unit 13

Definitely not, it's a little smaller than Lake Michigan so er…

Denmark?

Yes.

All of Denmark?

All of Denmark.

There's a new poll out about the happiest country on earth. Give a guess.

Anguilla, Italy.

Anguilla? Italy?

Finland, though I, one of those Nordic (close close close) Nordic countries. Sweden.

Getting closer.

Starts with a D, sounds like (Denmark) landmark…

Yeah.

Denmark, there you go.

What do you think is the happiest country?

It's my country.

It's your country?

It's Denmark.

You are from Denmark?

Yeah.

What are the chances! She's from Denmark.

You've heard that song, Don't Worry, Be Happy?

Yeah.

Is that your national anthem?

No, not yet.

But it could be.

Could be.

(Don't worry, be happy.)

How about my ma'am you're saying man mark? (I love it, love it)

But there is something to be said about the balance, you know, people who talk more about life and happiness (true) than work and in this country, we talk so much about work.

It's true.

I think that, and lunch of herring.

Herring is not as pickled as this. …

Herring and gulag (smog as board.)

But seriously, the question: You said the islands, all these places, would you want to live there? Would you want to live in Fiji instead of here?

Not forever.

But Denmark is a beautiful place. I have been there. (It is) (yeah). I have to say it is very very inspiring.

It is. …

We love America, but we love America.

It's joky we're happier?

Exactly

Contest desire.

· 199 ·

Keys:
Ex. 1 1. C 2. A 3. D 4. C 5. C 6. C
Ex. 2 Open

Dialogue 2

Matt Lauer: Dr. Gail Saltz is a psychiatrist and Today contributor and Money Magazine's Jean Chatzky is Today's financial editor. Ladies, good morning to both of you.

Both: Good morning, Matt.

Matt Lauer: So you, you look at this statistics, you say, OK, 25 percent of marriages right now, the woman earn, earns more than the man. Great for women, great strides. But if you also look at the fact that in those marriages the divorce rate is higher than in marriages where the man makes more, you realize you have a problem here.

Jean Chatzky: You absolutely have a problem. It's making people on both sides of the equation uncomfortable, women just as much as men.

Matt Lauer: Men are uncomfortable because cut to the chase, money is power.

Gail Saltz: Money is power and money, and power is masculinity. This has so much to do with what your view of it means to be masculine and feminine. It for both, it's very important for both because if you don't feel like your man as masculine, right? Then what does that say about your femininity?

Matt Lauer: OK, just wait a second, we understand why the men get freaked out. Just, because they've been taught to say I am the provider (Right!) I am the protector. But why exactly then are the women also (It's guilt.) uneasy with this guilt?

Jean Chatzky: It's guilt, it's guilt for leaving the household, going out, out-earning your spouse, depriving him of that masculinity.

Gail Saltz: I think it's that exactly that. Depriving him of that... it's, it's imagined women could get to, what am I really guilty about. They think they are robbing their husband of his masculinity.

Matt Lauer: And at some point, don't they start to question whether their husband's really trying as hard as he should be, and, and is he a slacker in some cases?

Gail Saltz: I think that's defensively somewhat to relieve their guilt. Well maybe he's been a slacker, it's not me robbing him a bit. But of course there is a wish to have an equal partner and feel provided for too on the part of the woman.

Matt Lauer: Let me get to some of the tips that you both come up with for how to make this work in an inner relationship. Think outside the box and I think what, what you mean there is redefine what it means to the terms: masculine and feminine.

Gail Saltz: Very much so. It's that and it's also come look for other ways to make each other feel masculine and feminine. So it doesn't have to be only about money, being power. There is time commitment, there is organization, there is nurturing. What else do you provide in ways you can make each other feel those masculine and feminine roles.

Matt Lauer: Control, contribute something else a value to the relationship.

Gail Saltz: Exactly.

Jean Chatzky: That's right.

Matt Lauer: Don't feel guilty. That's the other one.

Jean Chatzky: Well, and it's what that guilt makes you do, that's the problem. We've seen with women who out-earn their spouses, they come home and they take on a vast majority of the household chores which causes much more stress in the relationship and they hand their paychecks over, there is a new book out that shows women who out-earn their spouse just give the money to the guys and let them manage. That's no good for anybody.

Matt Lauer: So that they can have something that makes them feel masculine again. They, they are running the household finance, so even if they are not bringing in tho(se), that money.

Jean Chatzky: Right.

Gail Saltz: That's true. And that, and that might not be a bad thing to say. You could manage as long as the woman still knows where the money is and she has access to the money.

Matt Lauer: And by the way, you very rarely hear women who make a lot of money talking about the fact they make a lot of money. You hear men talking about that all the time. They avoid the subject, women?

Jean Chatzky: Right! We heard in the tape that women talking about the fact that she actually hides this. This, this couple goes out to dinner. She lets him pay the checks so he feels better.

Gail Saltz: You know, Matt, what matters so much is the roles of your family-of-origin. So a woman might not feel comfortable talking about the money she's making if her mother never would have done that and that wasn't the dynamic at home.

Matt Lauer: By the way, this subject gets very complicated when the wife becomes pregnant. And the baby arrives, now what about the maternity leave. If the wife is the, is the primary breadwinner, how comfortable is she gonna be even considering being a stay-at-home mom?

Jean Chatzky: Right and because you have to run the numbers in advance and you have to really explore the options. And we are not talking about the good point of this which is that this gives the family overall some additional flexibility (Options.) to figure out who should be working out which point and if your lines of communication/ are open, then you can really use these to your advantage.

Matt Lauer: But again, more of these marriages end in divorce than traditional types of marriages, so there are clearly some issues to be dealt with. Gail and Jean, thanks very much.

Jean Chatzky: Sure.

Keys:
Ex.1 1. D 2. B 3. B 4. B 5. D 6. C
Ex.2 Open

Part III Listen and Discuss

Passage 1

The first postal service in North America began in New England in the 17th century. All mail arriving in Massachusetts colony was sent to the home of the appointed official in Boston. In turn, he would deliver the mail from Boston on horseback to its destination, receiving one penny for each good article of mail. Later in the century postal services were established between Philadelphia and Delaware. In 1691, the British crown appointed the first postmaster general to have charge of the mail for all the colonies in North America. Later, Benjamin Franklin served as the postmaster general for the British government and then was made postmaster by the newly formed United States government. Franklin was responsible for establishing the United States postal system on a permanent basis. He increased the number of post offices, introduced the use of stagecoaches to carry mail, and started a package service system. Later, in the 19th century, as railroad and steam boats appeared, they were used to carry mail into the towns. Some communities, especially those out west, were far from the service of transportation. To serve them, the post office developed a system called "star routes". Private contractors were paid to deliver mail to the communities away from railways by horse and wagon. The postal service which was started over 3 centuries ago, has developed into an extensive government service with post offices in every city, town and village in the United States.

Questions:
1. What is the main topic of this passage?
2. What is the task of the first North America postal general?
3. Who appointed the first postmaster general?
4. Why did Benjamin Franklin deserve credit?

Ex. 1 1. B 2. B 3. A 4. D

Ex. 2 Open

Passage 2

Keys:

Ex. 1

1. ambition 2. Civil 3. creative 4. rough 5. staff 6. quitted 7. launched 8. applied
9. and most of them had seen a lot more of life than Zaslow, who was 28 and not married
10. His years in the advice business left him with a deep appreciation for people and their problems
11. I have much more faith in my fellow men than I had before and I'v read more letters to back that up

Ex. 2 Open

Part Ⅳ Watch and Debate

The two richest men in the world are dramatically different. Warren Buffett earned his 41 billion the old-fashioned way by investing in solid old-line companies that sell basic products—insurance, soft drinks, home improvement and shoes. Bill Gates is the modern genius who earned his 50 billion by creating the world's largest software company—microsoft. His innovative products include Windows, Office and XBox 360. In spite of their differences the two men are close friends and they share a common passion interacting with America's brightest students. Today, Buffett has invited Gates to join him in a dialogue with students from the University of Nebraska School of Business Administration.

Q1: Hi, My name is Christin Lovegrove. I'm a Senior Finance Major. And our society that's so material and you and your families are so well-off, how do you ensure that your children value things that aren't material and things that will truly mate them happy in the end?

Buffett: Well, I was a little lucky in that respect in that my kids didn't think I was rich. And I wasn't rich for a while, but even after I was, you know, we lived in the same house… There's one house they've known in their life in terms of a primary home and they went to public schools in Omaha. And we lived in a neighborhood where, and we still do, where the average income is probably more or less average for Omaha. So they really didn't have that problem.

Our kids are rich or are going to be rich by the standards of the world. They don't think they're going to inherit a significant portion of the fortunes of either of us. I mean 99% of what I have will—it'll go to philanthropy one way or another and Bill has the same attitude that basically… that we are not going to turn out some super wealthy, super-super wealthy cause they'll be wealthy. I mean there's no question about that. But the idea of dynastic fortunes, you know, I find it turns me off. I don't think it's what America's about. And I don't think… and if you talk about an equality of opportunity in this country and really having everybody with talents, having a fair shot at getting the brass ring and all of that, the idea that you hand huge positions in society on simply because someone came from the right womb, you know, I find that—I just think it's almost un-American.

Q2: Hello, my name is Paul Ternes. I'm a Senior of Business Administration and a Music Major from North Dakota, originally. I was wondering what is your definition of success and what has been your largest non-business success in life?

· 202 ·

Scripts and Keys

Gates: In my case, my goal for success outside of work is definitely raising a family. I'm just getting started with that, and I think there are some unique challenges when a parent is very visible and has money and things like that. It's not easy in any case to raise kids the right way, but I'd say, you know, I hope to be successful at that. So far, I haven't caused them any damage. They seem to be doing Okay.

Buffet: We get a lot a people that want to adopt them. He's working on his children, and I'm working on my great grandchildren, but otherwise I guess with the same approach. I would say that in terms of success. This will surprise you. But I would say, I've never known anybody that got to my age, close to my age, that had lots of people that loved them, that felt anything other than a success. I mean that you have lived a successful life if as you get older, the people that you hope love you do. That includes your family, your business associates— all kinds of people. And I... the converse of that is that I know people enormously wealthy, and they get schools named after them, and they get, uh, you know, they get dinners in their honor, uh, all that sort of thing, and the truth is that nobody thinks a thing of them, and I got, I have to believe they know that and that everything gets quite hollow in their life at that point. And they've got all these markers and there're people on the Forbes 400, you know that are in that category, and I won't name names. But they... but it's... I really... I can't think of anyone I've known, and I've known some, you know, a lot of people at this point in my life. I've seen them in very ordinary jobs, all kinds of situations, if the people around them love them, they feel very successful.

Keys:

Ex.1 1. C 2. B 3. A 4. D 5. A 6. B

Ex. 2

1. Music Major 2. non-business success 3. started with 4. visible 5. seem to 6. working on 7. the same approach 8. got to my age 9. other than a success 10. all kinds of people 11. named after 12. thinks a thing 13. gets quite hollow 14. in that category 15. around them

Ex. 3 Open

Part V   Extracurricular Listening

1. M: I'm tired of Bill's remarks. I don't know why he wants to look at everything in such a negative way.

   W: Why don't you do whats I do, John, and take his comments with a grain of salt.

   Q: According to the woman, what should John do about Bill? (D)

2. M: Allan has done some beautiful drawings of his dream home.

   W: So he has finished them.

   Q: What had the woman thought about Allan? (A)

3. M: I used to love this restaurant. For years, they have had the best Italian food in town.

   W: I agree. It was one of my favorites too until they redecorated and hired a new chef.

   Q: What did the man and the woman say about the restaurant? (C)

4. W: Susan never made a good grade on an exam until she began sitting beside Marsha.

   M: It sounds like you'd rather have Susan sit alone when she takes an exam.

   Q: What have the man and the woman suggested? (C)

5. W: You know, I've heard that Mr. Stanley inherited all of his money from his first wife and hasn't worked a day in his life.

   M: Oh come on. He was our mailman for more than ten years.

   Q: What did the woman say about Mr. Stanley? (B)

6. W: I certainly would like to buy the brown suit I saw in the department store, but I don't have enough money.

   M: Well, if you would budget your money more carefully, you would be able to buy it.

Q: What does the man say about the woman? (A)

7. M: When is Jack going to finish writing that program?

   W: I don't know. He's been working on it day in and day out.

   Q: What does the woman say about Jack? (B)

8. W: You didn't seem enthusiastic about the play.

   M: You must be joking. If I had applauded any harder, I'd have broken my hand.

   Q: What did the man think of the play? (B)

9. M: Don't you think John and Jim are telling the truth?

   W: It doesn't seem likely. It would be hard to write two compositions so much alike unless one of them were copying from the other.

   Q: What seems to be the woman's opinion? (C)

10. M: Have you finished your term paper, Alice?

    W: Not yet. Writing this paper turns out to be a bigger job than I thought it would be.

    Q: What's the woman's opinion of writing the term paper? (C)

Unit 14   No Environment = No Development

Part II   Join in the Dialogue

Dialogue 1

W: Hi, Jim. What are you doing?

M: Oh, Hi, Linda. I'm working on a report on energy sources for my environmental science class. But I'm having trouble finding enough information.

W: You know. We were talking about sources of fuel in my class today.

M: Yeah?

W: Prof. Collins. He is an authority on energy sources. He was telling us about a new way of getting fuel oil from coal.

M: I didn't know that was possible.

W: Eh… He said something about coal being set on fire and blasted with a mixture of steam and oxygen. This process produces a gas made up of hydrogen and carbon, the… hum, the basic elements of oil.

M: And then they do something to change that gas to oil?

W: Right. First, since coal contains fewer hydrogen atoms than oil, they have to add some extra hydrogen to the gas. Then impurities are washed out with methanol(甲醇), I think, before this gas is sent on to reactors where it's changed into oil.

M: Since coal is so plentiful I guess it won't be long till this new type of oil will be available all over the place, ah?

W: I doubt it. Prof. Collins said something about the process not being economically enough to use in this country. At any rate, you really ought to talk to him. He'll be able to help you more than I can and he's got office hours all afternoon today.

M: Thanks. He's over in Anderson Hall, right?

W: Right.

Questions:

1. What are the students mainly discussing?

2. How did the woman learn about the process she describes?

3. In the process described by the woman, why is the coal burned?

Scripts and Keys

Unit 14

4. What does the woman mention as a disadvantage of the process she describes?

Keys:

Ex.1 1. D   2. D   3. A   4. B

Ex.2 Open

Dialogue 2

Bob: Good morning, Madam, Sir. My name is Bob Smith. I'm doing a survey of people's shopping preferences, and how it relates to their thoughts about the environment. I'd be very grateful if you could spare a few minutes of your time.

Joan: The environment, you say. Well, I think it's very important. It's terrible what's happening. You can't pick up a newspaper without reading about melting icecaps and tigers going extinct. I'm very worried about my grandchildren's future.

John: Oh, don't carry on, dear. Are we going to help this gentleman, or do you have to get to your meeting?

Joan: It's the environment. Of course we're going to help him. My meeting can wait.

John: Looks like we can spare you a few minutes. By the way—what's your name again—Bob?

Bob: Right, Bob.

John: I'm John and this is Joan.

Bob: Great. Good to meet you.

John: You don't mind me asking who you are doing this for and what the purpose is? I don't want to go out giving information that will help those big corporations sell more junk food to children.

Bob: Don't worry, it's the opposite. I work for the Green Market Research company, based in West London. We specialize in helping environmentally responsible companies tell consumers why they should buy their products, rather than products that have a more damaging effect on the environment.

Joan: Well, that's a good thing. All those poisons the big companies are putting in our food and air. Have you read about the polar bears and seals in the Arctic having very high levels of PCBs, pesticides, and lots of other terrible things in them? And there are no factories where they live.

John: It's OK, dear. Why don't we see what the gentleman wants to know?

Questions:

1. What is Bob's survey about?
2. What does the old woman mainly complain about?
3. What does the old man want to know about Bob?
4. What does the old woman imply about food in the end?

Keys:

Ex.1 1. C   2. D   3. B   4. A

Ex.2 Open

Part III   Listen and Discuss

Passage 1

Let's talk about an environmental issue that has to do with how common household products have changed. More and more products contain bacterial killing chemicals these days. These antibacterial chemicals aren't just in products like soap. They are in all sorts of household cleaners and in toothpaste. And if you think about it for a second you will realize that most of those chemicals just end up going down the drain. But you are probably thinking that all that stuff go through a treatment plan that removes chemicals, right? After all that's what happens to stuff that goes down the drain. Well, waste water is treated, but that doesn't usually remove all the chemicals in it. The chemicals left in the treated water get into the aquatic environment. That is into the rivers and streams where plants, where fish and other animals live. Now to find out the effects of antibacterial chemicals on fresh water ecosystems, a study was done with algae, which are tiny plant like organisms. Different species of algae were taken to a lab and exposed to just a few of the antibacterial chemicals found in streams. And guess what? In the experiment, the overall gross of algae and the number of species dropped. This is not good and here is why. Algae are the base of the aquatic food chain, which means that other organisms depend on them for food. So if the chemicals kill algae at the bottom of the food chain, the whole system is being disrupted.

Questions:

1. What is the professor mainly discussing?
2. According to the professor, how have household products changed?
3. What does the professor say about the treatment of waste water?
4. What was the subject of the study mentioned by the professor?

Keys:

Ex. 1   1. C   2. D   3. A   4. B

Ex. 2   Open

Passage 2

Your professor has asked me to talk to you today about a topic that should be of real concern to civil engineers: the erosion of the United States beaches. Let me start with some statistics. Did you know that 90% of the coast in this country is eroding? On the Gulf of Mexico, for instance, erosion averages 4 to 5 feet per year. Over the past 20 years, there has been an increase in building along the coast, even though geologists and environmentalists have been warning communities about problems like erosion. Someway communities have tried to protect their buildings and roads and to build seawalls. However geologists have found that such stabilizing structures actually speed up the destruction of the beaches. These beaches with seawalls, called stabilized beaches, are much narrower than beaches without them. You may wonder how seawalls speed up beach loss. The explanation is simple. If the slope of a beach is gentle, the water's energy is lessened as it washes up along the shore. It is reduced even more when it returns to the sea so it doesn't carry back much sand. On the other hand, when the water hits the nearly vertical face of a seawall, it goes straight back to the sea with the full force of its energy and it carries back a great deal of sand. Because of the real risk of losing beaches, many geologists support a ban on all types of stabilizing construction on the shorelines.

Questions:

1. What is the speaker mainly discussing?
2. Why do communities build seawalls?
3. How does a gently sloping beach help prevent erosion?
4. What would the speaker probably advise engineers to do?

Keys:

Ex. 1   1. C   2. A   3. B   4. D

Ex. 2   Open

Part IV   Watch and Debate

Keys:

Ex. 1

1. grabbing stuff and protecting the environment are not compatible
2. compatible with what we need to do to survive sustainably in this 21st century
3. comes from knowledge and wisdom

· 206 ·

Scripts and Keys

Unit 14

4. comes from grabbing and appropriating
5. how many people you can keep on the planet, and how many people you can have living at a certain standard of living
6. put greater environmental strains on the world
7. want to remain in an undeveloped condition
8. are going to be concerned about what this all means
9. seven to eight billion people on the planet all of them living like Americans
10. we all accept that many more people are going to have to live in some parts of their lives in a much more constrained fashion

Ex. 2 Open

Part V Extracurricular Listening

1. W: How's your new job with the book company?
   M: It seemed promising at first, but I guess I'm no salesman. And to add fuel to the fire, the boss and I have our differences.
   Q: What do we know about the man from his statement? (B)
2. W: I used to be afraid of heights. Every time I was in a tall building or on a bridge, my knees would begin to shake.
   M: I had the same problem until I took up mountain climbing.
   Q: What can we learn about the man and woman from this conversation? (A)
3. W: I want to go to the concert tonight, but it starts at 7:00, and I have to work until 5:00. There won't be enough time to go home for dinner.
   M: I've got an idea. I'll pick you up after work and we'll eat downtown. That'll give us plenty of time to get to the concert.
   Q: What do we learn from this conversation? (C)
4. W: Bill, are you still planning to buy that nice red sports car you looked at last week?
   M: I'm afraid that is impossible because I haven't been able to come up with the cash and someone else has already made a down payment on it.
   Q: What do we learn about Bill from this conversation? (B)
5. W: Was this I heard about the Warcott Company, didn't their plans pan out for them?
   M: Well, if they'd stuck to their original plans, they would have made some money.
   Q: What did you learn about the company? (C)
6. W: How did Mr. Maclow's project turn out? I heard he had trouble with the financing and he couldn't get the land he wanted.
   M: It's true he did have difficulties. But all in all, he couldn't have turned out better.
   Q: What did you learn about Mr. Maclow? (D)
7. W: I have been waiting here for almost half an hour. Why did you take so long to park the car?
   M: I'm sorry, dear. I had driven two blocks before I found a place to park.
   Q: What can we learn from this conversation? (B)
8. M: Nothing went wrong with the new machine yesterday. You shouldn't stay up too late.
   W: Yes, but it's one of my habits. I seldom go to bed early in the evening and I never feel sleepy the next day.
   Q: What do we learn about the woman? (C)
9. M: I wonder what happened to Alice. I tried half a dozen times to call her but the line seemed to be always occupied.

W: Don't worry. There's nothing unusual. She likes nothing better than talking for hours on the phone with her friends.

Q: What do we learn about Alice? (C)

10. M: What do you think of the final exam?

W: I was expecting it to be easy, but at the end of the first hour, I was still on the first page, I barely had time to get to the last question.

Q: What can we conclude from the above conversation? (A)

Unit 15   Problems Are the Price of Progress

Part II   Join in the Dialogue

Dialogue 1

Brooke: Richard, you've studied the impact of inequality on health for a long time. Do any of your recent findings surprise you?

Richard: Oh, all of them. In fact, when we look at life expectancy, mental illness, teen birthrates, violence, and drug use, the problem becomes not just a little bit worse, but much worse, in more unequal countries. In fact, I'm still surprised that no one did look at them earlier. Once you know the relationship between income and death rates, for example, you should be able to predict what a state's death rate will be. What matters isn't the incomes themselves but how unequal they are. If you're a more unequal state, the same level of income produces a higher death rate. We know from the findings that it's the status divisions themselves that create the problems. It's almost impossible to find any other consistent explanation.

Brooke: It seems that we're all used to thinking of these problems as linked to poverty. To find out that they're not tied to the level of income is sort of an unexpected conclusion.

Richard: There are problems of poverty in the poorest areas of society, but in a country like the U.S., it's only the gaps between us that matter now.

Brooke: How do people think about these problems in terms of inequality rather than poverty?

Richard: I think people have been worried by the scale of social problems in our societies—feeling that though we're materially very successful, a lot of stuff is going wrong, and we don't know why. The media are always full of these social problems, and they blame parents or teachers or lack of religion or whatever. It makes an important difference to have an intuition for years that inequality is divisive and socially corrosive. In a way, the data show that the intuition is much truer than any of us expected.

Brooke: Your findings related to crime seem to be particularly illustrative of the way inequality can lead to social corrosion.

Richard: Yes. If you grow up in an unequal society, your actual experience of human relationships is different. Your idea of human nature changes: you think of human beings as self-interested. It becomes a trigger to violence and more intense in more unequal societies, where status competition is intensified.

Brooke: When I first heard about your work, I expected the book to deal with the material impacts of inequality. But your focus is different.

Richard: Yes. This is about the psychosocial effects of inequality—the impact of living with anxiety about our feelings of superiority or inferiority. It's not the inferior housing that gives you heart disease, it's the stress, the hopelessness, the anxiety, the depression you feel around that. The psychosocial effects of inequality affect the quality of human relationships. Because we are social beings, it's the social environment and social relationships that are the most important. For individuals, of course, if you're going to lose your home, or if you're terribly in debt, those can be more powerful stresses.

Brooke: What psychological impact does living in an unequal society have on people who are at the top of the scale?

Richard: Status competition causes problems all the way up; we're all very sensitive to how we're judged. People spend thousands of pounds on a handbag with the right labels to make statements about themselves. In more unequal countries, people are more likely to get into debt. They save less of their income and spend more. They work much longer hours. They experience themselves through each other's eyes—and that's the reason for the labels and the clothes and the cars.

Brooke: What's the effect of inequality on the way we perceive our communities—and how does that perception affect how they function?

Richard: Inequality affects our ability to trust and our sense that we are part of a community. In a way, that is the fundamental mediator between inequality and most of these outcomes, through the damage it does to social relations. For instance, in more equal countries or more equal states, two-thirds of the population may feel they can trust others in general, whereas in more unequal countries or states, it may drop as low as 15 percent or 25 percent.

Keys:
Ex. 1   1. D   2. D   3. D   4. A   5. C   6. A
Ex. 2   Open

Dialogue 2

Keys:
Ex. 1

1. incorporated   2. objective   3. appealing   4. associated   5. identify   6. visible   7. vital   8. impact
9. used in accordance with their appearance   10. by supplying food, warmth and mobility
11. be guided by satellite, enabling them to experience cities in a completely new way
Ex. 2   Open

Part III   Listen and Discuss

Passage 1

What Are Social Problems?

Social problems, also called social issues, affect every society, great and small. Even in relatively isolated, sparsely populated areas, a group will encounter social problems. Part of this is due to the fact that any members of a society living close enough together will have conflicts. It's virtually impossible to avoid them, and even people who live together in the same house don't always get along well. On the whole though, when social problems are mentioned they tend to refer to the problems that affect people living together in a society.

The list of social problems is huge and not identical from area to area. In the US, some social issues include the growing divide between rich and poor, domestic violence, unemployment, pollution, and many others. Sometimes social issues arise when people hold very different opinions about how to handle certain situations, while other members of the society remain strongly opposed to its use. In itself, strong disagreements on how to solve problems create divides in social groups.

Other issues that may be considered social problems aren't that common in the US and other industrialized countries, but they are huge problems in developing ones. The issues of massive poverty, food shortages, lack of basic hygiene, spread of incurable diseases, and lack of education inhibits the development of society. Moreover, these problems are related to each other.

It would be easy to assume that a social problem only affects the people whom it directly touches, but this is not the case. Easy spread of disease for instance may tamper with the society at large, and it's easy to see how this has operated in certain areas of Africa. The spread of AIDs for instance has created more social problems because it is costly, it is a danger to all members of society, and it leaves many children without parents. HIV/AIDs isn't a single problem but a complex cause of numerous ones. Similarly, unemployment in America doesn't just affect those unemployed but affects the whole economy.

It's also important to understand that social problems within a society affect its interaction with other societies, which may lead to global problems or issues. How another nation deals with the problems of a developing nation may affect its relationship with that nation and the rest of the world for years to come.

When it comes to tackling some of the problems that plague its society, there is diversity of solutions, which may mean that the country cannot commit to a single way to solve an issue, because there are too many ideas operating on how to solve it. Any proposed solution is likely to make some people unhappy. On the other hand, in countries where the government operates independently of the people and where free speech or exchange of ideas is discouraged, there may not be enough ideas to solve issues, and governments may persist in trying to solve them in ineffective ways.

The very nature of social problems suggests that society itself is a problem. No country has perfected a society where all are happy and where no problems exist. Perhaps as many people state, perfection many not be an achievable goal.

Questions:

1. How do social problems occur?
2. Why are people divided in society?
3. In what countries are problems of food, disease and education so commonly seen?
4. What is the effect of a social problem?
5. How to solve social problems?
6. According to the author, can we find good solutions to social problems?

Keys:

Ex. 1   1. A   2. D   3. B   4. B   5. A   6. C

Ex. 2   Open

Passage 2

Keys:

Ex. 1

1. yielded   2. encouraging   3. launched   4. injured   5. beneficial   6. approximately   7. Vehicles
8. endurance   9. Breach of speed limits is a strongly contributing factor to many road accidents
10. refers to drunk driving now being socially unacceptable
11. It really shouldn't matter to us if we are 30 seconds late for dinner

Ex. 2   Open

Part IV   Watch and Debate

Keys:

Ex. 1

1. It is facing health crisis.
2. Tens of millions of people will die of smoking-related illnesses.
3. No. It is important part of life. It is your surroundings, because everybody smokes.
4. Beijing Olympic Games was smoke-free. Smoking is banned in some public areas. Some restaurants now provide non-smoking areas. Hospitals and clinics help smokers quit.
5. It is a huge task. Because it involves not only health departments but also many aspects of the whole society.

6. We, as a whole society, need to increase our awareness of smoking control.

Ex. 2 Open

Part V Extracurricular Listening

1. M: I thought it would be fun if we all went to see that new movie downtown.
   W: Count me out. I've heard it isn't worth the money.
   Q: What does the woman mean? (A)

2. W: I feel very uneasy about trusting David with our money. How about you?
   M: Some people say he's not reliable, but others have a lot of confidence in him. I'm willing to give him the benefit of the doubt.
   Q: What did the man mean? (B)

3. M: You go ahead and sit next to Alan. I don't want him talking to me throughout the whole movie.
   W: And I do?
   Q: What does the woman mean? (B)

4. W: Professor Williams helped me so much that I'm thinking of buying him a book of poetry.
   M: I think you should get him a record. Just because he's an English teacher doesn't mean that all he does is to read.
   Q: What does the man mean? (B)

5. W: If Professor Thomson is willing to give us a three-day extension to finish the project, maybe she'll give us a few more days.
   M: Let's not push our luck, Mary! O.K.?
   Q: What does the man mean? (A)

6. W: Is that restaurant on the corner any good?
   M: I'll let you form your own opinion, but I should warn you that if you want to go there you'd better make a reservation in advance.
   Q: What does the man imply about the restaurant? (B)

7. M: I hear you're taking a painting class. I didn't know you were an artist.
   W: Oh, I'm not. But I've never had an art course before, so I decided to take the plunge now.
   Q: What does the woman imply? (B)

8. M: Are you sure you can't remember the name of that record?
   W: It's just on the tip of my tongue.
   Q: What does the woman mean? (A)

9. W: Oh, it's the third time I've had to wait for you. Why couldn't you call me?
   M: I'm sorry, dear, but every time I have to drive through very heavy traffic to get here.
   Q: What's the implication of the man's words? (B)

10. W: They just built some new apartments near campus, but a one bedroom rents for 500 dollars a month.
    M: That's a bit beyond the reach of most students.
    Q: What does the man mean? (D)

Unit 16 Cultural Diversity Shapes National Character

Part II Join in the Dialogue

Dialogue 1

People of the World——Interview with a Couple

Where are you from?

My name is Liz and I'm American, my husband is German and named Uwe.

Where did you meet?

We were both teaching at a language school in Germany, he teaches English and German so we got to know one another via the staff room. I conspired for lessons from him so we could spend more time together, so he was also my German teacher.

What language do you speak at home?

Oddly enough we speak English at home. Uwe spent time in the U.S. as a child and has traveled and lived abroad extensively, so his English is quite fluent. I've made a point of always using German with his friends and family, and now that we have moved back to Germany I'll use more at home too. It's important to get my German back up to speed.

Do you try to cook food from each other's countries?

We both are fascinated by international cuisine and love to cook, so any week will be extremely international. Uwe usually cooks the more European things, and German specialties of course. I cover the rest of the world. We eat a lot of Indian, quite a bit of Thai and Chinese, a lot of Moroccan, Arabic and Turkish. Italian of course, we really loved living there and exploring regional specialties. We went to Mexico and Central America for our honeymoon, so I have those ingredients and flavors on my mind. Maybe I should put up a map of the world on the wall and throw darts at it to decide what's for dinner tonight!

Can you explain one part of your partner's culture that you found surprising?

Cross-cultural awareness played a large role in my studies at university, and I studied German there so I had some knowledge and an intellectual basis for assessing German culture when I arrived.

The biggest surprise to me has been social and political. Another passion of mine is politics, and I remain heavily involved in American politics even though I've lived abroad for 15 years or so. The contrast between political systems and styles of governing, the campaigning and advertising, what beliefs are held by what groups of people is fascinating to me.

What's the best thing about being in a cross-cultural relationship?

Absolutely it's a chance to expand your horizons, your world view. Any two people in a relationship bring their lives together and build something, there's always learning involved. But the chance to have a close-up insider's view of another culture adds a wonderful element.

What's the hardest thing about being in a cross-cultural relationship?

Every cross-cultural relationship will have its unique dynamics, depending on the cultures and people involved. In our case I think the most difficult thing was adjusting communication styles in times of stress. Germans have a more direct style and easily separate discussion of an idea from personal feelings or ego.

Do you have any advice for other cross-cultural couples?

Be patient, understanding and respectful of other ways of doing things, the other values people have or different ways of looking at the world. Understanding the different frameworks used to analyze cultures helps offer insight into why your partner does some things certain ways. Communication is crucial, as is compromise! This is true in any relationship, but cross-cultural couples might need to work a little harder at it.

Scripts and Keys

Keys:

Ex. 1 1. D 2. C 3. D 4. A 5. A 6. D

Ex. 2 Open

Dialogue 2

Keys:

Ex. 1

1. represent 2. distinctive 3. exactly 4. symbolic 5. remote 6. geography 7. exposed 8. commerce
9. the Chinese follow not just in the preparation and cooking of food, but everyday life
10. a practiced philosophy where people learn to have a more well-balanced life
11. If you eat a balanced diet, and exercise, you'll be healthy

Ex. 2 Open

Part III Listen and Discuss

Passage 1

1. Learn about how your values, attitudes, behaviors and communication style may be perceived by someone from another culture, e. g. they may interpret humor as not taking things seriously. Seek feedback from the people you work with or from a friendly party in the other culture.
2. Relate to each person as an individual and not as a stereotype. Understanding the values, expectations and beliefs that drive behaviors in different cultures should inform your actions towards an individual, not direct them. Culture doesn't determine anything, but it shapes everything.
3. Understand who can make what decisions as it may be at a different level than in your own organization; be done more quickly or more slowly. In cultures where status is of more importance than in the UK or the U. S. , such as Spain/Italy/Greece/France, decisions are made nearer the top of an organization. In cultures where status counts for less, such as Sweden/Norway/Finland /Netherlands, decisions may be made at lower levels. Decisions may also be made more by individuals (e. g. U. S. and Australia) rather than through collective decision making (e. g. , Japan).
4. Identify if their management style is more typically masculine or feminine — assertive and competitive or modest and caring respectively. This will affect the style of negotiation and the type of relationship. An assertive approach in times of conflict may be greeted positively in the U. S. but negatively in Sweden. In a more feminine culture such as Sweden, a modest approach at a presentation may be viewed very positively, whereas in the U. S. the same presenter may be viewed as lacking commitment, passion or drive.
5. Understand if they have a short-term or long-term view as this will affect the way and the speed at which projects are assessed, justified and decisions made. Asian cultures take a much longer view than many Western cultures, e. g. the period over which a project is justified.
6. Identify their need for structure and certainty as this may vary and affect the level of control, definition, risk taking and governance. Agree on a common working approach that balances the differences, e. g. you may have to provide much more detail and information for a partner than you yourself would need for a decision to be taken.
7. Develop your empathy skills and show people you are making every effort to see and feel things as they do. Think of yourself as a "translator" of your own culture and protocols. Making a small change such as greeting people in their own language or showing knowledge of their culture and its customs will be seen positively.
8. If you are unsure what is appropriate, have more explicit communication rather than less. Remember that this is not everyone's preferred style, e. g. the Japanese have a much more implicit communication style than the British. When communicating remember to speak clearly and at an appropriate speed and level of language, but never

patronize.

9. Ask each person how they would like to be addressed and treated. Master the correct pronunciation and spelling of the names of people you work with. Talk to them about their expectations and how you can respect their position and the value they add.

10. Assume nothing — a smile and handshake are not necessarily an agreement, "yes" can mean "no", unsmiling may not mean unfriendly, silence may not mean disagreement. Ask questions and be ready to be flexible. It is much easier to change your own behaviors than influence someone else's.

Keys:
Ex.1 1. B 2. A 3. A 4. D 5. C 6. D 7. A 8. A
Ex.2 Open

Passage 2

Keys:
Ex. 1
1. interpret 2. aggressive 3. volume 4. impact 5. indicate 6. intercultural 7. competent 8. trustworthy
9. a standardized mental picture that one person or group of people holds in common about another person or group of people
10. Many people do it to justify their conduct in relation to the group they have stereotyped
11. How we interact with others is quite often based on our value systems and beliefs
Ex. 2 Open

Part Ⅳ Watch and Debate

Keys:
Ex. 1
1. Because information only takes the form in a container, but not change the form. It is more important to have transformation, because it changes the form, which means changing our mind.
2. The same information can give very different interpretation: one is a disaster, and the other is an opportunity; one leads to loss of energy, and the other one to increasing energy.
3. Happiness is more related to our mind than to our status or money.
4. We must get rid of our limitations, because it is our limitations that prevent us from fulfilling our potential.
5. Laozi's teaching: "In pursuit of knowledge, every day something is acquired; in pursuit of wisdom, every day something is dropped."——meaning: by learning, you increase knowledge; by getting rid of limitations, you get wisdom.
6. "Common sense is not that common", because you often do not realize and know how to apply the common sense.
7. The extraordinarily successful small groups have 1) more sense of confidence and 2) always ask questions.
8. Only by understanding ourselves can we better understand others, because "What is most personal is most general".
Ex. 2 Open

Part Ⅴ Extracurricular Listening

1. W: I only want to get a can of juice to take back to my room.
   M: You don't have to wait in the food line for that. There's a machine near that stack of trays.
   Q: Where does this conversation probably take place? (C)

2. W: Excuse me, where can I find the apartment manager? I need to see him right now.
   M: Sorry, I can't help you. I'm not familiar with this building.
   Q: What does the man mean? (C)

· 214 ·

3. W: Have you met our new next-door neighbor?
   M: What a beautiful car she has!
   Q: What can be concluded about the man? (C)
4. M: I forgot to bring my notebook.
   W: No problem. You can borrow some paper from me.
   Q: What does the woman tell the man? (B)
5. W: Maybe you lost your wallet in this room.
   M: I've searched it from top to bottom.
   Q: What does the man mean? (D)
6. W: Have you planted your vegetable garden yet?
   M: I'm waiting for it to stop raining so much.
   Q: What is the problem? (B)
7. W: You won't be able to get to the airport in time to catch the plane at four o'clock.
   M: I realize that now. I'll have to get my ticket changed.
   Q: What will the man do? (D)
8. W: What did Charlene say when you recommended that she not go jogging in this heat?
   M: Oh, she's perfectly willing to listen to reason.
   Q: What does the man say about Charlene? (D)
9. W: Is it true that the coach resigned yesterday?
   M: Yes, but why did is still a mystery.
   Q: What does the man mean? (A)
10. M: I didn't know till recently that Mike was going to move to New York.
    W: That took us all by surprise.
    Q: What does the woman say about Mike? (A)

Unit 17 Calamity Is Man's True Touch-Stone

Part II Join in the Dialogue

Dialogue 1

Can you tell us about the national response to the earthquake and tsunamis?

EO: It has been a massive response. Numbers are not very clear but we are talking about between 80,000 and 250,000 people, coming mainly from the Self Defense Forces but also from other emergency medical organisations as well as some other foreign and government aid groups.

What are the main medical issues in the places that MSF has visited?

EO: For the moment, in the 20 or 30 different evacuation centers we have visited, the main issues are chronic diseases among elderly people. Their treatment has been interrupted and our doctors are looking at restarting it to prevent the patients falling into acute situations. Communication has been very erratic over the past four days. It is getting better, but it is still quite difficult. Transportation is difficult too. Almost everywhere we have been, roads are blocked and there has been a shortage of fuel for our vehicles. There are a number of issues facing those people affected by the earthquake or the tsunamis. The cold weather is not at all nice. There is a lack of food and water, while the most urgent need is blankets.

Does MSF envisage a long-term involvement in Japan?

EO: It is too early to say. We are looking to expand the team, but no decision has been made yet. One thing is clear:

our flexible mobile teams are responding to the needs and we will continue with the same strategy. It may be that we bring in more teams, but we are not looking at a massive intervention with hundreds of international personnel coming from all over the world.

Why is that?

EO: First, because there is a massive deployment of aid from the Japanese government, as well as from foreign governments. It is not a humanitarian crisis at this stage, and the most urgent needs are covered. A number of hospitals still function in the area, there are drugs, and doctors are available in most of the hospitals.

What will MSF do in the event of a significant nuclear event or the situation in Fukushima getting even worse?

EO: We will evacuate our teams. We are monitoring the situation on an hourly basis. We have radiometers (radiation detectors) with each of our teams on the ground. We are cross checking the situation with various government and non-government agencies, in many different locations in the world, not just Tokyo. As soon as we reach a level that could become unhealthy or dangerous for our teams, we will evacuate the team. We have the means to evacuate quite rapidly, evacuation routes have been identified, so yes, that's what we will do.

What about treating illnesses caused by radiation, is that something MSF can contemplate?

EO: At this stage no. We are not experts on that. We are investigating the medical issue of nuclear radiation to try and see if we can help. We have some people amongst the 25,000 or 30,000 people working in MSF who have worked in this field of medicine, and we are collecting this expertise together. This is more the duty of the Japanese government and, from what we hear or read in the news, they are already trying to prepare for that.

Keys:

Ex.1   1. D   2. A   3. C   4. D   5. B   6. A

Ex.2   Open

Keys:

Dialogue 2

Ex.1

1. consequences   2. destruction   3. engaged   4. sustainable   5. spotlight   6. coordinated   7. necessity

8. decisive   9. to the extent that there is understanding and evaluation of accomplishment through planning

10. create and sustain public awareness that can make disaster reduction a policy priority

11. invest in resources that are dedicated to risk identification, assessment, and management

Ex.2   Open

Part Ⅲ   Listen and Discuss

Passage 1

From the point of view of many humans, the term "natural disaster" is a convenient scapegoat because it allows a person or a whole nation to blame nature for their own poor planning. Wherever we find so-called "natural disasters" around the world, we usually find a large group of people who have cut down the forests, paved over the grasslands that allow rain to soak into the soil, and built their homes right in the middle of natural drainage channels. When the floods come, they look to the sky and curse Mother Nature, shouting, "We got hit by a natural disaster!"

Most "natural" disasters are actually caused by poor human planning. That's a man-made disaster. Or, more accurately, it's just poor planning on the part of short-sighted humans. Generally speaking, people don't have a very long-term view of things. "Why does God punish us by destroying our home?" they cry. Maybe God was actually sending them an important message: "Don't build your home in a flood zone."

So how can we avoid these "natural disasters" on a personal level? It's easier than you think: Be aware of your impact on the world around you and the fact that you are connected with the world around you. Everything we do to world around us, whether destructive or creative, will eventually be reflected in that world. And especially be wary of contaminating the planet, destroying natural habitat or attempting to alter the natural cycles of nature. The best way to avoid natural disasters is to learn to live in greater harmony with the nature world, respecting its natural cycles of "destruction" which are actually crucial to life on Earth. Many "natural disasters" are really only disasters from the point of view of people who don't respect nature in the first place.

Keys:
Ex.1   1. B   2. A   3. C   4. D   5. A   6. C
Ex.2   Open

Passage 2

Keys:
Ex.1
1. resistant   2. witnessing   3. threatening   4. unwillingness   5. characterize   6. cause and effect chain
7. potential   8. emergence
9. When the Earth is in a healthy ecosystem balance, these diseases tend to be kept under control
10. Since the industrial revolution, we've thrown more particulate matter into the atmosphere
11. Either we learn how to respect nature, or we'll be wiped out and nature will make the adjustments for us
Ex.2   Open

Part IV   Watch and Debate

Keys:
Ex.1
1. We should be careful.
2. The possibility of blowing our life or living the wrong kind of life.
3. We'll 1) make bad choices in what we're aiming for and 2) fail to accomplish even if we make right choices. So, 1) we have to be careful in choosing our aims and 2) we have to be careful in the execution of our aims.
4. One, to pack as much as you can into life given that you have only a finite time and two, to live a life of accomplishment. Strategy One deals with small potatoes like "eat, drink and be merry" while Strategy Two deals with large potatoes like doing things more valuable.
5. To get the right mixture of strategy: To manage large accomplishments while assuring smaller things out of life.
6. Quality can trump quantity in that it has peaks or heights of life.
Ex.2   Open

Part V   Extracurricular Listening

1. W: That jacket suits you very well!
   M: Thank you! What I can't figure out is why I've never chosen this color before.
   Q: What does the man mean? (A)
2. M: I'm going to see if I can persuade Brian not to buy that used car.
   W: I doubt that will do any good. His mind is already made up.
   Q: What does the woman say about Brian? (B)
3. M: Are you doing research for Professor Adams this semester?
   W: Actually, I'm working as his teaching assistant.
   Q: What does the woman mean? (B)
4. M: Marcia looks like she's on cloud nine. Do you know what made her so happy?
   W: She just had a paper accepted for publication.

Q: What are these people saying about Marcia? (D)

5. M: Sue, have you given Doug's book back to him?

   W: No, and he's reminded me a thousand times, but I keep forgetting.

   Q: What does Sue say about Doug? (C)

6. W: Thanks for volunteering to drive me to the airport, but I'm taking the tube that goes there from the campus.

   M: It's no trouble. Besides, I'd like to see you off.

   Q: What does the man mean? (A)

7. W: I don't think our classmates should confront Prof. Simons with these issues.

   M: I know. I'm going to try to talk them out of it.

   Q: What will the man try to do? (A)

8. M: Janet, you're redecorating your apartment, aren't you? How's it coming along?

   W: I'm just taking it one step at a time.

   Q: What does the woman imply? (C)

9. W: I hear you're taking an advanced physics course this semester.

   M: I think I've bitten off more than I can chew.

   Q: What does the man mean? (D)

10. W: Martha seemed to know just the right thing to say to Bob in order to cheer him up.

    M: That's just like her.

    Q: What does the man mean? (C)

Unit 18　Science and Technology Revolutionize Life

Part II　Join in the Dialogue

Dialogue 1

You are going to hear a conversation between Dick and Sue who are two college students. They are talking about the history of flight.

Dick: Hi, Sue. Wow, this is great. The Smithsonian National Air and Space Museum. I'm really looking forward to doing this project on the Wright brothers.

Sue: Me, too. My dad was an air force pilot, always talking about the Wright brothers. If they hadn't invented the airplane my dad might not have had a job. What got them interested in flying?

Dick: It says here that their dad used to buy them lots of toys, and one was like a helicopter. And it seems that this toy helicopter first got them interested in the idea. Also, they read about this German guy who made himself a pair of large wings and managed to glide. Then they started to read everything they could get their hands on about flying, and began building a plane in 1900. Next?

Sue: Their first jobs?

Dick: Er... They started a printing shop, and also a bicycle shop. I guess they both needed some knowledge of mechanics—it helps if you want to make the world's first airplane.

Sue: I suppose so. Anything else?

Dick: Yeh.

Sue: OK, now the big question. When did they first fly their airplane?

Dick: Well, they made a glider and flew it in 1902. But the one that made them famous was—I'll read it to you—the first ever heavier than air, manned-powered flight in 1903.

Sue: Got the exact date there?

Dick: No, just the year. We can easily find it later. Hey, but listen to this: Government bureaucrats thought they

· 218 ·

were crazy, and some engineers thought that if two bicycle mechanics could build a successful airplane, they could do it, too.

Sue: Hey, you write down the answers now. Let me have a read. Here's the day they first tried to fly it: Monday, December 14, 1903. They tossed a coin, and decided that Wilbur would take the first turn as pilot. And, the plane weighed six hundred pounds. He started off, but turned the rudder too sharply, and the left wing hit the hillside. So they repaired it and Orville tried again on Thursday, December 17, 1903.

Dick: So that was the big day.

Sue: Yeh. The flight wasn't much—12 seconds, 120 feet. I'll read what it says: but it was the first controlled, sustained flight in a heavier-than-air craft, one of the great moments of the century. And on their third flight that day, Wilbur flew 852 feet in 59 seconds.

Dick: OK, time for a coffee.

Keys:
Ex.1 1. B 2. A 3. C 4. A
Ex.2 Open

Dialogue 2

John: Hi, Ann. How's it going? Thank goodness I've finished that survey on television watching and reading ability. What was your survey on?

Ann: I told you before. I wanted to find out if there is any relationship between how fat students are and how many times they eat at fast food restaurants.

John: That's right. I'd forgotten. Have you got your report finished, all the graphs and charts, that sort of thing?

Ann: Almost done. What about you?

John: All ready to present to the class, apart from one or two small things. Actually, my results are really interesting. Want me to tell you what I found?

Ann: Sure. If you promise to let me tell you what I found.

John: No problem. Anyway, look at this graph here. On the X axis I have the dependent variable, reading level.

Ann: How did you measure reading level?

John: I used the English Department test. And on the Y axis I have number of hours usually spent watching television every week.

Ann: 13 to 19, 20 to 29, 30 to 39, 40 to 49 and 50 to 59. What are these numbers?

John: The people's ages. I managed to get exactly 20 people from each age group to do the test. Took me ages!

Ann: And what did you find out?

John: Well, look at this. If we take the 100 people as one group, we see that the more television people watch, the worse their reading level.

Ann: That's not surprising. But did you find any significant difference between the different age groups?

John: You bet. OK. This is the curve for the group as a whole. These lines are for the different age groups. See what I see?

Ann: Wow, that's fascinating! The two youngest groups are very similar. Big difference between the oldest two groups and the youngest two. The older the people are, the less the correlation between reading level and hours spent in front of the TV. Why do you think that is?

John: Well, I need to do more research before I can say for sure. But from talking to the people it's clear that over the past thirty years most people have been watching more television and reading fewer books. But the older people…

Ann: Don't tell me. They spent more time reading when they were young than young people nowadays, so they learnt to read well and even though they spend more time in front of the TV than they used to, their reading levels stay the same.

John: Hey, you're pretty smart. That's exactly what I think. But I need to do more research before I can say for sure. How about your survey?

Keys:

Ex. 1   1. D   2. C   3. B   4. D

Ex. 2   Open

Part Ⅲ   Listen and Discuss

Passage 1

Listen to part of a lecture by a physics professor.

Today let's consider the neutrino(中微子) and the results of some experiments down in 1995 at Los Alamos National Laboratory in New Mexico, which bear on the neutrino. These results suggest that this little particle does indeed have mass, a tiny bit to be sure but measurable by the very sensitive instruments of that lab. The neutrino's origin has always been an interesting case, though a case not unusual in the history of physics. As you know, ordinarily scientific observation precedes scientific theory. Ocean tides are observed, ocean tides are explained; gravity is observed, gravity is explained. However, let's consider what happened in the neutrino's case. When the neutrino was proposed over sixty years ago, it was a convenient fiction. Scientists had not observed such a particle, nor even its effects. So what led them to conceive of this imaginary object? They had been writing equations about neutron decay in which the energy amounts on each side of their equations were unequal. In order to keep the energy amounts the same on both sides of the equations, they added a little particle named neutrino and gave it precisely enough energy to balance the equations. Years later, about thirty-five years ago real neutrinos were found. Now we have these more recent developments. Originally, the neutrino was thought not to have any mass at all. But Los Alamos experiments seem to disprove this premise. They indicate that neutrinos do have mass—about one-millionth the mass of electron.

Questions:

1. Why did the speaker mention ocean tides and gravity?
2. How did the concept of the neutrino originate?
3. What did the experimental results at Los Alamos show about the neutrino?

Keys:

Ex. 1   1. A   2. D   3. D

Ex. 2   Open

Passage 2

Listen to part of a lecture in a psychology class.

Today let's talk about synesthesia(副感觉). That's a brain condition in which a person's senses are combined in unusual ways. For example, a person with synesthesia may taste sounds. To them, a musical note may taste like a pekoe(香红茶). Many people who have synesthesia experience intense colors when they hear specific words. For example, they might see a flash of pink every time they hear the word "jump". For a long time, many scientists were unconvinced that synesthesia really exists. So in the 1990s an experiment was done to find out for sure. Two groups were studied. One was a group of people who claim to experience colors when they heard certain words. The other was a control group, people who experience nothing out of the ordinary when hearing words. Each group was asked to describe the colors they thought of when they heard a list of spoken words. When the test was repeated, the difference between the two groups was startling. After just a week, the control group gave the same answers only a third of the time. But even a year and a half later, the synesthetic group gave the same answers 92% of the time. Clearly, this is

· 220 ·

not just a matter of memory. Scientists are still not sure just why synesthesia happens. But certain drugs are reportedly able to produce it artificially. So we all probably have brains with connections that could produce synesthesia. It's just that the connections normally aren't used in that way.

Questions:
1. What is the main purpose of the talk?
2. What is one example of synesthesia that the professor mentions?
3. What was the purpose of the experiment the professor mentions?
4. What were some of people in the study able to do?

Keys:
Ex. 1   1. C   2. D   3. C   4. A
Ex. 2   Open

Part Ⅳ   Watch and Debate

Keys:
Ex. 1
1. there's a sequencing of events that imposes a certain structure to the story
2. we do not give the same amount of emotional significance to every event
3. how that particular experience connects with your effective systems of response
4. if something produces an undue amount of pleasure or undue amount of displeasure, it's going to be judged differently and it's going to be introduced in your narrative with a different size, with a different development
5. not on the basis necessarily of the time course, but rather on the basis of how it was valued by you
6. whether we want to do it because we want to have people to have a different idea of who we are or not, we do it naturally
7. You're not the same after, say, an incredible love affair that went very well or a love affair that went bad
8. sort of changes the weights with which memories are recalled
9. the weights with which something is more probably going to be or not recalled on the next instance, are going to be changed

Ex. 2   Open

Part Ⅴ   Extracurricular Listening

1. M: I'm so confused by my notes from Professor Johnson's lectures.
   W: How about reviewing them now over a cup of coffee?
   Q: What does the woman suggest they do about the notes? (B)
2. M: The lock on my front door is broken.
   W: Why don't you have Mr. Smith fix it? He's very good.
   Q: What does the woman suggest the man do? (D)
3. M: I really ought to buy some new shoelaces before these break.
   W: Why not some new shoes?
   Q: What does the woman suggest? (C)
4. W: I'd like to get away for the long weekend, but I don't know where to go.
   M: Have you thought of the beach?
   Q: What does the man mean by his response? (D)
5. M: Are there any tickets left for the concert tonight?
   W: Why don't you check at the box office? They may have something.
   Q: What does the woman mean? (A)

6. W: We could turn down this road to get to the shopping.
   M: Let's not go that way today because of all the traffic.
   Q: What does the man suggest? (B)
7. W: We ought to stop buying this kind of coffee. It always tastes terrible.
   M: Maybe we should get a new coffee machine instead.
   Q: What does the man mean? (D)
8. W: Shouldn't someone pick up the clothes from the cleaner's?
   M: Don't look at me.
   Q: What does the man mean? (B)
9. M: I can't remember the due date for our final paper.
   W: I think it is the last day of class. But Professor Murdoch told us not to wait until the last minute to hand it in.
   Q: What does Professor Murdoch suggest to the students? (C)
10. M: I don't know whether I should time my speech now or keep on revising my notes. What do you think?
    W: I'd carry on with what you are doing.
    Q: What does the woman suggest that the man do? (A)

Unit 19　Best Is Cheapest

Part Ⅱ　Join in the Dialogue

Dialogue 1

Listen to a conversation between two students.

M: Excuse me. I am looking for the textbook for a course called *Psychology of Personality*, but I can't find it anywhere.
W: Is that the book for Dr. Peterson's course?
M: That's right, Psychology 3601.
W: Yes, yes, I was afraid of that. It seems we didn't order enough books for that class. You are the 7th person today who has come in looking for one.
M: But classes begin on Monday…
W: I wouldn't worry. Dr. Peterson was aware of the problem, and we've got another shipment of books coming in before the end of the month.
M: Can I reserve the copy?
W: No problem. Just give me your name and phone number. We'll call you when the books arrive.
Keys:
Ex.1　1. C　2. B　3. A
Ex.2　Open

Dialogue 2

Listen to a conversation between two students.

M: What's up Marcy? You seemed to be in a good mood today.
W: I guess I am. It's the new printer I just bought for my computer.
M: Hey, that's terrific.
W: Thanks. It's good I can charge it to my credit card though. If I'd had to come up with that much cash on the spot, I just wouldn't be able to afford it.
M: You know, I'm doing a term paper on that for my economic seminar. I read that a lot people in the world would be

able to support themselves and their families much better if they could start their own businesses. But usually the bank won't lend them money they need to get started. Often, if you don't already have property or other assets, they won't give you even the smallest loan.

W: That doesn't seem fair.

M: Exactly. But now there's something known as microcredit. That's what they call very small loans that enable people to go into business for themselves. In Southern Asia microcredit programs were set up to lend to people that regular banks even wouldn't look at.

W: And the borrowers used the money…?

M: To buy tools and materials for producing clothes or food or whatever that they can sell to make a little money to feed their families and also start to pay back the loan, and then they can borrow a little more and make a little more profit. And…

W: And the lenders get their money back?

M: With interest. It's been so successful that now microcredit lending is spreading to other parts of the world too, even to North America. That's what my paper will be about.

W: Say, do you need someone to type it for you? My rates are reasonable, and it'll look really nice when I print it out.

M: On your new printer? Hey, how could I say "no"?

Questions:

1. Why is the woman happy?
2. What is the conversation mainly about?
3. Why does the man mention Southern Asia?
4. What will the woman probably do?

Keys:

Ex. 1   1. B   2. B   3. D   4. D

Ex. 2   Open

Part III   Listen and Discuss

Passage 1

In the 18th century French economists protested the excessive regulation of business by the government. Their motto was laisser faire. Laisser faire means let the people do as they choose. In the economic sense, this meant that while the government should be responsible for things like maintaining peace and protecting property fights, it should not interfere with private business. It shouldn't create regulations that might hinder business growth, nor should it be responsible for providing subsidies to help. In other words, governments should take hands off approach to business. For a while in the United States, laisser faire was a popular doctrine. But things quickly changed. After the Civil War, politicians rarely opposed the government's generous support of business owners. They were only too glad to support government land grants and loans to railroad owners for example. Their regulations kept tariffs high and that helped protect American industrialists against foreign competition. Ironically in the late 19th century, a lot of people believed that the laisser faire policy was responsible for the countries industrial growth. It was generally assumed that because business owners did not have a lot of external restrictions placed on them by the government, they could pursue their own interests, and this was what made them so successful. But in fact, many of these individuals would not have been able to meet their objective if not for government support.

Questions:

1. What is the talk mainly about?
2. Who first used the motto laisser faire?
3. What is the principle idea of the laisser faire policy?

Keys:

Ex. 1   1. C   2. B   3. B

Ex. 2   Open

Passage 2

Keys:

Ex. 1

1. the kids' education, that big house in the country you've always dreamed of, and of course retirement
2. the various types of investment you can make
3. you take out the cash you need every week from the bank, and keep a record of what you buy with your credit card
4. the higher the potential for making a fortune by buying shares of a particular company
5. made a fortune, but they got out before the market crashed
6. low-risk but low return things, to things like blue chip stocks that are somewhat less predictable, but which will probably provide steady, if not spectacular, returns for years

Ex. 2   Open

Part Ⅳ   Watch and Debate

Keys:

Ex. 1

1. evolve their management models faster than their competitors
2. on the basis of how many tickets have been filled against them, how quickly they are closed
3. do you innovate radically in management, without blowing up your organization
4. you do something radical and safe at the same time
5. give them six months, we ask them to kind of tear it all apart and put it back together again
6. there is a way of experimenting with management
7. have been made by senior executives; the heads of the big merchandising units there
8. sent an e-mail around to several hundred colleagues
9. predict the company's revenues in the last kind of six weeks of the year
10. really took just a couple of hours of time getting the e-mails together, the only incentive was $100 gift card for the best guess
11. innovation in management just like we think about innovation in products, services on our websites, anywhere else
12. experiment more with how they lead, organize, manage, structure

Ex. 2   Open

Part Ⅴ   Extracurricular Listening

1. M: The storm they predicted for last night turned out to be nothing.
   W: Didn't it, though!
   Q: What do we learn from this conversation? (B)

2. M: I'll bet that the competition for parts in the class play will be tough this year!
   W: Oh! An actor, are you?
   Q: What does the woman mean? (C)

3. W: Mark hasn't gotten up before noon once since he's been home from college.
   M: Catching up on his sleep, is he?
   Q: What does the man mean? (C)

· 224 ·

4. M: Are you going to replace the light switch by yourself?
   W: Why should I call an electrician?
   Q: What does the woman imply? (A)
5. W: The 10:30 train is late again.
   M: Why do they even bother printing a schedule?
   Q: What does the man mean? (B)
6. W: This course wasn't supposed to be hard.
   M: But it sure turned out to be, didn't it?
   Q: What does the woman think about the course? (D)
7. W: Janet insists she's coming to my graduation.
   M: But she has to work that week, doesn't she?
   Q: What does the man imply about Janet? (A)
8. M: Paul says he doesn't like television.
   W: Yes, but he seems to spend a lot of time watching it, doesn't he?
   Q: What does the woman think about Paul? (C)
9. W: We can ask Mark to help us set up the photography exhibit.
   M: When would he find time? He has exams next week.
   Q: What does the man mean? (D)
10. M: Let's ask Dan to introduce the musician to the audience at the beginning of the concert.
    W: Ask Dan? He'll be playing the violin.
    Q: What does the woman mean? (B)

Unit 20　The Present Is Pregnant with the Future

Part II　Join in the Dialogue

Dialogue 1

Earthwatch: What is the situation of today's species extinction?

E. O. Wilson: Today's extinction is not easy to see. In terms of scale, it's hard to put a figure on it. A lot of damage has been done, and it can be dangerous to us if we really just go on until half the species of organisms are extinct forever. One estimate has it that something like 20 percent of Pacific Island bird species has been extinguished by human activities. In fact most of those we won't even know about until we do studies. We know that the Hawaiian birds have gone from something like 125 species to present day 25 or 30 species through human activities.

Earthwatch: There are many environmental challenges facing the world today. How significant is species extinction in the face of these issues?

E. O. Wilson: The answer to that depends on the scale. In other words, if you're thinking ten years into the future, then clearly climate warming is more urgent. If you're thinking for 50 years, 100 years, species extinction is more important. Virtually, environmental change can be reversed by reduction in fossil fuel use. The environmental damage we're doing, such as the climate change and water shortage we can feel right now. Yet, you just can't reverse mass extinction. In the short term, it's not pressing in terms of our survival and immediate comfort. In the long term, it's the most important.

Earthwatch: Can we turn this global challenge into opportunity?

E. O. Wilson: Yes. If you just take what we're losing by our destruction of nature and put it upside down, then that gives you a description of what we gain.

Earthwatch: Why is it important to conserve biodiversity? What are the consequences if we don't?

E. O. Wilson: We will see diminishment in ecosystem services, which have been estimated to be equivalent to the world gross domestic product, roughly $30 trillion. We get these services scot-free. We'll see a reduction over time, so that we'll have to invest more and more of our gross domestic product into replacing those services. So we will see a lot of that going on. Choices made, and bad choices taken, that will diminish what we are already getting scot-free.

There will also be opportunity costs: so many species we can learn from, new products derived, wisdom obtained through scientific study, will be lost forever. That's a huge opportunity cost that's beyond measure.

Earthwatch: Why aren't people aware of the gravity of species extinctions?

E. O. Wilson: In my upcoming book, *The Creation*, I've addressed these particular issues. What I've done is made the following argument. There are three great problems that are overlapping and interlocked. One of them is that we haven't caught on about the environment. We still lack concern about the environment. It's only when you suddenly run out of water or you're in danger of being killed by an earthquake. People don't care. They certainly don't care about the living environment. That's one problem.

The second problem is the failure of science education. Even well-meaning television can't do the job of raising people's awareness.

The third problem is the explosive growth of biology as a science. Most of all the key issues are biological that we're talking about. Biological information is increasing so fast, and with deepening technical difficulty, that even biologists themselves don't know what's going on. They can specialize on one thing and get to master that but they don't understand most of what's going on. This has created chaos in terms of teaching biology. And it's also created new ethical problems that people can't handle. So it's not surprising that they can't understand what evolution is and what the meaning of life is. Anyway, those three problems overlap, and if we can attack them as one problem we can start to approach the issue of awareness.

Earthwatch: Much of the greatest tropical biodiversity is in developing countries, many of them economically challenged and with burgeoning populations. Will these countries be able to grow without sacrificing their biological wealth?

E. O. Wilson: There are so many countries now that are beginning to profit from nature and do much better about conserving their natural resources, designing their agriculture and industry accordingly. It should be kept in mind that tourism is the biggest industry in the world, a trillion dollar industry, and a larger and larger portion of it is ecotourism. A trillion dollars is nothing to be sneezed at. If you're lucky enough to have wild environments, you can build them into ecotourism attractions. You can have all sorts of attractions people will like, small animals, fish, and so on. I'll bet there aren't too many places in the world where you can't find some ecotourism potential.

Questions:

1. What is the situation of today's species extinction?
2. How significant is species extinction in the face of these issues?
3. Can we turn this global challenge into opportunity?
4. Why is it important to conserve biodiversity? What are the consequences if we don't?
5. Why aren't people aware of the gravity of species extinctions?
6. Will these countries be able to grow without sacrificing their biological wealth?

Scripts and Keys

Keys:
Ex. 1   1. C   2. C   3. D   4. A   5. D   6. B
Ex. 2   Open

Dialogue 2
Keys:
Ex. 1
1. ivory tower   2. stereotype   3. dimensions   4. ecosystem   5. planet   6. fundamental   7. essential   8. welfare
9. the origin and meaning of life   10. in terms of public consciousness turned into political action
11. are rising at an even steeper curve than awareness and action
Ex. 2   Open

Part III   Listen and Discuss

Passage 1
Space has always been quite enigmatic in nature and trying to know more about nature reveals that there is still a lot more to know. As you dive deeper into the realms of nature you find that the more knowledge you acquire the more is yet to come. This intriguing factor of space has inspired a lot of young men and women to seek the study of space and its exploration as an option of their higher studies to know and understand it more deeply. So today there are a lot of universities offering space technology as an option of study. With a degree in this, you can always opt for a job in the space exploration centers across the world.

There have been many benefits of space exploration and that is the reason why there is so much funding for it from the side of the government of ever developed and developing country. With the help of satellites, today nature's unpredictable nature can be harnessed and understood much earlier and this helps in preparing for the worst when it happens. Besides, communication has advanced in such a great way that today the distances do not matter and the world has become a global village. This was made possible only with the help of space exploration and using it for the benefit of mankind. Scientific research in the field of medicine, agriculture and technology has been encouraged to a great extent with the exploration of space. Even the facilities in the military have been enhanced with the exploration of space as this helps in identifying and locating war ships and aircrafts. The police too have been greatly assisted in locating lost or abandoned vehicles and criminals on the run.

With the help of the information from space exploration, the concerned agencies are now identifying climatic changes and the changes in the behavior of the oceans and other natural elements on earth. All these favorable results from the exploration of space has defied all the criticism. With such positive benefits, space exploration is not to be deterred nor ended as the benefits are far too many.

Questions:
1. How much do we understand our space?
2. What can universities do for space exploration?
3. What can the government do for space exploration?
4. What can satellites do for space exploration?
5. How does space exploration benefit mankind?
6. What is the future of space exploration?

Keys:
Ex. 1   1. B   2. A   3. A   4. C   5. D   6. D
Ex. 2   Open

Passage 2

Keys:

Ex. 1

1. surface 2. planet 3. launch 4. core 5. orbit 6. radiation 7. peak 8. fading

9. because his greatest contribution to science is the prediction of what's known as Hawking radiation

10. it's being accelerated by a mysterious force called dark energy

11. we're left with a sea of radiation that expands forever and ever

Ex. 2   Open

Part IV   Watch and Debate

I have a dream!

I am happy to join with you today in what will go down in history as the greatest demonstration for freedom in the history of our nation. Five score years ago, a great American, in whose symbolic shadow we stand today, signed the Emancipation Proclamation. This momentous decree came as a great beacon light of hope to millions of Negro slaves who had been seared in the flames of withering injustice. It came as a joyous daybreak to end the long night of their captivity. But one hundred years later, the Negro still is not free. One hundred years later, the life of the Negro is still sadly crippled by the manacles of segregation and the chains of discrimination. One hundred years later, the Negro lives on a lonely island of poverty in the midst of a vast ocean of material prosperity. One hundred years later, the Negro is still languished in the corners of American society and finds himself an exile in his own land.

When the architects of our republic wrote the magnificent words of the Constitution and the Declaration of Independence, they were signing a promissory note to which every American was to fall heir. This note was a promise that all men, yes, black men as well as white men, would be guaranteed the "unalienable Rights" of "Life, Liberty and the pursuit of Happiness." It is obvious today that America has defaulted on this promissory note, insofar as her citizens of color are concerned. Instead of honoring this sacred obligation, America has given the Negro people a bad check, a check which has come back marked "insufficient funds."

But we refuse to believe that the bank of justice is bankrupt. We refuse to believe that there are insufficient funds in the great vaults of opportunity of this nation. And so, we've come to cash this check, a check that will give us upon demand the riches of freedom and the security of justice. We have also come to this hallowed spot to remind America of the fierce urgency of Now. Now is the time to make real the promises of democracy. Now is the time to rise from the dark and desolate valley of segregation to the sunlit path of racial justice. Now is the time to lift our nation from the quicksands of racial injustice to the solid rock of brotherhood.

Now is the time. There are those who are asking the devotees of civil rights, "When will you be satisfied?" We can never be satisfied as long as the Negro is the victim of the unspeakable horrors of police brutality. We cannot be satisfied as long as a Negro in Mississippi cannot vote and a Negro in New York believes he has nothing for which to vote. No, no, we are not satisfied, and we will not be satisfied until "justice rolls down like waters, and righteousness like a mighty stream."

Let us not wallow in the valley of despair, I say to you today, my friends. And so even though we face the difficulties of today and tomorrow, I still have a dream. It is a dream deeply rooted in the American dream.

I have a dream that one day this nation will rise up and live out the true meaning of its creed: "We hold these truths to be self-evident, that all men are created equal."

I have a dream that one day on the red hills of Georgia, the sons of former slaves and the sons of former slave owners will be able to sit down together at the table of brotherhood.

I have a dream that one day even the state of Mississippi, a state sweltering with the heat of injustice, sweltering

Scripts and Keys

with the heat of oppression, will be transformed into an oasis of freedom and justice.

I have a dream that my four little children will one day live in a nation where they will not be judged by the color of their skin but by the content of their character.

I have a dream today! I have a dream that one day, down in Alabama, with its vicious racists, with its governor having his lips dripping with the words of "interposition" and "nullification"—one day right there in Alabama little black boys and black girls will be able to join hands with little white boys and white girls as sisters and brothers.

I have a dream today! I have a dream that one day every valley shall be exalted, and every hill and mountain shall be made low, the rough places will be made plain, and the crooked places will be made straight; "and the glory of the Lord shall be revealed and all flesh shall see it together."

This is our hope, and this is the faith that I go back to the South with. With this faith, we will be able to hew out of the mountain of despair a stone of hope. With this faith, we will be able to transform the jangling discords of our nation into a beautiful symphony of brotherhood. With this faith, we will be able to work together, to pray together, to struggle together, to go to jail together, to stand up for freedom together, knowing that we will be free one day.

This will be the day—this will be the day when all of God's children will be able to sing with new meaning:

My country 'tis of thee, sweet land of liberty, of thee I sing.

Land where my fathers died, land of the Pilgrim's pride.

From every mountainside, let freedom ring!

And if America is to be a great nation, this must become true.

And so let freedom ring from the prodigious hilltops of New Hampshire.

Let freedom ring from the mighty mountains of New York.

Let freedom ring from the heightening Alleghenies of Pennsylvania.

Let freedom ring from the snow-capped Rockies of Colorado.

Let freedom ring from the curvaceous slopes of California.

Not only that:

Let freedom ring from Stone Mountain of Georgia.

Let freedom ring from Lookout Mountain of Tennessee.

Let freedom ring from every hill and molehill of Mississippi.

From every mountainside, let freedom ring.

And when this happens, when we allow freedom ring, when we let it ring from every village and every hamlet, from every state and every city, we will be able to speed up that day when all of God's children, black men and white men, Jews and Gentiles, Protestants and Catholics, will be able to join hands and sing in the words of the old Negro spiritual:

Free at last! Free at last!

Thank God Almighty, we are free at last!

Keys:

Ex. 1

1. For the freedom of Negro
2. Still in poverty.
3. Because of racial discrimination.
4. Life, Liberty and the pursuit of Happiness.

Ex. 2

1. join   freedom   score   light   slaves   injustice
2. justice   opportunity   cash   demand   security   remind   promises
3. We hold these truths to be self-evident, that all men are created equal

4. they will not be judged by the color of their skin but by the content of their character

Ex. 3　Open

Part V　Extracurricular Listening

1. W: I hope you have a good flight.

   M: The weather's supposed to be clear all down the coast, so it should be pretty smooth.

   Q: Where is this conversation probably taking place? (C)

2. W: What did you do with your dog while you were away?

   M: Oh, he's a good traveler as long as he gets a chance to play.

   Q: What can be concluded from the conversation? (D)

3. W: Do you really have to work at the student center tomorrow night?

   M: I'm afraid so. I wish there were some ways I could get out of it.

   Q: What does the man mean? (C)

4. M: I didn't see your car outside when I drove up. Where is it?

   W: Brenda and I started commuting together in order to save money on gas.

   Q: What does the woman mean? (B)

5. M: I've been trying to get the furnace started, but I can't find the right switch.

   W: Here, I believe this one in the back will do the trick.

   Q: What are the man and woman discussing? (A)

6. M: Do you think Andy could help us plan the camping trip to West Virginia?

   W: Well, since he spends every summer there, he might know a thing or two about it.

   Q: What does the woman mean? (C)

7. M: Louise, do you want me to try to fix that broken camera of yours?

   W: Thanks, but I already had it taken care of.

   Q: What has happened to the camera? (A)

8. W: Did you ask Shirley to go to the dance with you?

   M: She is away at a conference until tomorrow.

   Q: What does the man mean? (D)

9. M: Were you able to get your own locker at the Gym?

   W: They're temporarily out of them. I've to check again next week.

   Q: What does the woman mean? (B)

10. W: I hear Sarah's been pretty successful in her new job.

    M: Pretty successful? That's the understatement of the year.

    Q: What does the man imply about Sarah? (A)